MAY DAYS

MAY DAYS

By Samuel F. Pickering, Jr.

University of Iowa Press ψ Iowa City

University of Iowa Press, Iowa City 52242
Printed in the United States of America
First edition, 1988

Book and jacket design by Omega Clay
Typesetting by G&S Typesetters, Austin, Texas
Printing and binding by Edwards Brothers, Ann Arbor, Michigan

The author wishes to acknowledge the following publications
in which essays in this volume first appeared: *Texas Review,*
"Outside In"; *Southern Review,* "At Cambridge"; *New Mexico
Humanities Review,* "Eating under the Stars"; *Chattahoochee
Review,* "Might as Well." He further wishes to acknowledge his
debt to the storytelling ability of Will R. Bird in his book *This
Is Nova Scotia* (Toronto: Ryerson Press, 1950).

Library of Congress Cataloging-in-Publication Data
Pickering, Samuel F., 1941–
  May days.
  I. Title.
AC8.P666 1988   081   87-34292
ISBN 0-87745-204-0

For LAURIE and DUDLEY who made Nova Scotia possible

Contents

MAY DAYS

Outside In

ON THE ROAD to Chestnut Mound just beyond the Buffalo Valley train station stood the Sewall place. Built in the 1870s by Walter Sewall for his two maiden sisters Miss Kitty and Miss Jo Sewall, the house was the most imposing building in Buffalo Valley. Two bulging bay windows overlooked the road while two others faced across fields toward Gentry. Above the windows tall gables ran to points like the ends of pencils, and around the roof lattices were carved into clubs, diamonds, and spades. By nature retiring, Miss Kitty and Miss Jo became reclusive as they grew old, so much so that by the turn of the century, the only person who saw them regularly was Comfort Shoaff, a grocer and meatman who twice a week made rounds from Carthage across Chestnut Mound and then down through Buffalo Valley to Middleton and New Middleton. Partly because their house was the biggest building in town and partly because they lived to great ages and were objects of curiosity, the sisters became landmarks on the Buffalo Valley road. Neighbors talked about them familiarly and never failed to point out their house to visitors. Thus when Miss Kitty died at ninety-six, it seemed as if part of the country had passed from sight, and people felt obliged to visit Miss Jo. In truth some folks behaved poorly and visited more to gratify curiosity about the inside of the house than to express condolences. Old Dr. Sollows, however, was not one of these. He didn't go by until after the funeral, and then he took a deep-dish peach pie, baked by Mammie, his cook. "I am so sorry, Miss Jo," he said. "I know how lonely you must be now that Miss Kitty is gone." "Lonely," Miss Jo exclaimed, "I am not lonely, and I'm not unhappy. This is the first time in my life I have had coffee made right. Kitty was four years older than me, and, until last week, we always had it her way."

Like Miss Jo, I think about changing the flavor of some things in life. Unlike her, though, no Kitty with a wisdom begot by longer experience blocks me. What stops me from altering the recipe for daily living is custom and her handmaiden anxiety. My ways have hardened, and, instead of attracting, change disturbs me, and I labor to ignore it. Occasionally, though, I stir things up a bit and decide to alter the ingredients of my days. What I usually decide is to become a naturalist, or if not a real naturalist, at least a nature writer. Almost inevitably I make this decision in May, just before Vicki and I and the children leave Connecticut for the remnants of a farm she and her brothers own in Beaver River, Nova Scotia. Fifteen miles up the Bay of Fundy from Yarmouth, the farm consists of an old house with attached outbuildings and barn and about thirty-five acres of meadow, bog, and shoreline. A thriving settlement of farmers and fishermen at the end of the nineteenth century, Beaver River is no longer a community. Consisting of but a score of houses, it is now an out-of-the-way, out-of-date, quiet arm of road. Because the land is not tilled and we are freed from the burdens of sowing and reaping, buying and selling, life on the farm is deceptively and alluringly simple. Far from the bustle of teaching and earning, summers are comfortable, and, as days fold silently one into another, I imagine resigning from the University of Connecticut and moving to Nova Scotia. Because there is little in Beaver River apart from the countryside, I dream about days spent wandering field and shore. Unconsciously I become privy to nature's secrets, and I imagine writing about them. Oddly enough, such thoughts don't lead to a simpler life. Instead they drive me to the bookstore, and, when Vicki and I set out each June for Nova Scotia, crammed into the back of the car is a box filled with information about things natural. This year most of the books were about wildflowers.

My interest in wildflowers took root in April during a visit to Nashville. Whenever I go to Tennessee, I dig through my parents' attic. This time I unearthed *How Plants Grow,* "Botany for Young People and Common Schools," written by one Asa Gray and published in New York in 1858. Gray began his preface by citing the sixth chapter of Matthew: "Consider the lilies of the field, how they grow: they toil not, neither do they spin: and yet I say unto you, that not even Solomon in all his glory was arrayed like one of these." "Our Lord's direct object in the lesson of the lilies was," Gray observed, "to convince the people of God's care for them. Now, this clothing of the earth with plants and flowers—at once so beautiful and so useful, so essential to all animal life—is one of the very ways in which HE takes care of his creatures. And when Christ himself directs us to consider with attention the plants around us,—to notice how they grow,—how varied, how numerous, and how elegant they are, and with what exquisite skill they are fashioned and adorned,— we shall surely find it profitable and pleasant to learn the lessons which they teach." When I found *How Plants Grow,* the semester was almost over. Having endured a winter of dry committee meetings, I was tired of academic Solomons. Already I anticipated wet summer and Beaver River. After reading Gray, I determined to study wildflowers, the daisies and buttercups of the meadow, certain that amid such simple beauty lay deep lessons.

All Nova Scotia seemed in bloom when we arrived, and after unloading the car, I walked slowly around the yard. About the barn were wild roses, tumbling and spilling over each other like fragrant potpourri. On the far side of the well pink and white phlox attracted bumblebees. A golden chaintree stood yellow in the sun at the edge of the meadow; beyond the stone wall in the damp, blue flag bunched together in tall slender clusters. Along the highway ran purple lines of lupin while down the lane toward the beach sheep laurel was about to bloom. The next morning I got up early, and, after bringing in wood from the barn and making a fire in the kitchen stove, I walked three hundred yards down the lane to a bluff overlooking the Bay of Fundy. At first fog hung low and wet, and the day was seamlessly gray. But then as I walked the fog began to blow off, and I noticed pitcher plants and moccasin flowers growing in the deep mosses along the lane. Suddenly the grass seemed silver with spiderwebs, reminding me of linen napkins crumpled and dropped carelessly to the ground at some gay garden party. Brightness leaped from the earth, and, as the fog lifted completely, the meadows were aglow with yellows, purples, reds, and greens, and I began dreaming about being not simply a naturalist but a farmer.

The meadow of dream has little to do with stony reality and its harrows and reapers. I know only one farmer, Jasem, and he lives in a small village on the Syrian coast. Before leaving Connecticut, I received a letter from him. "Now we are preparing ourselves to work in the field," he wrote. "The trees wait us to work. The oranges crop was not good this year because frost. We are living from the income of our field. Trees are like children. They are growing every year. They also need care to grow up in a healthy way. We have two donumes (2000 metre) of small orange trees now. After six years they will share the crop. The tree needs 9 or 10 years to give good crop. At this time it becomes young, but at 30 it will become old." Instead of moving to a large city, Jasem explained, "I stay at home. I prefer to live in wilderness for ever. I feel purgation, simplicity, and freedom in nature. Working in the field makes me glad and good." Now his family owned, he concluded, "one cell of bees, one ewe, and twenty hens and 60 chicks."

Walking back to the house that first morning in Nova Scotia, I remembered Jasem's letter. His words had roots in things, and his thoughts were strong and nourishing. Just before leaving Connecticut, I attended a meeting in which new areas of graduate study were discussed. On my desk at the university lay a proposal for "Adult and Human Resources Education." Forming the core of study were courses such as "Experiential Self-Assessment." "The process of self-assessment in Adult and Human Resources Education," the description stated: "Understanding and assessing personal and occupational experiences in Adult and Human Resources Education and relating these to a plan of study, degree requirements, and professional goals." Being able to cope with what life doles out is important. To do so, however, requires clear vision and a sense of reality with its oranges and chickens. Relying upon abstractions, language like that of the course description lacks a taproot and, instead of sustaining self-knowledge, nurtures withering confusion.

Full of sentiment and an almost righteous good spirit, I began my study of wildflowers. Unfortunately, changing ways hardened by years of soft living requires more than spirit. Besides writing about nature, I planned to lose weight in Nova Scotia. As I celebrated a simple life and studied the natural and the lasting, so, I thought, I would pare my appetite, peeling away all confection. The resolution was short-lived. Two miles from Beaver River in Port Maitland was Edna Churchill's bakery, and when I drove over to buy the children a treat, all thoughts of diet blew away like morning fog. During our first eighteen days in Nova Scotia, Vicki and I and the children ate three chocolate cakes, one fruitcake, two war cakes (a concoction of gingerbread and raisins, heavy as a brick but wonderfully suited to strong tea), two rhubarb pies, one mincemeat pie, two plates of frosted chocolate squares, two pans of chocolate candy larded with marshmallows and nuts, one batch of chocolate chip cookies, and several loaves of brown bread.

The natural world which I imagined while comfortable at my desk in Connecticut resembled Eden. Along its paths I strolled, sniffing and plucking like unfallen Adam, albeit an Adam in shorts. Since there are no poisonous snakes, not even poison ivy, in Nova Scotia, I envisioned hours of dalliance. What was missing from my dream, however, were insects: mosquitoes, black flies, and ticks. Around Beaver River small

farmers have sold their places to people like us, summer folk, "environ-
mentalists" who know little about the environment. As a result pastures
are fast being overgrown. First bay appears, then alder, and finally
spruce. Along with the plants come insects in hordes as bloodthirsty as
those Attila led out of the plains of Asia to prey upon the suburbanites
of Central Europe. Only on the first flower hunt did I wear shorts. After
that I wore a hat, long trousers, and a long-sleeved shirt, buttoned
tightly at the collar and wrists. Having a sweet tooth for children, black
flies made days miserable. Once Vicki counted fourteen bloody, swollen
bites behind the ears and up under the hair of Eliza, our fifteen-month-
old girl. The plague of ticks was even worse. After each walk we took off
our clothes on the side porch and, like monkeys hunting nits, we
searched for ticks. The porch was visible from the highway, and as cars
passed by I wondered if their occupants saw us prancing around naked.

Although they tempered my enthusiasm for things natural, the insects did not drive me inside. Every morning I searched for flowers, and
by noon the kitchen table was covered with specimens and books. Soon
I identified a long list of flowers. Unfortunately, I never went beyond
identity to the lessons Gray mentioned. I was a university professor.
Like the people who drafted the proposal for Adult and Human Resources Education, I inhabited a world in which words were not simply
currency but deeds of the realm. Truth was not so much action as the
description of it, and often what passed for rigorous probing of complexity was airy, wordy illusion. Still, the names of flowers were colorful
and had almost magical lives of their own. In the names was poetry, I
said to justify my inability to dig beneath words. As proof I often made
up lists and read them aloud: yarrow, devil's paintbrush, everlasting,
eyebright, starflower, swamp candle, garden speedwell, bugle, yellow
rattle, meadow sweet, angelica, and dame's rocket. Occasionally when
identifying a flower was difficult and I consulted three or four books, I
told myself that I was doing original research. Whenever I found deli-
cate flowers whose names seemed bumbling consorts, I felt a rush of
pleasure, almost as if I unearthed forgotten truth. Frequently I renamed
the flower. Hedge bindweed, a pink and white member of the morning
glory family, became riverwater pink. Of course in celebrating names
for themselves, I dissociated them from flowers. Consequently I was
rarely able to pin the correct name on a flower two days after first identifying it. Happily, Francis, my five-year-old, did better. He remembered
the flowers and drew pictures of them, often with bees or butterflies

hovering about. One night he gave me drawings of five butterflies. The blue butterfly, he told me, was named sky; the yellow, sun; the pink, rose; the green, stem; and the purple one, dark cloud. In thinking about the drawings now, I find myself hoping, like so many fathers before me, that my son will accomplish what I could not.

Throughout the summer, I identified flowers. But aware I was not suited to study natural things, I no longer considered writing about nature and began spending more time inside, not in the house, however, but in the barn. With thick seven-inch beams running like roots above ground, our barn was a comparatively simple functional structure of loft and stall. Despite the weakness for words, I have little use for abstraction, and the barn attracted me almost as much as the imaginary nature which I created in Connecticut. Of course the barn's function had changed. No longer did it house animals. Gone were the oxen and work horses, Ayrshires and Belgians, bigger than myth. Gone were hay and manure and the heavy sweet breath of cows. The only animals I saw in the barn were a family of red squirrels and then a prowling yellow cat. Near the end of the summer the cat was killed on the road in front of our house. The death puzzled Edward, our three-year-old. When he saw the body, he asked me why the cat had not been buckled in a car seat. I told him car seats for animals did not exist. "When I get a dog," he said later, "I won't go anywhere because there are no dog seats in cars and no dog seats in restaurants."

The floorboards of the barn were loose and moved up and down like keys on a piano. Rubbing against each other, they moaned, playing, like the barn itself, a discordant but human tune. Containing fragments of things, the barn resembled memory, a storehouse of oddments, worth little to society but invaluable to an individual. Everything in the barn measured man and men. Although oxen had disappeared, memories of them and their owners remained: shoes nailed to beams, bells hanging from a wall, and a red head yoke used in ox hauls. In the stalls was a jumble of lumber and bricks, wire, broken glass, and nails—the remains of hours of repair. Each summer on the side of a stall, Vicki's parents marked her and her brothers' heights. In 1953 the banker was forty-five inches tall; in 1954 Vicki was thirty-two and three-quarter inches "With Shoes!" In 1956 the lawyer was forty-five and five-eighths inches. Before the summer ended, Vicki and I added the names and heights of Francis, Edward, and Eliza to the markings on the stall. Although the barn contained mounds of clutter, its contents were finite.

From days of exploring the out-of-doors, I took away awareness of my ignorance and the knowledge that I could never break through the green surface of things to the rich dirt below. In just two weeks I sifted through the contents of the barn. Before going to Nova Scotia I hoped that studying nature would somehow transport me beyond ordinary concerns. Now, digging through the piles in the barn, I was happy, deep in the stuff of daily living.

From a clump of rusting gears, tools, tin cans, and old tea kettles, I removed a black glue pot and a crimping iron with "Geneva Hand Fluter" stamped on it and packed them in a box to take home to use as doorstops. Not everything I thought about using was usable. With the bedrooms in our house upstairs and the only lavatory downstairs, Nova Scotia nights can be inconvenient. And when I found an ironstone chamber pot, I carried it inside to Vicki, saying our nighttime difficulties were over. Vicki did not agree. Observing that I might have an accident carrying the pot downstairs, she told me to return it to the barn. Several boxes of china were in the barn, and in the loft was a set which we eventually used for meals. On the plates in green and white was the Turkish equivalent of the blue and white Willow Pattern design. In the far distance was a mountain; before it ran the Bosphorus. At water's edge stood a summer palace with a pagodalike roof and minarets hanging miraculously above it in the air. In front of the palace sat a workman and a fisherman, both wearing robes and fezes. While they talked the fisherman held a rod, and the workman's hands rested on a pole, at the ends of which were thick, heavy bags.

Unlike the out-of-doors, the face of the barn was human. In a trunk of old clothes were two prints. Published by Currier and Ives, the first was entitled "Little Sarah" and depicted a round-faced little girl with stovepipe curls. In her arms she held a marble cat. Wearing a blue dress with lace around wrists and neck and with a blue bow, bigger than a peony, Sarah was cuteness, the picture which parents try to take of daughters on bright Sunday mornings just before church. Published in London in 1808 by William Holland, number eleven Cockspur Street, the other print was "Young Burns at the Grave of His Father." Young Burns's knees were almost as plump as Little Sarah's cheeks. Wearing a kilt, he stood by his father's tombstone, a buttery little man holding his book and reciting poetry. Wildflowers never made me smile, but the contents of the barn, things like the prints, often made me grin. Take the humbug out of life, Josh Billings said, and you won't have much left to do business with. Quite right, and for that matter there won't be much left to make a person laugh. Happily humbugs nested throughout the barn, making it a jovial place. From under lumber in a stall, I dug up an old trunk. Lining the inside of the trunk were advertisements and newspapers. One end of the trunk was completely covered by a poster for "OLD PARR'S PILLS." The paper was black; outlined in the center in white was the face of the Ancient of Days. Forming an oval frame around the face were the words "Caution Beware of Imitation." Tom Parr was the British Methuselah. In 1635 the earl of Arundel brought him to London as a curiosity. Unfortunately curiosity killed poor Tom, and he died in London, supposedly at age one hundred and fifty-two or one hundred and sixty, there being disagreement on the matter. On his corpse humbug flourished as quacksalvers, promising an eternity of days, sold Parr's Pills.

The papers lining the trunk were pages from the *Halifax Times* of February 29, 1848. Humbug did a good business in them too, as advertisements urged readers to buy "Mrs. Gardner's Indian Balsam of Liverwort" and "Dr. Lemuel Warren's Enamel Tooth Powders." Half a column contained accounts of the "Astonishing Efficacy" of Holloway's ointment in curing "a Case of Ringworm of Four Years Standing" or "Dreadful Ulcerous Sores on the Face and Leg in Prince Edward Island." Most of the patent medicines advertised were versatile and cured a variety of ailments. "SIGHT RESTORED," one notice proclaimed, then added, "Nervous Headache and Deafness Cured by the Use of GRIMSTONE'S SNUFF." Although the bite of the humbug may swell, it doesn't hurt like that of the black fly. Instead of itching, all it leaves behind is a silly feeling. I was bitten when I found what appeared to be a very old letter glued to the side of the trunk. When English professors are not dreaming of leaving the university world, they imagine discovering a long-lost manuscript, one which will catapult them into instant renown. I peeled the letter carefully off the trunk and, taking it inside, began reading it with a magnifying glass. "I have sent thee a thing, such a one as the gentlefolks call a loveletter," I read. "It was written in the Roman joining hand by the schoolmaster who is clerk of the parish, to whom I gave sixpence for his pains." For a moment I thought a really old letter alive with memorable rustics lay before me, and I quickly scanned the page. Alas, what I read was not a letter but a schoolbook exercise in penmanship. Following the signature of "trusty Hodge the ploughman" were a tall tale set in Arkansas and a mildly bawdy account of a barrister traveling in a coach with a "pretty quakerress."

Although Francis accompanied me on walks, studying flowers was a comparatively solitary activity. Identification of a flower rarely led to the populated world of people and story. Made, sold, and used by man, the contents of the barn were associated with a village of anecdotes. In the barn was a carriage, most probably built by Perry Weebe, who owned a carriage shop on the Green Cove Road between Port Maitland and Beaver River. Weebe was a fine craftsman, and story has it that the only thing he ever made that wasn't good was his marriage. A mild, self-effacing man, Weebe seemed destined for comfortable bachelorhood. But then one cold winter he surprised Port Maitland by marrying Bertha Shifney from an inland sawmill and potato family near Hectanooga. In appearance Bertha was as soft as a hot-buttered roll. In character she was as sharp as the blade on a six-foot saw. Within a month after she moved in above the carriage shop, she held the whip hand or, more accurately, the car-pet sweeper hand. Whenever she was angry at Weebe, which was fairly often, she chased him about with a wooden carpet sweeper. Once she drove him under the kitchen table at lunch time and refused to let him out until after she had eaten. Halfway through the lunch, Weebe looked up from under the table. "What," Bertha exclaimed, lifting the sweeper, "do you dare peep out?" "Yes," Weebe answered, retreating back under the table, "I do, and I will peep as long as I am a man."

Although Bertha could neither read nor write, she did not let illit-eracy stand in her way and took it upon herself to provide unwanted advice. Whenever she heard that a ship carrying seamen from Port Mait-land was expected home after a long voyage, she visited the sailors' houses and gave their wives baskets of cucumbers, which she said "cooled carnal lust." When Peggy Doane reached fifteen and showed every sign of growing into a buxom woman like her mother, Bertha gave Mrs. Doane several bunches of lady's mantle, explaining that the plant kept "maidens' dugs from becoming great and flappy." On learning that Mrs. Coaldwell, president of the Port Maitland Stitch and Chatter Club, was a bird-watcher, Bertha attended a meeting of the Stitch and Chatter. When all the ladies were comfortably settled around the room working on a quilt, Bertha asked Mrs. Coaldwell if she knew why birds didn't evacuate "by urine." "The creature," Bertha explained before Mrs. Coald-well recovered her composure, "the creature, whatever it is, that don't suck, don't piss." Bertha outlived Weebe, and on his death ordered a monument from his brother Travis, who owned the Yarmouth Marble Works. Travis spent care on the stone, decorating it with roses and lilies, and then cherubs blowing trumpets. Knowing that Bertha had made his brother's life difficult and aware that she could not read, Travis also took pains with the inscription. "Rest in Peace," it read, "Until I Come."

This story might be apocryphal. I looked for Weebe's stone in the Port Maitland cemetery but couldn't find it. On the other hand, Bertha was just strong-willed enough to bury Weebe away from his people and alongside hers in Hectanooga. I did not visit the graveyard there; Hectanooga was a longish drive, and I was too busy in the barn. Actually, at the time I was outside following Mrs. Coaldwell's lead and watching birds. Unlike the study of wildflowers, the barn expanded my interests, and often it seemed that the whole universe, including all things natural, could be found in a pile of clutter. In a carton of books was an account Vicki's father kept of the birds he saw in the early 1950s. On August 20, 1951, he wrote, "This afternoon a flock of nighthawks overhead, appearing late just as last year. Also, as last year the sparrows have gathered in great quantities in the north wind-break whether in preparation for migration or because of the oats in George Hall's meadow I do not know." "Birds very rare this year," he wrote on July 1, 1954, "the catbirds much friendlier than ever before, hopping about lawn and bushes close at hand. Goldfinches in great abundance and exceedingly friendly—they make a lovely sight, swaying in the tall red-dock in the uncut meadows." After reading the diary, I watched birds for several days. I saw a kingfisher hovering above a stream and learned to identify the lonely cries of willets as they hunted along the beach at low tide. I found a raven's nest and followed a Canada jay as he flew from tree to tree through wet spruce woods.

In the carton along with the diary were seventeen volumes of the Nature Library, published by Doubleday and Page in 1920. The Library included studies of grasses, moths, frogs, fish, trees, and mosses and lichens. Entitled *Game Birds, Bird Homes,* and *Bird Neighbors,* three of the books focused on bird life. These volumes didn't interest me, however; and the only book I removed from the barn was *The Spider Book,* a weighty 700-page study. By the time I began looking at the Nature Library, I had practically stopped watching birds. Not only was poor sight preventing me from seeing much, but I began bird-watching too late in life for peace of mind. As I grow older, thoughts of anything flying, birds or time, frighten me, and I am more comfortable around and sympathetic to things stationary. In the corners of almost all of the windows about the house were spider webs. After dinner Edward and I carried chairs outside and watched spiders repairing webs. Although we eventually decided most were gray cross spiders, we had trouble fixing identities. Despite its great size, *The Spider Book* was not very helpful. Not only was it out of date, ignoring the brown recluse and maintaining the black widow was harmless, but it did not contain color plates. Instead of, however, undermining Edward's enthusiasm, the lack of pictures increased it. Saying he was going to be a Spider Man when he grew up, he drew a group of colorful bugs and inserted them into the book.

Gradually I paid less attention to spiders, and after a few evenings on the porch returned to the barn, itself a kind of spiderweb, along whose strands hung not dried husks of insects but lively remnants of Nova Scotia life. In the nineteenth century shipbuilding was important in Beaver River, and many villagers were seamen. Although years had almost washed away practically all traces of their activity along the beach, their footprints were still visible in the barn's dusty sands of time. Here and there were buoys, barrels for shipping fish, bits of netting, coils of rope, spikes, hooks, lobster pots, rigging blocks for sailing ships, and pictures—pictures of captains, always young and serious, and pictures of crews, tough and hardy. In one picture eleven men posed on deck of a three-masted sailing ship. In back of them loomed the main mast; behind it on an upper deck were two lifeboats upside down, looking like turtles in their shells. Two of the men wore leather aprons; one had a mallet. All were in their twenties, and most wore rough work shirts, heavy boots, suspenders, and thick woolen trousers. Also in the barn was a seaman's chest with handles made out of wood and thick coils of rope. Inside was a rotten yellow sheet on which was woven "Royal Mail Steam Packet Cobequid." During a storm on January 13, 1914, the *Cobequid* struck Trinity Ledge off Port Maitland. The ship was doomed, but, before it broke up, local scavengers had a field day, and for years many families in Port Maitland ate off of *Cobequid* plates and slept on *Cobequid* linen.

Besides pushing me outward to community, the barn turned my thoughts inward. There, much like the barn's very contents, lay memories buried under an accumulation of years. Like the wreck of the *Cobequid*, they were not so much forgotten as neglected, and just a little digging or a chance remark was all that was needed to bring them to the surface. After they had gone through the rigging and the nets and had selected things for their treasure chests, Francis and Edward asked me to take them fishing. Practically without thinking, I said, "No, boys, I am sorry. Daddy's fishing days are over." "And well over," I thought, remembering my first trip to Nova Scotia. In 1969 I was a member of the Princeton Tuna Team, as we called ourselves. Each year the Nova Scotia Department of Tourism ran the "World's Intercollegiate Deep-Sea Fishing Championship." Ten or twelve universities sent teams. For the most part the teams were sponsored by undergraduate outing clubs. Somehow, though, the Princeton team had slipped into the hands of graduate students, and every spring six or seven stalwart, deep-drinking aspiring professors headed for Yarmouth and three dry days of floating on the water and three wet nights of drowning on land. Ostensibly the teams fished for tuna; unfortunately, the tuna had almost disappeared from waters off Nova Scotia, and few were ever caught. In the contest, though, every pound of fish counted and, after making token attempts to catch tuna, teams spent their days jigging cod off the bottom.

The first day of the contest went easily. We dozed in the sun, ate lobsters, and caught forty-nine pounds of fish, a total which put us an expected and comfortable last in the championship. On the second day we also caught forty-nine pounds of fish and made ourselves at home in last place. That, though, is all the two days had in common. When we left Wedgeport that morning, small craft warnings were out. Within an hour we were draped over the gunnels. It was the second sickest I have ever been, and I spent hours praying that our boat would founder on the Rock of Ages and pitch me into that land where small craft warnings never fly and all sailing is smooth. Thankfully, the third morning of the contest broke sunny and calm, and we went to sea, cheerfully expecting to eat more lobster, perfect our tans, and catch another forty-nine pounds of fish. Things did not go according to expectation. Around noon we sailed into a university of cod. Contest rules stated that only four members of a team could fish at one time. Such a rule, we quickly decided, was for landsmen and maybe for the other teams, but not for old salts like us. Within minutes all of us, including the captain and his mate, were jigging cod up from the bottom. That afternoon we caught over fifteen hundred pounds of fish, setting a record for a single day's catch and in the process rising from the lower depths to steal the contest.

After our return to New Jersey, the Nova Scotia Department of Tourism invited us to a banquet in Philadelphia and presented us with blue blazers monogrammed with the Nova Scotia coat of arms, a shield supported on one side by a unicorn and on the other by a Micmac Indian. Traffic was heavy and the drive from Princeton was choppy. An open bar, though, soon poured oil on our nerves and the evening began smoothly. Alas, just as I was pushing off under two whiskey sours, an official told me that dinner was going to be served in fifteen minutes. Warning that becalming speeches lay ahead, he advised me to turn back to port and load up on rum, "unless, of course, you don't mind the doldrums." Not one to neglect the advice of an experienced sailor, I tacked over and took three stiff ones aboard, enough, I reckoned, to enable me to steam through any and all speeches.

Unfortunately, my seaman friend made a navigational error. Instead of fifteen minutes, dinner was an hour and fifteen minutes away. By the time fruit cocktail appeared on the horizon, I had lost my rudder, and the first sip of wine knocked me on my beam ends and I slid slowly out of my chair into the dark beneath the table. Once there a transformation occurred. All the rigging of manners washed away, and miraculously I turned into a fish, most certainly a cod, and spent the rest of the meal wiggling along the floor, rising from the grit only to nibble thin ankles and shapely calves. From the deck above several fishermen tried to jig me up, but they were not members of the "World's Intercollegiate Deep-Sea Fishing Championship" team and had little luck with a wary fish like me. Not until crème caramel and coffee floated above did I break surface. By then I felt like a fish out of water and could only breathe hard, stare goggle-eyed, and wave my tongue at the dessert. "What ho," my friend Frank said, when I beached myself in a chair, "here is the Ancient Mariner." Would that I could have traded places with the mariner. Compared to the things that wiggled across my vision, the sea snakes that so upset the mariner were things of beauty. To have had an albatross around my neck would have been a joy. Woe, alack, the albatross was nesting in my stomach. Not only that—he was fluttering about testing his wings. Later that evening outside a doughnut shop in New Hope, Pennsylvania, he took to the air, leaving me the sickest I have ever been. "Yes, yes, indeed, boys," I said to Francis and Edward, "my fishing days are over."

The farm buildings in Nova Scotia were linked like houses in the old nursery rhyme beginning, "Big House, Little House, Back House, Barn." Joining the little house or kitchen to the barn, the back house traditionally contained the tool room and shop and, at the end farthest from the kitchen, the privy. Many important activities took place in the back house. Harnesses and tools were repaired, and, if the farmer had a business, he ran it from a shop in the back house. Almost as long as the barn but not so wide, our back house had become the shed. Although tools were kept in the shop, the privy was filled in, and the shed was a storehouse for things too good for the barn. Without a loft, the back house did not convey the barn's open, expansive feeling. After rain, smells rose from the wood and clung heavily to the boards. When I walked through the back house on damp mornings to fetch firewood from the barn, I smelled age and decay and sometimes imagined that death lurked in a dark corner. Actually, I had good cause. Along one wall of the back house was a shelf of poisons: Flit, Hudson Spray Dust, Black Flag Sprayer, Slug Bait, Rose Dust, DETH Rat-Mouse Exterminator, and something chillingly labeled Bordeaux Mixture.

Once I finished examining the barn's contents, I turned my attention to the back house. More like an attic than a shed, the back house was such a conglomeration of flowerpots and watering cans, scythes and hand mowers, that I seemed to spend more time climbing than walking and digging. Almost immediately I found a wooden carpet sweeper, probably the very kind Bertha used on Weebe. Sold by W. L. Harding, "Dealer in Crockery China Silver and Plated Ware," the sweeper was decorated with yellow stenciling: dots, triangles, circles, and things which sometimes resembled flowers and other times birds. In a washtub were two table clocks, one dated 1840 and made by Daniel Pratt, Jr., of Reading, Massachusetts, the other undated but manufactured by the New Haven Clock Company of New Haven, Connecticut. Ranged along one end of the back house and blocking the door to the privy were several iron stoves. The most ornate was the "No. 233 Orient," made in 1888 by the Burrell Johnson Iron Company in Yarmouth. Above one another on each side of the fireplace were three yellowish ceramic profiles of children. The bottom profile was that of a Roman girl with hair bound behind her head; over her was an Elizabethan wearing a ruff collar and with a wreath entwined in her hair. Above her was the modern girl, Little Sarah adorned with bonnet, lace, and sentiment.

One of the most intriguing items I found was a hatbox, woven out of birchbark with latches made from reeds. Inside the box was a brown scrap of paper. On it in a formal nineteenth-century hand was written "Clara Jolly." Probably she was one of the Jollys from Sunrise, a family of hard-drinking, shiftless men and capable, strong-willed women. Clara might have been the sister of Pate Jolly, who worked for Weebe until Bertha appeared and chased him off, saying he had a bad influence on Weebe and was doing "the devil's own handiwork." Known around Port Maitland as "Addle," Pate was not evil; he was just simple. Simplicity, however, never corked a jug; and about once every fortnight, Pate got dead drunk. One Friday he took a wagon of lumber to Yarmouth. As could be expected, he used the occasion to pick up a keg of rum. By the time he got to Sandford, he was so drunk that he tumbled over his seat into the back of the wagon and fell asleep. While he was out, somebody stole his team of horses. The next morning when he came round, he peered over the seat and, not seeing any horses, supposedly said, "Either I am Pate Jolly, or I am not Pate Jolly. If I am Pate Jolly, then I have lost two horses. If I'm not Pate Jolly, then, by God, I have found a wagon."

The back house was crammed with things waiting to be found, many like the hatbox, fermenting with intoxicating stories. After opening the hatbox, though, and thinking about Pate, I stopped exploring. Although the summer was not entirely successful and I had not become a naturalist, the summer was not a failure either. The contents of barn and back house now attracted me as much as, maybe even more than, the out-of-doors. Their contents, though, were finite. Once I had gone through and studied them, I knew I probably would not return to them. And so, deciding to save the back house for another summer, I stopped digging and began spending more time on the beach, poking about in tidal pools, trying to learn something about periwinkles and limpets, watching the shore birds—sandpipers, whimbrels, turnstones, sanderlings, and cormorants—and more than anything else waiting for the glorious August flowers: purple orchis, skullcap, jewelweed, seaside goldenrod, little hop clover, and riverwater pink.

May Days

L IKE ROBINS hunting for earthworms early in the morning, the girl was a sign of spring. The long white dress washed around her, ebbed, clung for a moment, and then fell away in the breeze. As she walked along the path, she carried her shoes in her left hand. Soundlessly her heels touched the ground; then with a pat the balls of her feet smacked down, pushing small brown clouds of dust out over her toes. In her unconscious sensuality, the girl was part of budding May, that quiet contemplative moment when all the greens are softly tinged with yellow and every day seems light blue. In the silence of that morning, though, raucous days were gathering. Just ahead were redwing blackbirds posturing on fence posts and the deep purple blooms of iris, their throats yellow and busy with bees.

A week later when my friend Neil and I were jogging, we found a dildo on the shoulder of the Gurleyville Road. " 'Tis the season to be jolly," Neil exclaimed and stopped. On our runs Neil and I come upon many things; usually they are not so jolly. In March and April we see dead squirrels; in May broken groundhogs and opossums; and in August the bodies of small garter snakes. The snakes always startle me, and I jump aside. Later I feel sad and somehow diminished. Although its size gave me a qualm or two, the dildo did not sadden. Instead it provoked curiosity, and Neil and I turned it over with a stick. For a while I thought about wrapping it in a leaf of skunk cabbage and taking it home. "To plant in the garden between the tulips and windflowers," I told Neil. "Once I water it and cover it with peat moss, there's no telling what it will do." The Gurleyville Road, though, is narrow, and Neil and I run single file. Since he is faster, Neil always runs ahead of me. Although the skunk cabbage would have protected my hand, I could not find a leaf big enough to hide all the dildo. What would people think, I wondered, if they saw me running after Neil with the dildo in my hand? They would probably think I was chasing him trying to poke him in the behind. Better at my age, I concluded, to keep such things out of hand

and out of mind, and I left the dildo on the shoulder of the road. The next day it was gone; the busy time of May, however, was upon us with all its heat and in all its force.

Like daffodils, UPS trucks suddenly appeared outside every house in my neighborhood. The woman next door ordered a closet of new shoes, and Tom, the delivery man, practically became a resident of our street. Telephone calls interrupted every dinner. The *Hartford Courant* urged me to subscribe. If I visited a condominium on Cape Cod, I was told, I stood a good chance of winning a new car and was practically assured of a color television or at least a set of designer luggage. Investment houses knew just what I should do with my savings, and insurance companies advised me to buy an annuity. Jacques Cousteau explained that important new environmental studies depended upon people like me renewing our memberships. In order to confirm the information they had received, the publishers of two college directories called and in the process suggested I buy their leather-bound volumes. Increasing my gift, World Wildlife informed me, would buy more time for the gorilla while Mothers Against Drunk Drivers sent me a ring for my car keys. Like a bud swelling in the noonday heat, my mailbox burst with catalogues: Banana Republic, Vermont Country Store, Old Pueblo Traders, Gump's, the Crow's Nest Book Shop, Williams-Sonoma, Childcraft, Johnny Appleseed's, Land's End, the Metropolitan Museum of Art, and then—forwarded from old addresses and sent to me, to Vicki, and to Vicki's mother—six L. L. Bean summer catalogues.

I renewed memberships, donated to colleges and charities, and read catalogues and, since the sound of the UPS truck pulling into the driveway always excites me, I bought some things. Mostly I bought flowers; during May I ordered one hundred and seventy-two dollars and eighty-five cents' worth of flowers from Breck's. This October I will have three hundred and thirty-four bulbs to plant: one hundred and six tulips, a hundred and two iris, and one hundred and twenty-six daffodils of sundry hues and names: pistachio, Salome, Jules Verne, Limerick, sweet charity, and ice follies. Spending so much on flowers did not come easily, but May was in the air.

During the fall I write a great deal, almost, it sometimes seems, in an effort to hold winter at bay. In spring I stop writing and, instead of fending off cold mortality with words, I tend to the yard. I rake leaves off the periwinkle so rust won't set in, and in May when days are warm enough, I plant the Easter lily. So birds will be able to line their nests with soft

material, Vicki fetches the lint she has saved from the dryer in the basement. In the backyard she sticks it loosely on chicken wire which I have
wrapped around a big shagbark hickory. Around the middle of the
month I remove the Havaheart mousetrap from the attic and store it in
the garage. From Thompson and Sons in Mansfield Depot, I buy fertilizer, grass seed, and hay to cover the bare spots in the yard. And this
year I purchased flowers from Breck's. I didn't spend all the money at
once; I made four separate orders and by doing so created the fiction
that I considered each purchase carefully. Down one side of my yard
runs a small, shady dell; each year I plant flowers in it. Sometimes I
wander through woods searching for wildflowers like Jacob's ladder
which I can dig up and bring home. Other times I buy from nurseries.
In early May flowers attract me like budding girls and, sitting on a rise
just above the dell, I look down through the yard and dream of colors
forever blowing in the breeze. Every spring I struggle against the urge to
buy a wild profusion of flowers, much, I suppose, as I struggle against
barefoot beauty. Somehow I know that everything May proffers should
not be seized. The good gardener, and man, always leaves gaps for next
year's flowers. Still, when Vicki read our checkbook, she said, "You sure
spent a lot on flowers; next year I am going to hide the Breck's catalogue." Anyone who writes, even if he doesn't write much in spring, can
always fashion a fictional response, and I was ready for Vicki. "Don't
worry about the money," I said, "I am going to write an article about
flowers and then deduct them from the income tax as a business
expense."

May is a time of beginnings. After reading the Sears catalogue, I decided to order new trousers and then, after talking to Vicki, determined
to lose weight. "I don't want to be married to a man with a thirty-eight-
inch waist," Vicki told me when I filled out the Sears order. May is also
the month for second marriages, not the fabled May-December marriage
but the May-October marriage. In June the marriages of young brides
and grooms crowd church calendars. In May a few dates are always
available for girls embarking on first marriages with older men. Making
plans as ornate as their dreams, decorated with frilly cakes, white dresses,
and sunny island honeymoons, the bride explains to her husband to be,
"I am only getting married once, and I want to do it right." Having been
divorced, the groom would prefer the county clerk's office to the chapel,
but he goes along with the plans. Before the marriage he spends evenings stripping off the wallpaper he and his first wife hung in the house

twenty years ago. At fifty, the future holds little mystery for him. Love and life seem fragile, and he would have preferred something more impressionistic on the walls. Nevertheless, he hangs the paper the bride selected, an early American pattern, stamped with clean solid images of domesticity: a farm house surrounded by tall trees and a long yard full of children and a dog, a high wagon being pulled by big horses along a shady country lane, and a broad field stretching out to a horizon of clouds, haycocks, and a brown reaper.

May days are also the time of college graduations. In a scrapbook I found an invitation to the "Commencement Exercises" of Cedar Bluff Female College in Woodburn, Kentucky. The exercises were held on May 13, 1888, and there were seven graduates: five from Texas and one each from Indiana and Kentucky. Would that I could attend such a small ceremony. I am tired of big graduations and of hearing thriving, well-connected people describe the ills of society, all of which, they say, can be cured with a strong dose of cash. In general, May makes me content with things as they are, and I tolerate mistakes. Last Sunday at 6:45 in the morning the telephone rang. "I am calling from Danielson, Connecticut," a woman said when I answered. "Would you play the 'Polish Lullaby' for Florida?" At another time in the year, the wrong number would have irritated me, but not in May. Still, although the season dulls my reactions to simple mistakes, it sharpens my exasperation with people who don't look about themselves and who think the things they haven't got are the only things worth having. At a recent graduation address which assured students that there was little good in the world as it now existed, I thought about stealing a few lines from George Washington Harris and asking the speaker a question. "Is the fool-killer in your part of the country doing his duty," I wanted to say, "or is he dead?" "What?" the speaker answers. "I have never heard of such a person." "That's what I thought," I say, turning away abruptly. Of course I did not say anything. I just went home and planted perennials in the dell.

In a commencement is the ambivalence of ending and beginning. Some of this ambivalence is in May itself. Near the end of April my father always becomes despondent and, after telling me that Pickerings die in May, provides me with instructions for his funeral. This year I telephoned Father at the end of May. "Daddy," I said, "I have gone through all the family bibles and have discovered you are wrong. Pickerings don't always die in May; they die in every month." Oddly enough, the information did not shore Father up, and all he said was, "Small comfort." Attitudes toward May used to be more ambivalent than they are today. When I was a boy, May was prelude to hot summer and the polio season. Early in June my mother and I left Nashville and went to my grandfather's farm deep in the Virginia countryside. We stayed there until just before school began in the fall. In late August Father drove up from Tennessee to take us home. One summer there was a late outbreak of polio. Wytheville, Virginia, was particularly hard hit. The road from Nashville to Richmond ran through Wytheville. Before reaching Wytheville, Father rolled up the car windows. Somehow, though, as he drove through town a June bug got into the car. Once beyond Wytheville, Father lowered his window, and the June bug flew away. When Mother heard about the bug, however, she would not let me get into the car until after the inside had been scrubbed then wiped off with rubbing alcohol.

With the end of polio epidemics, May has grown benign. On May 8 Francis, my older boy, was five, and the next week Vicki and I took him to Northwest School for a kindergarten orientation. As we looked at him, skinny and eager in his new sneakers, red shorts, and crisp blue and red striped shirt, we were proud yet apprehensive and sad: sad because our little boy is growing up and years seem to be running away from us like rain into dry ground, apprehensive because Francis is a gentle, sweet child, too sweet, maybe, for bus and playground. When he finds a green inchworm on the driveway, Francis picks it up and puts it in the grass. Neither Vicki nor I care if he learns anything useful; all we hope is that he will get through unscathed, something we know is impossible.

Memory which grows dimmer year by year burned white when I entered the school. The halls seemed unchanged from those I walked forty years ago. Outside each room was a familiar line of coathooks, each with a child's name written on tape and pasted above it. Along the walls were pictures of fat orange teddy bears and thin purple cats. The kindergarten room itself was warmly cluttered, and much of my anxiety fell away when I saw the jumble of books, watercolors, crayons, games, and musical instruments: a set of drums, two xylophones, and a tambourine like the one I played at Mrs. Little's when I was five. In the windows were an anthouse, an aquarium teeming with tadpoles, and a tray of small paper cups, each with a plant sprouting in it. Forty years ago the plants were zinnias. At the end of the school year, students took them home and gave them to their parents, gifts that led to some frustration as mothers and fathers carefully nursed the plants through the summer into bloom.

Francis sat down at a low table. When a brown-haired little girl sat next to him, he didn't look up. "Ah, my boy, you'll have to do better than that," I thought, "if you want your shoes tied." Then I remembered that Francis's sneakers used Velcro instead of laces, a real improvement upon the past. Until the second grade I could not tie my shoes and, before going to school for the first time, I made myself sick, worrying about what would happen if my shoes came untied. And untied they came, but happily Linda was assigned the chair next to mine at the table. Linda was my first-grade angel, and whenever I stumbled back from recess, laces dragging, she bent over and tied them for me without saying a word. Suddenly Francis looked up and, smiling, said something to the little girl beside him. When she smiled back, I knew Francis would be all right, and in my mind's eye the little plants in the window grew into giant zinnias, red and yellow in the bright sunlight. A little later the children went outside and got on a school bus for a trip around the block. When Francis and the little girl sat beside each other, Vicki and I held hands, glad that May had arrived.

Old Papers

I HAVE NEVER subscribed to a newspaper. Every six months or so, the *Hartford Courant* offers me a ninety-day trial subscription. I always turn the offer down, saying newsprint is so dirty that I would have to wear blue jeans and rubber gloves to read the paper. "I don't like to scratch my nose and later look in the mirror and discover 'Libya' and 'Margaret Thatcher' printed on it," I explain and hang up. I don't really have anything against newspapers; not reading them is just part of a general indifference to current affairs. Our radio is broken, and I would not own a television if Edward's birth had been easier. My wife Vicki and I have not given each other presents for years, and when Edward disagreed with her about entering the world and argued with her long and hard, I wanted to perk her up. Aside from a pocketbook or an umbrella, neither of which seemed adequate, I couldn't think of anything to give her except a television.

Of course, not keeping current can be embarrassing. Not long ago in a telephone conversation with a friend in Sewanee, I asked what was happening at the college. "Giving an honorary degree to Bush," he said, "has caused turmoil. The Secret Service is everywhere, telling us to do this and not do that." I was puzzled; the only Bush I could recall was a literary critic, and I thought he died years ago. Even if he were still alive, critics rarely, I thought, received much attention from the Secret Service. "What Bush are you talking about?" I asked. "George Bush," my friend answered. Even that was not enough information. "I am afraid you have left me in the dark," I said. "What does George Bush do?" "Don't worry about it," Vicki said that night when I told her about the conversation. "Politicians come and go. How many vice-presidents can you name from the 1920s and 1930s?" she asked. "See?" she said, when I could not name one. "It's not important. Shame on Sewanee for wasting a degree."

Keeping up is distasteful to me, and I prefer the company of people who are out of date. Indifferent to modernity and rarely prey to hustling, fretful ego, such people put me at ease. Not only that, but they themselves become subjects of stories, not brittle stories that whet the mind but gentle tales that soothe. Years ago Harriet Tilly was one of the most active women in Carthage, Tennessee. Head of the Christian League, associate matron of the Eastern Star, and president of the Carthage Garden Society, Mrs. Tilly was present at every community gathering. Except to go to the bank or see about his insurance, her husband Anable Tilly rarely came to town. Content to grow tobacco, he left, as he put it, "all the gadding about to Harriet." Forever worried whether or not he had enough insurance, he visited my grandfather four times a year to discuss policies. On those days, he brought his lunch and after taking care of business sat in Grandfather's office and visited with everyone who dropped in. One winter Mrs. Tilly, along with the Kettlewoods, the Merrithews, and Widow Tinkham, decided to go to New York on the theater train from Nashville. Mr. Tilly didn't want to go. With some misgivings, Mrs. Tilly left, not without, however, leaving him the telephone number of the Biltmore Hotel, where she was staying. At dinner time four days after his wife left, Mr. Tilly appeared at Grandfather's house. "A man came by the farm and told me I needed lightning rods on the tobacco barn," he said after Grandfather invited him in. "I want to talk to Harriet and see what she thinks," he said, "but I don't know how to reach her. All she left me was a piece of paper with a number on it." "What you have to do, Anable," Grandfather explained, "is call that number on the telephone and ask for Harriet." Mr. Tilly paused, looked down at the number, and then looked up at Grandfather and said, "Gracious, is Harriet that well known? I knew that everybody in Carthage, even folks in Red Boiling Springs and Gordonsville, knew her, but I didn't know that people in New York knew her too."

Too many stories in newspapers seem significant; they are for people trying to learn something or get somewhere. They are not for people just thankful to be where they are. To me the best stories are not meaningful or informative; they simply brighten the fleeting moment. Sometime ago when E. W. B. Childers was fishing off the bridge over Difficult Creek, he caught a small catfish with a white mark the shape of a foot on its head. Normally, E. W. threw little fish back, but the mark was unique, and he took the fish home to show to his wife Mae and their two boys Juba and Origin. After showing it to the boys, E. W. was going to throw the fish out, but Origin had read about an aquarium in his school reader and he asked his father if they could keep the fish in a washtub in the woodshed. Mae didn't object, so E. W. tossed it in the tub, and for the rest of the summer Juba and Origin fed it, first worms and grasshoppers and then slops as the weather turned chilly. The fish ate everything: orange peels, chicken bones and once, after Juba misbehaved and was sent away from the table before dessert, a piece of strawberry shortcake with whipped cream on top.

Throughout the winter the children played with the fish, dropping it on the ground many times. The fish was hardy, though, and thrived on exercise and kitchen leavings. By March it had grown so big that E. W. put it in the rain barrel. Jumping out of the barrel was easy, and by late spring the fish was spending more time out of water than in. On warm days it liked nothing better than stretching out in the grass and dozing. After a nap it often played tag with "Dog," an old beagle who had appeared at the Childers' back door some years before, covered with cockleburs and ticks as big as plums. Staying out on the grass for hours at a time gave the fish a huge appetite, and that summer it grew monstrously big eating turnip greens cooked with hog jowl, watermelon, corn on the cob, and apple turnovers. The fish had such an appetite that E. W. said he didn't know how he could keep it. Then one day in October he saw a poster for a catfish derby in Gordonsville, advertising a thirty-dollar prize for the biggest fish. E. W. reckoned he could win and, when the day of the derby arrived, Mr. Harwell from next door helped him hoist the fish onto the wagon, and he set out for Gordonsville. All went well until he started across the bridge over Difficult Creek. Then because the wagon was so heavily laden one of the planks on the bridge cracked and the wagon tilted sideways, dumping the catfish into the creek, just at the spot where E. W. had originally caught it. As soon as the fish fell into the water, E. W. jumped out of the wagon and ran down the bank to haul it out. Alas, before he could pull it on shore the catfish drowned.

My family and I spend summers on an old farm in Beaver River, Nova Scotia. Beaver River is sleepy, and summers there are peaceful. I spend hours with the children, roaming woods and fields identifying wildflowers. On rainy days we root through a hundred and twenty years of clutter in the back house and barn. The only radio in the house has been broken for a decade, and unless one buys a receiver resembling a huge scallop shell and beaches it in the front yard, there is no television. In contrast to Connecticut, however, I read newspapers in Nova Scotia. Behind a pile of rigging blocks in the back house I found a tattered stack of newspapers. Published from November 13, 1862, through May 7, 1863, the papers were numbers of the *Yarmouth Herald*. Established in 1833, the *Herald* advertised itself as "a Family and General Newspaper." Appearing every Thursday, it consisted of four 18- by 24-inch pages and cost two dollars a year if one paid in advance or two and a half dollars "when not paid in advance."

I shook the papers so that dust would fall off and carried them into the kitchen. I pushed the lazy Susan aside and, spreading the papers out under a print covered with fat robins and the inscription "What Is Home without a Mother," sat down at the kitchen table and began reading.

Old things, particularly those no longer useful, attract me. Because they are not immediately associated with and thus limited by function, such things stir the imagination. Like Aladdin's battered lamp polished into life by dream, the seemingly worthless can magically transform drab moments. For their part, the papers themselves were anything but drab. Columns of print and advertisements were neatly, even artistically laid out, and the newsprint did not rub off. Unlike today's papers that appear to suffer from a virulent strain of pulp-begotten hepatitis and turn yellow within six months, the *Herald*s had remained white, spotless aside from brown watermarks and a stain where a spider once laid eggs. For me, the contrast with present-day papers increased the *Herald*'s attraction. Much smaller than a single *Boston Globe,* the stack of *Herald*s was finite. Moreover, the *Herald* was a weekly. If I were ever to subscribe to a paper, it would be a weekly. Relentlessly arriving every morning, a daily fosters a sense of passing time and guilt over lost opportunities. Since I get little done in a day, a morning paper with its accounts of what some people accomplished during a mere twenty-four hours would depress me. Finally, the papers attracted me because I found them; no subscription manager with designs upon my wallet telephoned and interrupted my dinner.

As a person ages, he grows comfortable with inconsistency. Long separations punctuate the marriage between Philosophy and Deed, and, despite my celebrating the useless and nonfunctional, what first drew my attention in the papers were items which touched, if not on everyday existence, at least on my personal life. Of course, it may be that all wanderings through the past eventually lead to the present. By providing diversion, the wandering, however, often makes the present appear less significant. As a skilled wordsmith can tell sharp truth in ways so gentle that all bite is lost, so the indirect approach to the present softens reality. Some years ago in Carthage the Vergy family supplemented their income by petty thievery. What they took didn't amount to much, and people ignored it until Thomas Vergy stole a prize leghorn pullet from Ben Pinkney just before the state fair in Nashville. Ben prided himself on winning blue ribbons at the fair, and when he learned that Thomas had fried and eaten his best chicken he was furious and took him to court. At one time or another the Vergys had taken something from just about everyone in town and at the trial folks found it difficult to say much good about Thomas. Even that most forgiving of men, Dr. Sollows, who never said a harsh word about anything, not even "Dog" who nipped him on the calf when he was vaccinating Juba, could not white-wash Thomas's character. "I do not say," Dr. Sollows testified, "that Thomas is a thief, but I do say that if his farm joined mine I would not try to keep poultry."

Be this as it may, what first caught my attention in the *Herald* were accounts of the Civil War. In the 1950s when I was a boy in Tennessee, the Civil War seemed more recent than World War II. Not only did trenches still run through yards and across fields, but its effects were forever subjects of conversation as people blamed southern problems on northern politics. Taking a fierce pride in anything southern from segregation to football, regional nationalism fermented under the surface of life. "We might be poor as Job's turkey hen," a man from Alabama told me, "but, by God, we have the best football team in the country."

About the only world news in the *Yarmouth Herald* concerned the Civil War, and the first articles I read were dispatches describing the Battle of Fredericksburg and "The Doings of the Alabama," the Confederate raider. For a moment I was back in sixth grade lamenting the lost cause and angry that I as a southerner had to memorize the Gettysburg Address. As maturer years taught me that the lost cause was fortunately lost, so the flash of anger vanished when I came to accounts of the Battle of Murfreesboro. According to a correspondent, Murfreesboro was "one of the most ferocious battles of modern times, maintained by both sides with splendid determination." "Shell and Shot fell around like hail. Gen. Rosecrans," the Union commander, the dispatch stated, "was himself incessantly exposed. It is wonderful that he escaped. His Chief of Staff, the noble Lieut. Col. Garesche, had his head taken off by a round shot, and the blood bespattered the General and some of his staff. Lieut. Col. Kirk, just behind him, was lifted clear out of his saddle by a bullet which shattered his left arm." The discrepancy between the bloody battle and the words used to describe it made me pause, but not for long. My great-grandfather William Pickering was from Ohio and fought under Thomas at Murfreesboro. Later, as family story has it, he became Thomas's secretary, writing when asked for a sample of his penmanship Longfellow's "Lives of great men all remind us / We can make our lives sublime, / And, departing leave behind us / Footprints on the sands of time." At Murfreesboro he had not yet been made Thomas's secretary. Just a soldier under the general's command, he must have been present on January 2, 1863, when at "almost one o'clock on Wednesday Gen. Thomas threw his entire corps de armee against the centre of the enemy's forces, and breaking it, drove it back over a mile in great confusion."

What was the stuff of splendid determination and death for some became the matter of humor for others as the papers occasionally included light fillers. "'Well what next?' said Mrs. Partington, as she interrupted Ike, who was reading the war news—'The pickets were driven in five miles! Bless my soul, but that will make a strong fence. I suppose they had to be driven in deep to keep the sessionaders from digging out from under them.'" Like most news, accounts of battles are ephemeral; what remains is commerce. Advertisements filled two of the four pages of each *Yarmouth Herald*. Only occasionally did the war touch buying and selling. Along with "Hoop Skirts, 8 to 30 Hoops" and "Sozodont (Teeth Preserver), a new and unequalled preparation for the Teeth," Charles Brown, a Yarmouth merchant, advertised "Superior Tobacco, loyal citizen and 'Secesh.'" Under "RE-ENFORCEMENTS!!," in bold letters, Corning and Gray announced they had received "a large Stock of GOODS, of every description," while John Murphy of Tusket Village drew attention to his "new and commodious DRY GOODS STORE," headlining his advertisement "NOTICE. AMERICAN WAR AT AN END."

The stages of our lives may be marked more clearly by advertisements than by events. My childhood was a time of highway signs, particularly those on the roads from Nashville to Richmond. Before Lebanon, just east of Nashville on Highway 70, Burma-Shave signs began. "Many a wolf," one related, "Is never let in / Because of the hair / On his / Chinny-chin-chin." Somewhere between Crab Orchard and Rockville was "the Zoo." "See Wild Mountain Lion at the Zoo," "Don't Miss the Bear at the Zoo," "See Snake Pit at the Zoo," "Get Your Pecans at the Zoo," signs read. For sale outside the Zoo hung towels decorated with red and blue Confederate flags and bedspreads, alive with peacocks, their tails spread in luminous display. At my request we stopped at the Zoo once, and although Father bought half a bushel of winesap apples, the visit was disappointing. The bear was stuffed, and the mountain lion turned out to be a bobcat. In a cage were three or four rattlesnakes; all had stopped eating and their flesh was collapsing over their bones like slack sails in the doldrums. On a shelf inside the Zoo was a rooster in a jar. The owner said he dropped the rooster in when it was a chick. Although he had tried to raise chickens in jars before, this was the first time, he told us, he had been successful.

After reading the articles on the Civil War, I started studying advertisements. In almost every number of the *Herald* was an announcement for a pamphlet written by one Dr. La'Mert with offices in London at 37 Bedford Square. The good doctor was available for consultation every day from ten until two and from six until eight. Patients "residing in the colonies," the advertisement promised, could be "successfully treated by correspondence, with remedies forwarded in secrecy and safety." Secrecy was important because the ailment the doctor treated was potentially embarrassing. Indeed, I would not have had nerve enough to purchase the pamphlet, but since *Self-Preservation* was advertised week after week, customers must have existed. The pamphlet was, the doctor claimed, "a popular Essay on Nervous and Physical Debility, resulting from injurious habits contracted in youth, or excesses in maturity, which, by prematurely exhausting the functions of Manhood, destroy the happiness of Married Life, or prevent fulfillment of engagements that constitute the most cherished objects of existence." La'Mert's concerns aside, the *Herald* ran few medical advertisements. Occasionally a physician announced that he was setting up practice, and among available goods merchants listed patent medicines like Ayer's Pills, Atwood's Bitters, Cherry Pectoral, Holloway's Ointment, and Woodill's Worm Lozengers.

At the end of the nineteenth century Yarmouth's fleet of ocean-going vessels was second in Canada only to that sailing out of St. John's, New Brunswick. Yarmouth captains traveled over the world, and many advertisements addressed them. Ships' chronometers, watches, sextants, quadrants, barometers, telescopes, compasses, and charts were available, Francis M. Moore stated, "to those visiting Belfast, or neighboring ports." As reference Moore listed two Yarmouth businessmen and twenty-nine captains. Everyday supplies were always on hand in Yarmouth itself. In 1863 Ryerson and Moses informed fishermen that among other things at their wharf were twenty-five thousand bushels of salt, one thousand fish barrels, sixty barrels of mess pork, two hundred bolts of gourock canvas, two hundred gross of fishhooks, five hundred dozen cod lines, fifty kegs of cut nails, a ton of bolt rope, and two tons of manilla rope and cordage, all of which, the advertisement stated, "will be sold low on the usual terms."

Milliners, ship-brokers, auctioneers, tombstone makers, saddle and harness makers, cobblers, tailors, photographers, booksellers, all the small and large business folk of a bustling seaport advertised in the newspaper. Larger merchants listed their stocks. From the schooners *Lydia, Loyal,* and *Monitor,* W. H. Moody received "a large supply of AMERICAN GOODS," including five "trunks Ladies' Kid, Prunella and Enamelled Leather Boots, Shoes, Buskins, and Slippers—single and doubled soles, with and without heels," and one case "Men's Cloth and Furred Winter Caps, Men's and Boys' Black and Colored Hats; Black, Blue and Fancy Cassimeres and Satinetts, Red and White Flannels, Shirting, Bed Ticking, Denims." I enjoy lists, and I read them like a child digging into a Christmas stocking, hoping to pull out something unfamiliar like "Satinetts" or "Cassimeres." Many of the advertisements in the paper were for food: "50 Bottles Mixed Pickles, Chow-Chow, Onions and Piccallily; 50 boxes Sardines, John Bull Harvey and Worcestershire Sauce; Sage, Summer Savory and Sweet Marjoram; Tomatoes and Oysters, in cans" ran a notice from Corning and Gray. For me, old advertisements for food are the staff of reading. Not only do I read at the kitchen table, but whenever I read I usually drink tea and eat fruit, invariably managing to leave both clothes and book awash. Although my reading snacks rarely change from apples or oranges and milk colored by a pinch of Earl Grey, the various advertisements for food intrigued me as I wondered what people ate a hundred years ago. In May 1863 J. W. H. Rowley listed seeds in stock in his store: Dwarf, China, Marrow, and Mohawk beans; Champion of England, Daniel O'Rourke, Canada, Black Eye, Marrowfat, and Potato Peas; "Blood Beets, Cucumbers, Mangel Wurtzels, Orange Carrot, White and Yellow Turnips, Premium Dutch Cabbage, Lettuce, Radish, Ruta Baga, Squash, Somer Savory," and "one barrel Potato Onions."

Raisins were popular, and merchants advertised their arrival. The citizenry of Yarmouth, however, did not breakfast upon raisin bran. Indeed, if W. H. Townsend's notice provides a hint of culinary preferences, people in Yarmouth liked their mixtures to have a bit more body. In black type, Townsend proclaimed that "BRICKS AND RAISINS" were available; ten thousand bricks, twenty-five whole boxes of raisins, fifty half, and a hundred quarter boxes. All sorts of notices appeared in the paper. On January 15, 1863, under "BONES WANTED," W. Kinney offered to "purchase Bones of all descriptions." "Pick them up," he advised, and "keep them out of the snow." Bones were not the only item wanted. Merchants had trouble collecting debts, and throughout the year "MONEY WANTED" advertisements appeared. "All persons indebted to the subscriber over six months either by Note or Bank account," Robert Brown advertised in October 1862, "are hereby notified to call and settle the same on or before the first day of December, 1862." Rum may have contributed to the difficulties merchants had collecting debts. Although advertisements for molasses and sugar from the Caribbean appeared in every *Herald,* rum was conspicuous by its absence. In the early days of Yarmouth, a historian wrote, the amount of rum sold "was simply enormous, and, in some accounts rendered by traders of the day, liquor of some kind forms every second or third item." Only indirectly did the advertisements acknowledge drink. "The Rev. W. N. Burton," a notice read, "will give a Lecture before the Plymouth Total Abstinence Society, on TUESDAY evening 25th inst. A cordial invitation to the public is extended." "Wanted, a Boy about fourteen or sixteen years of age, to serve as an apprentice to the Tailoring Business," a notice stated, "none but those of good moral principles need apply." Men were not the only creatures to stray in Yarmouth. "All persons are hereby requested to prevent their cattle going at large in the street or commons after this date, or they will be dealt with according to the law," Henry Thurston, the cattle reeve, warned on April 2, 1863.

A seafaring family built our house in Beaver River, and flotsam from voyages still clutters nooks and crannies. In the back house was a print of the harbor at Rio de Janeiro. Someone, probably a captain, had written "City," "Cemetery," and "Hospital" on the print and marked their locations with small crosses. Above three hills he wrote "Mound Garvia," "Corcovado," and "Shugar Loaf." Behind a stack of lawn chairs I found a long thin wooden chest containing charts of the Pacific and Indian oceans. A captain had marked his journeys in pencil. At noon on Christmas Day, 1885, he was slightly south of latitude 33 and midway between longitude 138 and 139, on the way to or from Simoda Harbor on Japan's Idsu Peninsula. On February 16, 1886, he was north of Borneo and west of the Seahorse Reefs.

In my childhood in landlocked Tennessee, adventure did not lay beyond a rolling blue horizon or gleam in the deep sand. Instead it lay over the crest of the next green hill, buried amid the snakelike roots of a hollow tree. Exploring the back house resembled hiking through thick brush. Climbing over rusting stoves as big and as rough as lichen-covered stones and pushing through piles of thorny, snaring tools resembled roaming hills in Middle Tennessee. The Bay of Fundy seemed far away, and even though the print and charts intrigued me, I was such an inlander that I did not immediately associate them with the sea.

By the same token, when I first read the *Herald,* I paid practically no attention to the most important columns in the papers, the "Shipping Intelligence." Only when I started through for the third time did I read it. What I found were the currents of story, both treacherous and calm. "Advices from Tobermory of Dec. 11, received per steamer Africa from Liverpool," the *Herald* reported, "state that a bottle has been found on the shore of Gometra (an island on the west of Mull) containing the following memorandum:—'On board the *Mariner,* of Nova Scotia, J. Wilson, passenger, struck an iceberg on the 14th Sept., 1862; vessel going down.'" In the paper for March 19, 1863, Captain Gilliat of the brigantine *Conductor* reported coming upon the wreck of the schooner *Gypsy* out of Port Maitland. From the wreck he saved the captain and the mate. "As it was blowing a gale of wind, with a very heavy sea," Gilliat reported, "could not get a boat to them, but succeeded at last in hauling them on board in bowlines, barefooted and nearly naked." The *Gypsy,* its captain recounted, sailed from New York carrying a general cargo to Demerara. Sixty-six hours out of New york, the *Gypsy* was "knocked down" in a heavy gale and waterlogged. The captain himself escaped through the cabin window. Except for the mate, the rest of the crew was lost overboard. "Their names," the account ended, "are as follows:—David Hoys cook; Wesley Bonnel, Alexander Nelson, William Temple, all of Maitland."

Port Maitland is two miles south of Beaver River. In evenings when the tide was low, I walked along the shore to the wharf at Port Maitland. On foggy days I often explored the town cemetery. In the nineteenth century most of Port Maitland's inhabitants earned livelihoods at sea. A good many of them died there, and throughout the cemetery are markers to their memory. Above the graves of Lemuel and James Raymond, two brothers who drowned together in 1842, is engraved, "As billows roll to meet their fate, / And break upon the shore, / So rolls that billow, human life: / So breaks, and is no more." Captain J. G. Perry once owned our house. While his boat was taking on a load of guano off the coast of Peru in 1876, the ship's cook went crazy and stabbed him to death. In the graveyard is his marker; on it is written, "My body lies with strangers / But my spirit's home with God." Unlike the tombstones, the "Shipping Intelligence" described as many rescues as losses. On January 30, 1863, Captain O'Brien of the barque *Helen Campbell* out of Weymouth "saw a boat ahead, which, on being picked up, was found to contain the officers and crew, twelve in all, of the Spanish brigt. Leon, of Bilboa, which had foundered after being beset with ice. She was from Newfoundland to Cadiz, fish laden." The men had spent sixty hours in the lifeboat with no food and only four gallons of water. Shortly after they were rescued, the paper stated, "a very heavy gale arose, in which they would doubtless have perished."

Like the back house, the front page of a newspaper is often a miscellany. Unlike the back house, though, which yields treasure to the persistent explorer and often raises spirits, front pages make me melancholy. By placing the absurd and the tragic, the sensational and the thoughtful, side by side, a front page trivializes and makes life meaningless. Consequently, on finding the *Heralds,* I skipped articles on the front pages except accounts of the Civil War and only examined the front pages closely after I had read everything else. I was surprised. The *Herald* tried to provide family entertainment, and, instead of being disturbing and dislocating, the front page was an entertaining mixture of fact and fiction. On it appeared articles on turkeys, the Russian steppes, arsenic, and the Empress Eugenia, "probably the most extravagant woman living." In the *Herald* appeared the Reverend D. A. Randall's account of climbing the pyramids. Two Arab guides accompanied his climb, chanting all the while, "Ya ah, ya ah, ya ah ha! / Away, away, and up we go, / American gentleman berry good man, / Give us backshiesh, ya ah ha! / Yankle doodle dandy." On the summit of the Great Pyramid, the cries of the guides fell on deaf ears as Randall experienced the conventional moment of truth, writing, "Then History came, and lifted the gates of memory, and opened long vistas through the winding and intricate mazes of the past."

The lead columns on the left side of the paper were literary, featuring "Select Tales," short stories of various kinds. "Chased by a Pirate" was a straightforward miraculous escape, while "Not Perfect" preached the evils of slander. "The Wife Tamer" was himself tamed, while a man who disliked children was the butt of "What Took Place in the Bazaar." Several tales were inspirational; "Poverty and Pain," for example, was an uplifting account of an old coal seller who after inheriting a hundred thousand pounds devoted the remainder of his life to decency and good deeds. In deepening understanding, formal study creates preferences. While teaching readers to appreciate the subtle and the complex, university education often neglects and undervalues the simple. Outside the study, however, complexity is not something to be celebrated but avoided, as day-to-day happiness depends upon living simply and learning to appreciate the simple for its simplicity. My favorite tale in the *Herald* was "The Duellist's Revenge," the only excuse for which was that it entertained. On the restoration of the monarchy after the Napoleonic Wars, the tale began, "bitter animosity existed in France between the royalists and imperialists." In Paris the two factions often met at the Palais Royal, where "a saucy look, a grimace, or a smile of contempt" was liable to provoke a duel.

One morning a former officer under Napoleon, "one Capt. Honitan, who was suffering from gout, was slowly hobbling along under the famous wooden galley" of the Palais Royal "when being somewhat pressed by the crowd, and fearful of being injured in his suffering limb, he took a sudden step aside, and accidentally trod on the foot of an officer of the royal guard. Quick as lightning the latter, a young man of spirit and fire, seized the former by the nose, and then cuffed him on both sides of the head." Honitan's face turned "deadly pale, as he said, quite calmly and politely, evidently controlling his passion by a master effort of will, 'I would have apologized for what really was an accident, had not Monsieur put it out of my power.'"

"I do not want an apology from such as you," replied the young man, Lieutenant Henri Duvais, "the youngest son of an ancient and honorable family of royalists." When Honitan said he would remember the incident, Duvais said, "Pray do not forget"; then, to insure that the day did not slip from the captain's memory, he trod heavily on Honitan's foot, "drawing from him an involuntary cry of pain." After several days passed during which he did not receive a challenge, Duvais was puzzled. "What could you expect of a man who doubtless disgraced himself at Waterloo?" one of Duvais's companions sneered, exclaiming in disgust, "Bah! this comes of plebeian blood, Henri!" Several months passed; Duvais fought two duels, was himself promoted to captain, and then got engaged "to a beautiful lady of rank." On the morning of the wedding day while Duvais was "engaged at his toilet," preparing "for the nuptials that were to make him the happiest man in Paris," his manservant announced a visitor. Just as Duvais said he could see no one, the visitor entered the room, saying, "I beg your pardon Monsieur le Capitaine, but I know you will see me." Turning with a "proud and haughty air" and seeing a "middle-aged man in plain citizen's dress," Duvais asked, "And who are you, sir? and why this intrusion?"

"Monsieur le Capitaine seems not to know me," the visitor replied, "but yet Monsieur may have the happiness to remember the pleasure he once had in pulling the nose, boxing the ears, and treading on the foot of a quiet-looking gentleman, under the gallery of the Palais Royal, some twelve months since." The speech was said "with the most freezing politeness; but there was something awfully wicked in the cold gray eye of the speaker, as it all the time rested quietly and steadily on the other." When Duvais flushed and said Honitan should have appeared sooner if he wanted to save his reputation, Honitan answered, "My reputation, fortunately, was not in the keeping of a rather forward boy," adding, "I have come at last to ask the pleasure of Monsieur le Capitaine Henri Duvais to a little quiet walk, thinking the beautiful bride elect might be pleased to hear of the prowess of her lover on his wedding day." After observing that he would be justified in putting Honitan off "for the present," Duvais said he would not "balk" Honitan's "kind intentions" and bringing out small swords invited him to enter the garden twenty paces away. The captain is so obliging, Honitan responded, "perhaps they lied who said Monsieur was a coward and would not fight." The remark enraged Duvais, and "bursting with suppressed passion," he answered, "Coward or no coward, I have sent your betters to the ——, and you shall soon follow." In less than ten minutes they were fighting. In contrast to Honitan, who was cool and self-possessed, Duvais was almost "blind with rage." Anger, however, was not enough. Although Duvais was the best swordsman in his corps, "in less than a minute he discovered to his horror that he was only a mere child in the hands of his antagonist, who seemed rather disposed to play with him than fight. In the course of five minutes, however, he received a disabling wound; and then like lightning, the blade of the other flashed close before his eyes and severed his nose clear down to his face."

"Monsieur le Capitaine did me the honor to pull my nose," Honitan said. "I have done myself the honor to cut off his. Good-day, Capitaine," Honitan concluded. "When you are well, I will call again. My compliments to the bride, and how does she like your beauty?" Unfortunately, the loss of a nose affected not only Duvais's beauty but the ardor of the bride to be, who "declined to marry a man whose features were so terribly disfigured." For his part, Honitan disappeared until Duvais regained his health. Then one day after Duvais had fully recovered from his wound, Honitan reappeared. "I have been expecting you," Duvais said, bringing out a brace of dueling pistols. "Monsieur le Capitaine does me too much honor," Honitan said, gracefully adding, "I hope my visits do not prove troublesome." In the first exchange of shots, Honitan was wounded in the left shoulder while Duvais lost part of his right ear. "'Monsieur le Capitaine did me the honor to box my right ear,' said Honitan coolly; 'I have done myself the honor to shoot off his.'" In the second volley Honitan received a neck wound, and Duvais lost his left ear. As they took their positions for another round, Honitan said, "Now, then, Monsieur le Capitaine, I will remember the foot." Unfortunately, Honitan did not carry out his threat. When he finished speaking, both pistols cracked, and the story ended abruptly as the "antagonists fell back dead—the one shot through the heart, and the other through the brain." Both characters were, of course, doomed from the beginning of the tale, but the editor of the *Herald* killed them prematurely, probably because the story had already filled two columns and space was needed for a consideration of the commercial possibilities of an Atlantic Telegraph Cable and for Burnside's and Lee's accounts of Fredericksburg.

One winter afternoon not long after Mr. Tilly's death, Dr. Sollows visited Mrs. Tilly to see how she was getting along. "I am doing just fine," Mrs. Tilly said as she and the doctor sat in the parlor before the fire and drank tea, "but I do worry about Mr. Tilly, especially now that winter is here. Poor soul, how he loved a big fire. I do hope he has gone where they keep good fires." I am not quite so keen on fires as Mr. Tilly, but if I do go anywhere soon, I hope that there are piles of old papers about. Around here avoiding new papers is getting more difficult. Just yesterday I received an advertisement in the mail, not one for raisins and bricks but for the *Hartford Courant.* "Starting this September the *Courant*'s going to be all around *your* town as never before," the advertisement proclaimed. "We'll be covering more of what matters to you about your town, community, and region." "Don't miss a thing!" the ad urged. "Subscribe to the *Courant* Every Day!"

Picked Up

POD MALONE was the worst stutterer in Smith County, Tennessee. One evening after a meeting of the Knights of Pythias, Dr. Sollows, who had just read about a new treatment for stutterers at Vanderbilt Hospital in Nashville, met Pod outside Read's drugstore. "Pod," he said, "have you ever attended a clinic for stutterers?" "No," Pod answered after pulling his left ear and thinking a bit, "I just pi-pi-picked it up on my-my own."

Most learning is like Pod's, picked up informally beyond the high rail of rule and regulation. Bound by focus, formal education forces one to crop a narrow path and by preventing a person from ranging leads not so much to thoroughbred intellect as to absurdity. It just so happened that one night, so the old but illustrative story goes, a long-haired professor, a bald-headed man, and a barber were traveling together through a forest inhabited by packs of ravenous wolves. Before dusk the travelers stopped, gathered wood, and built a fire to keep the wolves away. To insure that the fire would not die during the night, they set up a watch. The barber agreed to watch from eight until midnight. Then, he said, he would wake the professor, who would tend the fire for the next four hours. Finally, the bald-headed man was supposed to watch the fire from four until the sun rose the next morning. Traveling through the forest had been difficult, and by eight o'clock the bald man and the professor were sound asleep. Quickly the barber grew bored. No wolves appeared, and made out of hard, dry wood, the fire burned easily and did not need much attention. To pass the time, the barber propped the professor up against a tree and shaved his head. When he finished, he laid the professor back on the ground. By midnight when it was time for the professor to stand watch, the barber shook him. Tired from the day's journey, the professor sat up slowly then rubbed his hands across his face and back over his head to help him wake up. As he pushed his hands across his head, the professor noticed that he didn't have any hair. For a moment his face was blank and he looked puzzled, then suddenly, as knowledge seemed to break upon him, he nodded and spoke. "What a fool you are, barber," he said. "You have awakened the bald-headed man instead of me."

If the professor had spent more hours in the woods and less in the office, he would have grown accustomed to odd things and the absence of a little hair would not have confused him. Grazing unblinkered across years, a person doesn't pick up ideas so much, though, as he does facts. As he grows older, many of the facts are, alas, necessarily medicinal. By fifty, one usually knows more medicine than an intern. I have spent much time roaming through libraries, reading books more neglected than the most forbidding part of any forest. In the process I have accumulated a medical school of knowledge, much of it, I am afraid, pertaining to digestive matters. "Great harmes have growne, and maladies exceeding," John Harington wrote in 1624, "By keeping in a little blast of *wind:* / So *Cramps, & Dropsies, Collicks* have their breeding / And *Mazed Braines* for want of vent behind."

In gathering medical knowledge I followed the lead of Henry Lyte, who in 1619 wrote in the introduction to *A New Herbal* that "a good thing the more common it is, the better it is." In *A Rich Store-house or Treasury for the Diseased* (1596), A. T. suggested that one who was "costive and bound in his body" should take a suppository of "boyled Honny and little fine Powder of Salt." If this did not work, one could, *The Treasure of Poore Men* (1550) advised, "take a morsel of Larde as much as thy finger" and powder it with sage and "put it to the fundamente." For the opposite sort of stomach affliction, I found many remedies. "The doung of a Camell dried & dronke" or "the liver of ani beast sodden in vinigar," Humphrie Lloyd (1585) wrote, "doth binde the belly mightely." The best thing for a pain in the side, Lloyd thought, was "the doung of a Wolfe, if it bee newly made." According to William Warde (1560), the best way to cure "the paine of the side" was to keep a dog in a chamber for ten days "and give him only lambes or motton bones to gnawe, then take of his excremendes and drie it in the sunne, and make thereof a powder, and give the patient to drinke of it every morning halfe an unce in white wine hote." If one didn't have a dog handy, "the like effect" could be achieved by making a "warm glister." "Take the dung of a blacke asse as hot as you maie find it whan it commeth from him," Warde instructed, "and seeth it in white wine that is not sweete, wringing well the dunge into the wine."

While searching for cures for various digestive ailments, I came upon useful remedies for all sorts of afflictions. For "leprosie," T. Bright (1615) recommended "*Hedgehogs* dryed and drunke"; for cankers, "the flesh of *Snayles* boyled, *Crayfishes,* greene *Frogges.*" For "the stone," L. M. (1588) recommended the "Oyle of scorpion," while "Millipede, the loop, or the worme with many feet drunk in wine cureth the Jaundice." Often, of course, one remedy is about as good as another. Some years ago a drummer appeared in Carthage and, setting up a table on the courthouse lawn opposite the Smith County Bank, started selling bottles of flea powder. With each bottle came a page of instructions on how to kill fleas. For best results, the drummer explained, reading the instructions, the flea was to be held in the left hand between the thumb and index finger. With the thumb and index finger of the right hand, one was to take a pinch of the powder and apply it "to the flea's trunk or blood-sucking proboscis." Afterward, the drummer declared, "if any flea to whom this powder has been administered can be proven to have bitten the purchaser, I will give that person another bottle of flea powder free." Vester McBee, a country woman from Gladis, a hill and hog hamlet up the road from Carthage, bought the first bottle. Vester listened carefully while the drummer explained for a second time how to use the powder. When he finished, she raised her hand slowly and then innocently asked whether—when she had caught the flea and had it in her hand between her fingers—killing it with her nail wouldn't do as well as the powder. "Yes," the drummer said, folding up the table and packing his bottles away, "that's a good way too."

The person who ambles through days picking up out-of-the-way learning rarely sets goals for life. Content to idle along without a purpose, he is usually not ambitious and collects observations, rather than possessions. For such a person, experience is an end in itself, the stuff of tale and conversation, not the means to advancement or growth. Along with medical knowledge, I have picked up many creatures during my wanderings, including a flea or two during my dog days. Much as some people return from travels with clothes or jewels, I bring back memories of creatures. Years ago I visited Kos, the birthplace of Hippocrates, the great physician. Early one morning I bicycled out from Kos Town to the ruins of the Asklepion, the medical sanctuary built in the fourth century B.C. in honor of Asklepios, the god of healing.

As I walked through the terraces, I hoped to see a snake. Asklepios himself was represented as a serpent and the serpent is still, of course, the sign of a doctor. I climbed through the pine woods to a hill behind the sanctuary. Below me the pines were yellow in the sun. Beyond them lay the blue sea and to the northeast Bodrum, a white speck, I thought, on the horizon. In the pines cicadas chattered, but on the hill all was quiet until something on the ground rustled. I looked down expecting a snake; instead a large tortoise crawled out from under some briars. He stopped at my feet and wagged his head back and forth. Then he scraped one side of his head through the grass. The right side of the tortoise's head puffed out, and the eye was shut, buried beneath a pillow of proud flesh. Seeing something sticking out at the corner of the tortoise's eye, I reached down and, wrapping my hand around his neck, held the head steady while I pushed back the swollen skin. In the corner of the eye was a thorn. At first when I tried to pull it out, the thorn would not give, but then it slipped free, hard and glistening. Behind it burst a thick brown cream, spotting my shirt then dripping down the tortoise's neck and over my hand. I held him while the sore drained. It took a long time, but when it stopped the tortoise blinked his right eye. Seeing the eyeball had not been damaged, I freed the tortoise, and he crawled noisily away through the grass. Unlike Asklepios, I had not restored life to the dead, but I had saved a tortoise's eye, and, walking back through the sanctuary to my bicycle, I felt in harmony with time and for a moment thought myself part of a natural process, green and healing.

Snakes have attracted me since childhood, and I was disappointed not to have seen one on Kos. Over the years, though, I have collected a den of memories. My interest began when I spent summers on my grandfather's farm in Virginia. A dirt road passed in front of the farm, and occasionally cars ran over snakes. Because the road was soft, the snakes were not badly crushed. Whenever I found a fresh one, I took it back to the house and, when Mother took her afternoon nap, I carried it upstairs and curled it in the hall outside her door. Nowadays when I explore ruins, I look for snakes. Their presence quickens the dead rock and invigorates me. Just before going to Kos I saw two snakes in Syria. Early one morning as I walked sleepily through a maze of gray fallen columns in Palmyra, I stopped and unaccountably looked at the ground. A step ahead a snake lay partly buried in the sand. For a moment the snake was still, then it slipped silently under a column. Initially I thought the snake a Palestinean viper, but later I realized it was too long and was probably a harmless whip snake.

For the rest of that morning, though, I was alert and little in the ruins escaped my sight. Three days later I explored Marqab, a huge castle

looking out over the sea above Baniyas. Marqab is made from black
basalt and on overcast days seems to hang above the coast like a heavy
cloud. Inside the castle the keeper had a one-barrel shotgun beside his
desk. He used it to shoot snakes, he explained and warned me that the
castle was infested with kufi, the Arab name for the Levantine or blunt-
nosed viper. Stout and sometimes five feet long, the kufi is dangerous,
and the thought of coming upon one excited me. If I walked softly, I
thought, I might see one, and sure enough, as I crossed stone fallen
from a broken rampart in the middle of the castle, I found one sunning
himself. I tried to creep up on him, but as soon as I got within four feet,
he wrinkled and sliding off the rock disappeared into a patch of yellow flowers.

I am not sure why snakes attract me. Not only do I look for them in
ruins, but I pick up stories about them. According to ancient account,
Noah is responsible for there being snakes in the world today. Although
God told him to take some "of every thing that creepeth upon the earth"
into the ark, Noah disobeyed. Because of the serpent's treachery in
Eden, Noah refused to allow snakes on the ark. As a result, all the
snakes on earth drowned during the flood. When the waters receded,
Noah immediately started building a new and better world. Over six
hundred years old, he did not know how many years he had left and he
did not want the lesser things of life to distract him from ploughing and
planting. Above all he did not want to fritter time away pursuing fleeting
pleasure. Despite resolution and age, however, his penis kept obstruct-
ing his plans, drawing him toward sweet grapes and ripe music. One day
while sowing grain, he had thoughts so amorous and distracting that he
became disgusted and tearing off his penis threw it into an acacia tree.
Immediately the penis turned into a giant viper, thorns from the acacia
its fangs and its belly swollen with young.

Although I often try to catch the snakes I see, the truth is that I am
relieved when a snake glides out of sight. Other creatures, though, I
pick up and bring home. One October several years ago, I found a monarch butterfly lying in the grass in the front yard. Because the butterfly's
wings were still intact, Vicki said we ought to revive him. I took him
into the house and put him on a bowl of chrysanthemums in the living
room. In the kitchen I dissolved cane sugar in boiling water and, taking
two small cup-shaped ketchup containers from Wendy's, I made "honey
pots." After placing them under the chrysanthemums, I urged the butterfly to drink. For a while he seemed to regain strength. That night I

told Vicki that we would probably find Mr. Butterfly sitting on the mantlepiece the next morning. Instead I found him on the rug, lying on his side and slowly wiggling his legs. I picked him up and carried him over to a honey pot, where he drank a little. For six days Vicki and I fed the butterfly. No matter how we "stuffed" him, however, he was always on his side in the morning. Finally on the seventh morning I found him on the rug dead, lying on his back, legs drawn into his body. Vicki put him in a red matchbox, and after breakfast we buried him beside some goldenrod.

"That's the last wild creature I bring home," I said after crumpling the honey pots. Three years passed, and Francis and Edward were born. One night six weeks after Edward's birth, Vicki and I sat at the kitchen table eating chocolate chip cookies. Suddenly Vicki glanced outside, then jumped up and jerking open the back door ran into the yard. The dog next door had broken up a rabbit's nest and after scattering the baby rabbits was trotting home with one in its mouth. "Damn it, Coke," Vicki yelled, "drop that rabbit; drop it right now." Seeing Vicki rushing after him, Coke paused, then dropped the rabbit and ran home. Vicki picked up the rabbit; at the same time I looked out at the road. Crouched in the middle was a baby rabbit so little and awkward it could barely push its way along. Thirty minutes later the two rabbits were buried under a pile of shredded paper in a box under the kitchen table, and I was at the mall in the CVS drugstore buying an eyedropper and cans of soybean baby formula. Every four hours, night and day, for nine days I fed formula to the rabbits. Vicki wasn't able to help because she was busy with Edward. At two and six every night Edward woke up wailing. After handing him to Vicki, I staggered downstairs and warmed up formula for the rabbits. Once they were fed, I took Edward from Vicki and put him back in his crib. At the end of nine days the rabbits had grown considerably and were trying to jump out of the box; I then fed them clover and grass along with the formula. After eighteen days the rabbits were fat and vigorous and too much to handle. The next morning Vicki and I with Francis afoot and Edward in a "Snugli" walked to the university farm and turned the rabbits loose under the briar patch at the edge of a wood.

Since feeding the rabbits, I have avoided close involvement with neighborhood wildlife. After roving cats destroyed the nests of catbirds, I chopped down two yews which stood in the front yard. Hearing noises outside the bedroom window one night, I rushed into the yard and managed to save one fledgling from the cats. I wrapped the bird in a heating pad, but it died the next day. In thinking about it, I suppose I am more inclined to pick up animals than most things, particularly things mechanical. For example I dislike cars. I walk to my office at the University of Connecticut and have refused good positions at other universities because I would have to drive to work. I don't know how to use a computer and recently have stopped answering the telephone. When I started writing, I eagerly answered the telephone, hoping that someone was calling to praise a piece I had written or, better, to ask me to write an article or book. Years have passed and I have received little praise and no invitations to write books. So much time has passed that I don't want anyone to call me. A call now would only awaken resentment. Instead of being pleased with the present, I would think about the barren past and my day would be ruined. To insure no one telephones, I insert stories into my writings in order to keep people from taking me seriously.

Although I pick the stories up everywhere, from magazines and books or from conversation, I usually place them in my father's hometown, Carthage. Not long after she bought the flea powder, Vester McBee became housekeeper for Mrs. Hamper, widow of Morris Hamper, who sold lard and grease and manufactured linseed oil. Mrs. Hamper lived on Main Street in Carthage in a big Victorian house with purple and yellow stained glass in the door and above the front windows. Active in the Eastern Star and Ladies' Book Club, Mrs. Hamper was one of the grande dames of Carthage. She wore heavy hats with thick black ribbons and even put on perfume, something Vester had rarely smelled in Gladis. "Has that toilet water come?" Mrs. Hamper asked one morning when she was getting ready to call on Mrs. Eaves, a neighbor and treasurer of the Book Club. "Yes, ma'am," Vester answered from the kitchen. "I put it on the back of the commode." "Was it scented?" Mrs. Hamper asked, adjusting a ribbon on her hat. "No 'am, it won't sented," Vester said. "I went to Read's drugstore and brung it home myself."

The person who ambles along informally picking up learning and other things is usually content. Generally such a person has few wishes. Focused on actual objects, wishes lead to dissatisfaction, for failure to obtain a wish often brings unhappiness while a wish achieved frequently turns out to be a wish lost. With no desire thrusting him forward toward a goal, the "picker-upper" begins each day curious and expectant, and relaxed. Always willing to poke about in this and that, such a person can be a meddler. Two years ago an acquaintance in the English Department spent nine months in London. Before returning he mailed a cart of books back, and for a week each day's mail brought six or seven packages to the English Department. Curious about what my acquaintance was mailing, I sorted through the packages and read the customs declarations. Most boxes contained books; one or two, though, contained items less academic. On one declaration my colleague stated that the box contained "Books, Running Shoes, Sweat Suit." After the words "Sweat Suit," there was a gap on the customs form. The space offended my aesthetic sense, so I took out my pen and to the declaration added "One Jockey Strap (Very Small)." I put the box on top of the other boxes and made sure it stayed there until my colleague appeared to remove his belongings.

Things of interest turn up almost everywhere. Besides reading customs declarations, I listen to conversations. Much that I overhear is dull, but occasionally I hear something useful. This past summer after we had been in Nova Scotia for eight weeks, I read in the local paper that a ten-kilometer road race was going to be held that afternoon in Yarmouth, twelve miles away. Although I had not run all summer and had put on ten pounds, I decided to race. Since my running clothes were in Connecticut, I wore a white undershirt, a purple bathing suit, a pair of brown, stretch, knee-length, insurance salesman's socks, and the pair of battered tennis shoes which I wear when mowing the grass. "I might not be fit," I told Vicki, "but Yarmouth is flat. I might even win a prize. Not many hotshots are liable to show up here." For three kilometers I bounced along, but then my feet began blistering, the bathing suit started chafing, and a summer of shortcake afloat in cream and wild strawberries began percolating. Although I wobbled toward the end of the race, I was alert enough to hear a boy say to his father as I passed, "Daddy, look at that man. He is going to fall. He shouldn't be running." The boy was right. I put away my socks and bathing suit after the race and have not run since. Despite finishing ninety-third out of one hundred and two runners, I retired in style, however. Because I was from Connecticut, I was awarded the medal for the runner who lived farthest from Yarmouth. Unfortunately, the medal was not inscribed. McDonald's sponsored the race, and instead of the date of the race on one side of the medal appeared Ronald McDonald, his hair crinkly like fungus on damp wood.

The discipline and the labor necessary to complete a task or master learning often stamp impressions upon memory. In contrast, things which are picked up informally or require little effort to learn can just as

easily be put down and forgotten. Occasionally being able to drop something quickly is convenient. Not long ago I decided to write an essay
about my hometown, Nashville, Tennessee, and in a conversation with
my father mentioned the idea. "That wouldn't be nice for your mother
and me. We have to live here," Father said. "Besides," he added, "Peter
Taylor has already written about Nashville and he has done it better
than you could ever do it." Father was right. That night I tore the page
with "NASHVILLE" written at the top out of my notebook and began
taking notes for a piece called "Horse Sense." "You can find more horse
scents in a stable than anywhere else," I had read recently and thought I
might write about the relationship between Nature and Reason. I didn't
write the essay; something interrupted me and by the time I returned to
the subject a fresh breeze had blown my thought away. Actually, most of
the ideas and learning which I pick up get away from me, even medical
knowledge. Having heard that I knew something about stomach problems, a friend came to my office in the English Department last week.
He told me he felt poorly and then after describing his symptoms asked
me if his difficulties originated in his stomach or his liver. I had nothing
to say. If I had remembered Wynkyn de Worde's *Judycyall of Uryns*
(1512), a book I read four years ago, I could, however, have helped him
diagnose himself. "Uryne thyn and somewhat reade and cleare with a
bright cyrcle," de Worde wrote, "betokeneth a bad stomach."

The loss of learning does not bother me. Rarely do I regret forgetting
about a book like de Worde's *Judycyall;* most of the time I don't remember such books well enough to realize that I forgot them. What does
bother me, however, is the loss of the gentling effect of culture. At best
culture is a veneer, but it is one which took effort for me to acquire.
Sadly, anger can melt it in a moment. Three years ago I attended a performance of *La Traviata* at the Royal Opera House in London. The rich
music moved me, and I left the opera thinking that if human beings
could produce such beauty we were not doomed.

"Maybe someday," I thought, hope ringing through me like music,
"good really will triumph over evil." Even the descent into the underground and the loud, dirty ride on the Northern Line to Hampstead did
not affect my feelings. As Germont's "Who hath won thy heart away
from fair Provence's sea and soil" played through my mind, I imagined
rock roses pink and rich with myrrh and didn't see the metallic cars,
cigarette butts stamped out on the floor, and advertisements for temporary jobs pasted around the ceiling. At the Hampstead station, I got out

and walked along the platform almost oblivious to the crowd around me. Suddenly noise broke my mood. Near the elevator four drunken louts leaned against the wall, screaming obscenities. While we waited for the elevator, one of them urinated. Then another swayed into us and put his arm around the waist of a woman beside me. All traces of the music died out. Grabbing the man's arm, I jerked him through the crowd and, spinning him like a child playing crack the whip, I slammed him into a wall. "I'll throw the next bastard that moves," I yelled, turning to the others, "down the goddamn elevator shaft." They didn't move, and when the elevator came the passengers got on silently. Halfway up the woman turned to me and said, "Thank you." "Forget it," I said, not wanting to talk. Outside on the street, I took three or four deep breaths, hoping cold air would bring the opera back, but like the hopes of Violetta and Alfredo, beauty had died, and I strode aggressively down the street to my apartment on Rosslyn Hill Road, spoiling for a fight.

As one grows older, he realizes life is fragile. Time seems to pass quickly and one is no longer willing to commit years to mastering a subject. Instead one learns names, in my case the names of flowers. Not only does learning names create the comforting illusion that I have learned deeply and well but it makes me feel less temporary. Instead of being an alien, insignificant being, I feel part of larger enduring nature. Most flowers have had many names. In the past the common yellow and white daisy, today generally known as the ox-eyed daisy, was called, among others, moon penny, dog blow, butter daisy, and poverty weed. Names change perception, creating character and stimulating observation. Not until I learned its many names did I pay attention to the yellow mullein growing in a ditch along Eastwood Road, not far from my house. Now, whenever I walk along Eastwood, I stop and looking at the mullein marvel at the appropriateness of torches, hare's beard, velvet plant, Jacob's staff, shepherd's club, and Adam's flannel. A pink and white member of the morning glory family, hedge bindweed is one of my favorite flowers. Because the name hedge bindweed did not appeal to me, I refused to plant it until I learned that the plant has also been called bell bind, harvest lily, Rutland beauty, creepers, and lady's nightcap. In general I prefer older to newer names. Contemporary names often reflect advertising glitter. Recently Breck's sent me a description of their "Exclusive New Premier Daffodil Collection." For me the daffodil is a wholesome, homey flower of bank and brook and, no matter how ornate the blossom, it should not be named Palmares, Ambergate, Oriental Express, and Paola Veronese. Instead of budding spring, swelling with light and life, Breck's descriptions smacked of Hollywood and titillating lingerie advertisements. "For the first time ever a Butterfly Daffodil," Breck's wrote about Palmares, "with a diaphanous apricot-pink frilly cup subtly accented against pristine petals." I will probably order bulbs from Breck's but I won't call them Paola Veronese or Oriental Express. I will plant them in the side yard near the squill and Jacob's ladder and call them something familiar like girl's love or bright-eyed Eliza after my little daughter.

In learning the names of flowers, I also picked up remedies for stomach ailments. To cure "windy outgoings," John Gerarde (1597) recommended the marsh mallowe. "Whosoever is troubled with breaking of winde and weakness of stomack," Barnaby Googe suggested in *The Whole Art & Trade of Husbandry* (1596), should "use *Betony,* either the hearbe and flowre boyled in wine." Flowers even provided cure-alls for injured snakes. Being run over on the dirt road in front of Grandfather's farm was not certain death. To survive a snake had only to drag itself off the road and stretch out on moneywort or, as it was once known, herb twopence, yellow myrtle, creeping Joan, and wandering Taylor. I even discovered what to do if I fell asleep while exploring ruins and a snake crawled down my throat. On waking, Googe suggested, I could not do better than to drink "destilled water" of the "blessed Thistle." "A boy," Googe recounted, "into whose mouth as he slept in the feelde happened an Adder to creepe, was saved by the drinking of this water, the adder creeping out behind, without any hurt to the child."

Despite my interest in things digestive, most of my picking up is not done in libraries. I spend more time bent over in the front yard picking up sticks than I do hunched over old medical books. My trees, alas, are professionals and manufacture woodpiles. I sometimes think that if American industry would send workers to study my hickories and maples, domestic productivity would shoot up and hundreds of plants in the Far East would wither. Actually, I have learned a lot picking up sticks. Unlike facts discovered in libraries, this knowledge has resulted from experimentation or field work, as I say to acquaintances with scientific bents. When I bought my house and began research, I naively thought a lawn mower would grind most sticks into mulch. I was wrong; the lawn mower only broke big sticks into small sticks and scattered them over the yard. The way to get rid of sticks, I then decided, was to cart them away. Parking the lawn mower in the garage, I went into the house and got a sheet from the linen closet. I took it outside and, after spreading it on the ground and carefully placing rocks on all four corners so it would not take flight, I dumped a vast quantity of sticks on it. Even if I had been able to pull the four corners together, getting the sheet off the ground was impossible. I kicked two-thirds of the sticks back on the grass and managed to carry what was left into the woods behind the house; unfortunately, I only made two trips to the woods. Sheets are soft and thin, sticks hard and sharp; after my second trip the sheet was ready for the rag bag in the basement. This, I am afraid, led to some domestic discomfiture as experience proved me unable to distinguish a good from a bad sheet.

Next I bought a tarpaulin. Thick and sturdy, tarpaulins are stick-resistant. They are also heavy, and unless one is young and fit and believes a hernia is a bird that lives in marshes and eats frogs and minnows, and the occasional baby snake, he ought to avoid tarpaulins. After the tarpaulin I purchased a wheelbarrow. A red wheelbarrow looks good sitting next to a lawn mower in the garage. On a late spring evening when the tulips are blooming, the poppies swelling, and the rabbits nibbling, I feel competent and wonderfully handy when I look in the garage and see my wheelbarrow and lawn mower nestled side by side like eggs in a nest. Unfortunately, wheelbarrows nest better than they carry. At every mole run, my wheelbarrow lurched, tipped, and dropped a stick or two. By the time I dumped a load of sticks in the woods, the wheelbarrow was half empty. I did not lose heart, however; in field work, failure and improvisation are the parents of invention. In the garage was a plastic garbage can in which I had once kept grass seed. The can was not handsome; part of one side and both handles had been torn off. Its faults, however, proved virtues. Because carrying the can was awkward, I could not overload it and strain a muscle. Actually, the temptation to overload did not exist. If I put too many sticks in the can, they fell out through the side, pulling handfuls of other sticks behind them. I now keep the can by the garage door, and, whenever my trees start turning out groves of sticks, I trundle it out, load it, and drag the sticks off to the woods.

People who wander through life picking things up informally rarely develop obsessions. Mastering one yard of knowledge, however, can affect behavior. Last May a limb fell into a patch of poison ivy in my backyard. I did not know there was poison ivy near the house, but, allergic to it since childhood, I should have stayed away from the limb.

Having mastered sticks, I was not about to worry about a little poison ivy, and, mumbling "mind is superior to matter," not only did I carry the limb away but I ripped up the poison ivy bare-handed. Two days later I was in bed, swollen and itching. Of course, if wild touch-me-not or jewelweed, as it is often known, grew on Eastwood, I could have cured myself. Not only do the plant's juices stop poison ivy from itching, but they dry it up.

Eventually people themselves are picked up. Blown from the tree of life, they fall to the ground where they are gathered then carted off through the sky to that town with jasper walls and golden streets. While tarrying here, however, most folks get picked up for many things and in many ways. Perhaps the most common thing people are picked up for is driving too fast. I was once stopped for speeding; happily, some of the language I picked up reading hymnals got me out of the ticket. I had driven from Nashville to Hanover, Virginia, to spend Thanksgiving with my grandmother. We ate our Thanksgiving meal on Saturday rather than Thursday and instead of turkey had goose with relatives in Louisa. The goose must have hung too long and lost its patience, for soon after lunch it began honking. By midnight I was certain I had been poisoned and longed for angelica, a sure remedy not only for poisons but for the plague. There being no angelica in the yard, I had to endure until dawn when the goose suddenly rose, circled once, and headed south. Once the goose was out of sight and body, I recovered rapidly and at nine o'clock left for Tennessee. Leaving four hours later than planned, I drove faster than usual and near Cumberland Courthouse whipped through a radar trap eleven miles above the speed limit. Despite the goose, I was ready when the patrolman pulled up behind me. "Praise the Lord," I said, getting out of the car to shake the policeman's hand, "God's in his heaven this sabbath." When the policeman stopped and looked at me, I knew he was as good as in the collection plate, and I launched my appeal.

"Brother, do you follow Jesus?" I asked. Then before he could reply I answered my question. "Yes," I said, "you do. From your soul the sun shines more glorious than that glowing in any earthly sky. In that bright sun isn't there pardon for me?" "Don't you think, Christian brother," I continued, stepping forward again, opening my arms, fingers outspread in benediction and familiarity, "don't you think that on this the seventh day you could rest and forgive me? When your summons comes to meet the blessed Savior and you put on the Crown of Glory, no jewel will shine brighter than that of Forgiveness." At first the policeman did not speak. He glanced at his watch and then as I took another step forward said hurriedly, "The Justice of the Peace has gone to church, and she won't be out for two hours, so you can go." "Hallelujah," I exclaimed, raising my hands and rolling my eyes heavenward until the whites showed. By the time I looked down, the policeman had gotten in his car, turned around, and was racing back along the road toward the world, speed traps, and sanity.

Vicki and I have three small children. This fall when one entered kindergarten and another started nursery school, we began talking about education. Rarely did we mention courses or technique. What we talked about were the children's abilities and characters, specifically what they picked up from us and our families. Although there has been some disagreement on the matter, I think it fair to conclude that the children inherited good looks, generosity, and genius from their father whereas any tendency toward the untoward probably broke off from their mother's family tree. At dinner last week Edward, who is four, announced, "In my house there will be no coffee, no tea, no beer, no alcohol, no drugs, no Coca-Cola, no smoking, no hamburgers, and no french fries." "Almost as discriminating as his father," I said to Vicki when Edward completed the list. Francis, who is five, is a thread off the old cashmere too. Just yesterday he refused a bathing suit which Vicki bought him, explaining it looked like Hawaii. Francis resembles me a great deal. When I was a sophomore in high school, I went to the state mathematics contest in Algebra II. Not only has Francis completed first-grade math, but he is interested in the computer, and the school has set up a special class for him. Although most of my colleagues own computers, I don't have one. In truth, I am not comfortable typing and have been afraid to touch a computer. Still, if Francis can use one, then the ability is in the blood. Come the fall I am going to pick up one.

Schooldays

WHENEVER I return to Nashville I visit my old high school, Montgomery Bell Academy on Harding Road. Usually I go on a day when students are not around. I walk over the grounds and sometimes look through a window into a building. In part I go because the visit gives my children something to do outside. There are no sidewalks where my parents live in Belle Meade, and Mother tells me that Percy Warner Park has become the haunt of drug dealers. At MBA the children run free, rolling down the long hill in the front yard. At the bottom they find scraps of wood and build bridges across the creek. Bouncing up and down, they pretend they are prisoners on a pirate ship, forced to walk the plank. During my last trip to Nashville, Edward, my four-year-old, asked when I attended MBA, so I showed him the yearbook for 1959, my senior year. "Daddy," Edward said that night at dinner, "you did lots of things. You were a baseball man, a football man, and a student man." "But Daddy," he continued, "football is bad. People get hurt and take drugs." "Yes," I said, "football is bad. But it wasn't bad when I went to school. It was fun. Things change."

As I wander over the grounds at MBA, I think about the changes which have occurred since I entered the school as a thirteen-year-old in 1955. Some of the changes like those which have ruined football make me uncomfortable. The crisp blocklike gymnasium and the green weedless playing fields bordered by tracks and bleachers, all enclosed within a high gleaming silver fence, seem emblematic of the pressures which have lessened play, transforming sport into business and even corrupting learning itself. I don't spend much time near the playing fields, however. Their symmetrical neatness seems sterile, and I prefer the front yard where thoughts grow like crabgrass, random and unkempt. Atop the hill overlooking Harding Road, Civil War cannons have been allowed to rot. Their wheels and carriages have fallen away, and barrels sink into the dirt, the metal flaking off brown and brittle. At the bottom of the hill, the old spring house has been torn down, and most of the artillery shells which lined the road up to the school have disappeared. Those which remain slump against the ground or lean crazily out toward Harding Road, held in place by mossy bits of cement.

In the yearbook for 1957, a student wrote he hoped that when "the night" drew near a traveler would find "the paths I leave behind." Unlike thought, change is unsentimental and comes rapidly, and paths disappear in a season. Amid neither modernity nor neglect is there a trace of me at MBA. During my final year I won two awards, and my name was affixed to plaques hung in the main building. The awards are no longer given at MBA, and the plaques have been removed. A friend found one in the trash and gave it to my mother, thinking she might like it. The plaque is pitiful and shoddy. For the first six years of the award the names of the winners were dutifully recorded. After those initial years, however, affixing names became arbitrary. Even though the award was made every year for another decade and a half, two- and three-year gaps appeared during which no name was added, and the plaque like the cannons in the yard fell away into fragments.

Named after Montgomery Bell, an ironmonger, MBA's origins were commercial and prosaic. With some stretching the school's lineage could be traced to the nineteenth century and the old University of Nashville. Such origins, however, seemed too ordinary to inspire, and in discussions of education Nashvilleans often evoked a romanticized antebellum South, not the heat and fire of Montgomery Bell's smelters. The picture was never clearly drawn but was always genteel, slow-paced, and seductive. It was at odds with the bustling industrial world of Bell and then my mid-South of the 1950s. This rarely bothered anyone, though, for references to the past were more habitual and emotional than considered and practical. Much as parishioners genuflect before entering pews in highish Episcopal churches, then sit down and settle comfortably into the serious business of looking around to see who is with whom, so Nashvilleans made ritualistic gestures toward a fictionalized old southern order then went their ways building malls and subdivisions.

In 1955 MBA consisted of three buildings, a small red-brick gymnasium with locker rooms and a basketball court, a classroom building housing a study hall on the second floor and rooms for mathematics and science on the first, and the Ball Building containing an administrative office, a room for the library, the seventh and eighth grades, rooms for English and language classes, a cafeteria in the basement, and on the

first floor a reception room cluttered with sofas and tables, athletic tro-
phies, pictures of graduating classes, and an assortment of oddities including an old jukebox. Forward of the other two buildings, the Ball
Building sat high above Harding Road, six white columns towering over
holly and magnolia, a flagpole, and two howitzers, used, I was told, by
Grant at the siege of Vicksburg. For Nashvilleans, the columns evoked
not simply a celluloid South of cavaliers and camellias, but also a Greece
of the imagination, learned and cosmopolitan, a Greece far different
from that peopled by the barbaric tribes who bled before Troy. "From
Hellas' learned men," a student poet wrote in 1956, "were our first memories." Reality was cruder and less Athenian. Beside the Ball Building
was a parking lot for students' cars, old Mercurys with bulldozed hoods
and moon discs, black 1950 Fords, tail ends pulled down to the asphalt
by lowering blocks, and new two-toned Chevrolets, spinners on the
wheels and long silver exhaust pipes running out from under motors
and along the sides of the cars. Mufflers were not popular, and at the
end of the class day students sat in their cars, gunning motors, before
dragging out of the lot, tires shrieking and hands held high above the
windows making obscene gestures.

Along with "Hellas' learned men," the columns, the poet stated, sym-
bolized "a form of life our fathers lived and loved, the life of gentlemen."
From small towns in and around Middle Tennessee, few of our fathers
and grandfathers rocked their lives away in graceful patrician idleness.
We had not been sent to MBA to become cultists devoted to an old
order. The gentleman was an ideal to which people had grown accustomed to praising, so much so that they actually believed in its existence, albeit it did not influence daily life. Out of custom, platitudinous
and reflexive, Nashvilleans regularly declared that shaping a gentleman
was the purpose of good education. Much like the concept itself, however, the practice was more gesture than substance. In the hall of the
Ball Building hung a portrait of Robert E. Lee. At MBA nothing was ever
said about Lee; somehow, though, we realized he represented the gentleman. If asked we would have praised his life; at the same time we suspected that the gentleman was merely decoration to grace a hall, sensitive and attractive but nevertheless bloodless.

Indeed, despite the portrait and the cannons, the magnolias and the
columns, we knew little actual southern history. In college I would hear
that I was fortunate to live in the section of the country which lost the
Civil War. With the pain and suffering of defeat, so the argument ran,

came hard-won knowledge and understanding. No other part of the nation had lost a war; consequently people raised outside the South were soft and glib, given to superficial sociological formulations and practically incapable of looking into the dark recesses of the human heart. Defeat made ours a privileged birth, raising us above the simple material concerns which corrupted the rest of the nation and initiating us, I was told, into profound insight. The argument was not so unconvincing as it was beside the point. Alight with the natural energy of youth and convinced that pots of gold and lust lay before us, my friends and I eagerly burned through adolescence, hardly nodding at the marmoreal past. Of more importance to us than ghosts at Chickamauga and Shiloh were Christmas dances and golf and tennis lessons at the Belle Meade Country Club.

In the late 1950s controversy over integration raged in Nashville and over the South. Few MBA students thought much about it, and, repeating what they heard at home, they pushed quickly on to other, usually more fleshly, topics. In contrast to students, however, adults found the matter deeply disturbing, and, along with advice to acquire athletic and social skills, I began receiving books about the Civil War as presents. In an oblique way a halfhearted attempt was being made to make me aware of southern history with, I suppose, the general intent of making me conservative. The plan, if ever thought out clearly enough to be a plan, didn't work. The books of Bruce Catton and Douglas Southall Freeman piled up. After lying about unread, they were eventually put on shelves in studies and living rooms, places where they could be seen and taken as a sign of interest in and commitment to the southern way of life. At school I learned that Sam Davis had attended one of the early forerunners of MBA. Tennessee's Nathan Hale, Davis was born outside Nashville in Smyrna, a town known in my schooldays for speed traps and now known for a Japanese car manufacturer. Caught delivering messages for the Confederacy, Davis refused to betray his comrades and, although "only a boy," was hanged, his nobility moving his Yankee captors to tears. Attitudes toward Davis's "martyrdom" mirrored Nashville's attitudes toward things southern in the 1950s. An abstraction which could be praised without risk, Davis's life was held up as an exemplar of integrity, patriotism, and devotion. When it came to actual living, however, no parent recommended that a child behave like Davis. Good enough for lip service, Greek, genteel, and antebellum ideals were not things to govern daily life, and when the draft for the Vietnam War threatened my friends, those who were not married with a family, safely in the navy, or in graduate school like me pushed extravagant gesture out of mind and rushed to join units of the National Guard, the Belle Meade Army and Air Force as they came to be known.

In 1955 two hundred and thirty students, forty of these in the seventh and eighth grades, attended MBA. School life was comparatively rude, and a number of students dressed rough, appearing in the now-comic uniform of motorcycle boots, jeans, T-shirt, and red James Dean jacket with a fluffy white lining. During my first year at MBA the high point of school days was the noon brawl. All classes were dismissed for lunch at the same time. After eating, students milled around outside the Ball Building. Often a group of juniors would gather and chant "the juniors rule the school." Inevitably this precipitated a brawl in which students hurdled into one another, eventually falling to the ground in great wrestling piles. Frequently trousers were run up the flagpole, and occasionally bones were broken.

Outside class hours the scrapping continued, usually with pupils from other schools and provoked by MBA's athletic success. In 1955 MBA won the state championship in football. With only two coaches and one hundred and ninety boys in the high school, MBA's athletic triumphs caused envy and astonishment. A few people also resented MBA because it was private, and, although the school did not cater to the sons of the wealthy, there not being the wealth that exists today, MBA students were occasionally labeled "rich boys." All this—the midday brawls, the athletic successes, the taunting, plus the general aggressiveness of adolescent boys—translated into the attitude that "we beat the crap out of you in football, and we can beat the crap out of you in any other way." During my first year rumors of fights with local schools—Dupont, East, Cohn, Ryan—abounded. In my second year the school quieted down, in part because the athletic teams were not so successful. In part it calmed down because my class and those immediately following contained boys more homogeneous and less athletic than classes ahead of us. At the center of my class were boys who had gone to elementary school together and who suspected they could not beat anything out of anybody. At one hundred and eighteen pounds my first year and then one hundred and forty-five my second, I was not eager to argue, much less fight. Still, even I occasionally went to rough spots. I stopped going to such places my junior year.

One night I went to Cherokee Orchard, an old barn in Flat Rock off the Nolensville Road. A rock band played and tough boys from all over town gathered there to fight and pick up girls. I went to Cherokee Orchard more out of curiosity than anything else. Terrified of both fights and fast girls, I hung about the edges of the dance floor, a safe voyeur, I thought, until a huge boy, muscles rippling in my memory like waves, tapped me on the shoulder and said, "Excuse me, but would you like to fight?" "No, thank you," I said backing swiftly away through the crowd toward the door, "I have to go home."

At a time when it should have been expanding and becoming more academic, MBA deteriorated. A bright and once competent administrator, the headmaster had aged and become ineffective. The midday brawls and a series of ludicrous confrontations resulted. One morning a heavy granite rock appeared on the desk of the study hall monitor. When no one came forward to remove the rock at his request, the headmaster said that if the rock were not taken away by ten o'clock, he would convene an assembly and we would remain in study hall until whoever was responsible for the rock's appearance came forward and took it away. At ten o'clock the rock was still on the desk, and accordingly the bell rang for study hall. The headmaster began the assembly by lecturing us. He droned tonelessly on until interrupted by a voice from the back of the room, shouting, "You son of a bitch." Identifying the speaker was not difficult, and, after the laughter subsided, the headmaster stared sternly at the boy and said, "What did you say?" "I said," the boy replied standing up, "that the square of the hypotenuse is equal to the sum of the squares of the other two sides." I cannot recall what happened next. Whatever occurred, however, was anticlimactic. The assembly was dismissed, and by the end of the day a student geologist had hauled the rock away and rolled it down the hill into the creek.

In the fall of 1957 Francis Carter became headmaster. Blue jeans and T-shirts were banished from campus. Ducktails and long hair became grounds for dismissal. Cars without mufflers were not allowed into the parking lot. The lunch hours for various classes were staggered and the brawls ended. The rule against smoking was enforced and smokers were expelled. In fact, enrollment seemed to dip as numbers of boys were expelled. By the end of a year MBA was a different and better school in which the most vivid moments were academic and athletic, not chaotic. Not only had he attended or taught in a number of good private schools—

St. Paul's, Gilman in Baltimore, and Episcopal in Alexandria—but Mr.
Carter was strong and energetic and enjoyed the reputation of having
been a college athlete, the Yankees having offered him, so tale had it, a
minor league baseball contract. In addition he was from Virginia. In the
1950s the social pecking order in the South was marvelously complex.
In general, however, Tennesseans looked down upon the lower South
and Southwest, saying that, although nice people lived in places like
Mississippi and Texas, they were "not our sort." In contrast, Tennesseans felt slightly inferior to Virginians and were willing to defer more
to Mr. Carter's wishes as he remade the school than if he had been a
native of Alabama, for example.

After Mr. Carter's death, the old science building was gutted and after
being rebuilt was named the Francis E. Carter Building. A dedicatory
stone was affixed to the side of the building and on it tribute was paid to
Mr. Carter as "Scholar, Athlete, and Gentleman." Alas, the tribute was
formulaic and just as false as empurpled evocations of Athenian education and the antebellum South. Instead of truth, something education
should encourage people to pursue, the inscription on the stone was
platitudinous. Mr. Carter was not a scholar, and although rumors of his
athletic ability in college initially may have eased his way at MBA, his
bat and glove had long gathered dust by the time he moved to Nashville.
He was a good man, but no gentleman could have remade MBA. He was
more than words without meaning. He was Headmaster, Teacher, and
Friend; and in truth he was Yardman, Boilerman, and Trashman, forever going to school at midnight or at dawn to put some aspect of the
plant to rights.

Conventional gestures satisfy, however; unlike truth, they rarely provoke inconvenient dissent. Despite the portrait of Lee and the story
about Sam Davis, little history was taught when I entered MBA. Consequently southern mythology with its ideal of "the life of a gentleman"
could exist in a soft imagination, undefined and unchallenged by truth.
During my first year I studied world history and memorized facts about
Babylon and Hammurabi. Never did I study American history. Actually,
as an adolescent I was almost incapable of thought, and if I had studied
southern history all I would remember today would probably be odd
facts about Andrew Jackson or Henry Clay. Moreover, the society in
which I grew up stressed manners rather than thought, and for that
matter social graces rather than social concerns. We learned quickly
who we were and how we were supposed to behave. At home we were

forever being told to be polite and warned not to speak back. This kind of intellectual repression did not bother us; it made our world stable and practically no one suffered through an "identity crisis." On the other hand, we were not particularly analytical and rarely tested ourselves or questioned society. We learned how to mix with and judge people. Rating manners too highly, however, we undervalued ideas and as a rule were not interested in abstractions or problems not closely identified with an individual. In the long run the lack of interest in abstractions, the environment for example, minimized concern and allowed exploitation and ruination to occur. In the short run it shaped students sensitive more to form than substance, ultimately turning out adults concerned more with rule and law than spirit.

At MBA I took the normal course, four years of English and math, two of Latin and two of French, three of science, and one of history. Despite tests being given almost daily, I enjoyed math, particularly the kinds which relied heavily on formulas. My sophomore year I competed in the state mathematics contest in second-year algebra. After the morning examination which relied exclusively upon formulas, I led or very nearly led the competition. In the afternoon, however, I did poorly on word problems and finished twenty-seventh. Solving word problems necessitated a little original thought, and that did not come easily to someone with my upbringing. Plane geometry was my favorite mathematical subject. I liked shaping the odd, ornate proof, digressing logically from the straightforward then suddenly turning and rushing to a conclusion. Not only did mathematics have an almost innate appeal to someone from a background like mine, obsessed with form, but in retrospect it proved good training for a certain kind of writing, the *Reader's Digest* sort built on simple, declarative sentences and raised on the premise that truth is easily discernible and can be expressed clearly.

A dead language, the rules of which were not in flux, Latin appealed to me in much the same way as mathematics and I was disappointed that only two years of Latin were taught. Partly because of mediocre teaching but also because the language was alive and unreliable, I disliked French. Although science was competently and enthusiastically taught, the sciences never appealed to me. With emphasis upon law and element, science should have attracted me. No character, however, is consistent, and what I missed in science was the wonderful irrational poetry of earth. As a boy I spent summers on my grandfather's farm in Virginia, catching and studying the small creatures of field and woodland. I wanted science to do the impossible and capture the excitement I felt on finding a box turtle, its shell completely yellow, or on discovering a patch of fox grapes running blue and full down the slope of an embankment.

The success and reputation of a small school often depend upon one or two individuals, the teacher or coach who by force of intelligence or personality startles and sometimes influences a generation of students. During my years there was one fine teacher at MBA, Mrs. Lowry, who supervised English studies and taught junior and senior classes. When science disappointed me, I turned to her courses for excitement. Mrs. Lowry knew that practice bettered, and, every two weeks from my freshman year on, I turned in a theme, each with two rough outlines and drafts. Remarkably bright and always kind, Mrs. Lowry liked teaching and believed it important. We soon realized she thought both students and subject mattered. Not only did that flatter us, but it gave her power over us. Today I remember almost nothing read in Mrs. Lowry's classes except, mundanely enough, Kenneth Roberts's *Arundel* and *Northwest Passage* and the only thing I can recall from these particular books is the account of a character who went insane and hid a human head in his back pack, pulling it out and gnawing on it whenever he felt hungry. Yet Mrs. Lowry had a long influence upon me. From her I learned that studying literature could be a joy and a challenge and that teaching was a worthwhile occupation.

Despite Nashvilleans' emphasis upon manners and the constant evocation of a cultured, high-principled antebellum South, MBA provided no aesthetic or moral education as such. Art and music were the province of women. Typically, a girl studied French and art in secondary school and college. The summer after her junior year in college she went on an eight- or nine-week guided tour of Western Europe. After college she married, joined the Junior League, at first doing charity work then becoming active in the arts, sometimes focusing on the symphony or a community playhouse, but usually on restoration. Eventually she became a member of the Colonial Dames, and every year thereafter sold beaten biscuits stuffed with country ham at the Dames' annual fair. Although the Dames, for example, brought in male experts from outside Nashville to assist in restoration and the experts were almost always well thought of and well entertained by the community, a career in the arts was not something Nashville boys ever considered. Music and art were not so much thought to be unsuitable as they were simply not parts of our youth. Later in life as monied successes some men would be pulled into the arts to be board members or fund raisers.

The annual for my sophomore year was dedicated to the retiring headmaster. In the dedication the headmaster was called a "true Christian gentleman." Like "gentleman," "Christian" had little meaning for us, being simply a baggy complimentary term sufficient to most ceremonial occasions. Although my schoolmates and I attended church youth groups on Sunday nights, we attended for social not religious reasons. Religion was a private matter apart from our world of manners, so private, in fact, that it played no active role in our lives. If asked whether or not we were Christians, and certainly no one from the right background would have posed such a question, we would have said yes, not as affirmation but as the gesture most likely to end the conversation. At MBA religion was not mentioned in the classroom, and morality as a subject for discussion usually arose only when a speaker from outside the school addressed a morning assembly. Probably out of a sense of courtesy or maybe from the conviction that education ought to shape the moral man, speakers who had been making the rounds of Nashville schools were sometimes invited to MBA. Often associated with a local church or the Fellowship of Christian Athletes, most appeared countrified and naive. When they testified how they discovered Christ, fourth down and inches from the goal line, I cringed in embarrassment. When they did not talk about scoring touchdowns on the field of life, speakers spooned out versions of *The Little Engine That Could,* more often than not trotting out the inspirational story of Glenn Cunningham, the champion miler who had been so badly burned as a boy that doctors thought he would not walk again.

In her intensity and enthusiasm, Mrs. Lowry was almost moral. Herself offering no simpleminded program for spiritual betterment, her classes demonstrated the importance of commitment and intelligence. Unlike speakers who had designs upon students, she succeeded because she had no uplifting schedule. Too naive to convince, most overt moral teaching fails and even repulses, and the only affecting "moral" instruction forced upon students at MBA was repulsive, if not immoral. In 1955 the honor system had been established at the school for a decade. Copied from the University of Virginia, it purported to promote honor among students by punishing stealing, lying, and cheating. Honor and the honor system were part of that southern mythology of the gentleman, Robert E. Lee, white dresses on the veranda, and black hands in the kitchen. Unlike other portions of the myth which remained vague, things worthy only of allusion and gesture, the honor system took hard shape. A flawed, cruel presence enabling people to weigh fault by rule rather than mind, the honor system had little to do with living and coping and should never have been applied to adolescents. After having been caught cheating on more than one occasion, a student was usually forced to apologize to the entire school at assembly. Ostensibly corrective and edifying, the scene was destructive. Not only did it affect the boy apologizing, stripping him of dignity and privacy and often reducing him to tears, but it marked those forced to listen, making me aware of the inhumanity of rule and principle and souring the word "honor" forever.

At graduation I wondered how well MBA had prepared me for college. Later I realized that for the most part age rather than schooling prepares one. In truth I needed little academic preparation for Vanderbilt. So shoddy was the instruction there that I soon lost interest in things academic. In mathematics I was placed in a freshman logic course taught by a graduate student. The teacher was well-meaning but dull; moreover, he suffered from mannerisms. During a single fifty-minute class period, he cleared his throat one hundred and twenty-one times and said "all right" fifty-five times, or so I calculated. Before he appeared at the next meeting, I entertained the class with an imitation, snorting and all-righting with fervor, not knowing, alas, that the poor man's wife was enrolled in the course.

Bedeviled not by mannerisms but by a growing family and his own academic work, the graduate student who taught English handled the lyric poems from the hackneyed Brooks and Warren anthology with the enthusiasm of a funeral director in a graveyard. "That man," I said one morning walking to class, "couldn't teach his way out of the shithouse." Unfortunately, the teacher happened to be walking right behind me and overheard my remark. Shortly afterward my grade itself began to have an unpleasant aroma. The graduate student who discussed history with a group of us once a week was much better. The professor, though, who lectured the course twice a week was an alcoholic. Forced to cancel more than a third of his lectures, he frequently dismissed class early on the days he appeared. Attending zoology was unnecessary. The professor rarely strayed from previous years' lectures, and most students bought old notebooks and cut class. When the professor did change the order of things, he apologized, saying, "If you are following last year's lectures, don't worry. What I am going to say next will appear five pages over in your notes." The only event of zoological interest which occurred in class was that one day I discovered that some small green worms had colonized the crepe soles of my saddle shoes, tunneling up from the toes into the heels. The single good teacher I had was Mr. Phillips in French, a subject for which MBA had prepared me miserably. Unfortunately, an ulcer ate through the wall of Mr. Phillips's stomach midway through the semester and he disappeared from the course. Knowing that I would be at Vanderbilt, Mr. Carter asked me after graduation if I would help coach freshman football in the fall. I was happy to assist and eagerly began work in August. At registration at Vanderbilt I was arbitrarily assigned to a gym class which met three afternoons a week. Not only did the dean refuse to grant that the exercise I got while coaching was equivalent to a gym class but he refused to transfer me to another section so I could continue to coach. "No exceptions can be made," he said. Not realizing that exceptions were made all the time, I took him at his word and stopped coaching. At the end of the year I left Vanderbilt.

If I had taken gym at another time and continued coaching at MBA, I might have stayed at Vanderbilt. Having few expectations about college, I was neither disappointed nor surprised by the mediocre instruction and assumed teaching was similarly lax at other colleges. Coaching gave me pleasure, partly because sports were as important to me at MBA as studies. Although specific events would be forgotten and would "mean but little in the spiralling years to come," participation in athletics, a student wrote in the 1958 yearbook, formed that "rock on which we build our strength." While adequate grades came easily to me at MBA, athletics were more difficult. Would that I now could claim a great deal for athletics and write that they kept me out of trouble during adolescence. Although they kept me tired and at home, I was not the sort of adventuresome boy who got into real trouble. All I am sure that sports did was make me happy. Although the student was correct in writing that particular events would be forgotten, a general memory remains, not, however, cold and formidably hard like the rock of character, but warm and light, a greening southerly breeze blowing smiles.

If Mrs. Lowry was the dominant woman in the school, the dominant man, aside from the headmaster, was Coach Owen, during my time basketball, football, and track coach. Quiet and skillful, he coached and in the process taught like Mrs. Lowry not a particular lesson but a way of

behaving and ultimately of thinking. If Mrs. Lowry showed us that reading was an activity worthy of intelligence and commitment, Coach
Owen taught us that participation in athletics was worthy only if it
bettered us by involving our better selves. How the game was played
mattered to Coach Owen. He believed that hard work and fair play on
the athletic field helped shape a decent adult. Because of Coach Owen's
high, almost moral vision of athletics, boys took sports seriously and
pushed themselves for him. As a result his teams generally had winning
seasons although frequently matched against schools with enrollments
vastly larger than that of MBA. Ironically, Coach Owen's notion of athletics as elevating has made it practically impossible for me to enjoy
sports today, except those like road racing in which most participants
are amateurs, running for fun and companionship, not profit.

Although football was important to me at MBA, I don't remember
much about it. The smells of the locker room, showers, damp equipment, powder, tape have all vanished. Perhaps I recall so little because
football mattered, and I accepted the world of the game uncritically. As
a poor athlete I wanted to play so badly that making the team drained
all thought. When I was put on the first team on defense, I sensed it
was likely to be the only time in my life I would be first team in anything. Toward the end of the second game of the season, someone
kicked me in the elbow. The next morning my elbow was the size of an
orange, and I went to our family doctor. After studying an x-ray, he said
my elbow was full of bone chips and told me not to play for six weeks. I
did not repeat what the doctor said to my parents. Instead I soaked the
elbow in cold water, and on Monday the student trainer made me a large
doughnut bandage out of foam rubber and I practiced that day and all
other days.

Most of my recollections of football are fragmentary, at best the odd
glimpse or two. I remember wearing number seventy-five when I was a
senior. Embarrassingly but naturally enough when I recall the concerns
of teenage boys, I remember who on the team had the longest and who
had the shortest penis. In a kind of joyous way, I also remember when I
didn't play by the rules, foreshadowing, I suppose, eccentricity or low-
level rebelliousness: biting a player in a pileup, provoking him to hit me
and thus draw a fifteen-yard penalty, and grabbing the ankle of an opposing player so our back could slip past on a kickoff for ninety-two
yards and a touchdown.

Actually, I remember more about baseball than football. Until my junior year I had never played organized baseball, and I only played it then to fill spring afternoons. Unlike football, I never took it seriously. Consequently I was not so much a participant, part of and involved in a moment, as I was an observer, watching myself and in the process pressing particular occurrence into memory. What I remember are not victory and loss but moments ludicrous in the discrepancy between expectation and event. I played right field and first base, usually the latter because I could not catch fly balls, inevitably losing them in the sun. In a game against a school owned by the Church of Christ, an opposing player singled to left field. "Good hit," I said when he reached first. "Your team," he answered, "ain't worth a shit." In truth, we weren't very good, but we did manage to beat his school. I may have even scored the winning run, getting on base after being hit by a pitched ball. Since I could not really hit, once striking out seven times in a row, I tried to get hit. Successful, I got on base five times more often as a hit batsman than as a hitter. Our coach was Charlie Matlock, the assistant football coach. I liked him immensely. From East Tennessee, he was out of place at MBA—Middle Tennesseans looked down upon East and West Tennesseans, seeing the former as yokels and the latter as no better than Mississippians. Spontaneous and sometimes silly and careless, Coach Matlock lacked Coach Owen's stature and skills. But he was always nice to me, and he made playing fun by being unpredictable. At MBA good athletes ran track or played tennis or golf in the spring while nonathletes played baseball. The school did not have a baseball field so we practiced a mile away behind the Veteran's Hospital off White Bridge Road next to St. Mary's Orphanage.

Keeping the field in playing shape was MBA's responsibility, and one afternoon, after deciding that the grass was too high, Coach Matlock decided to burn off the infield. As soon as he lit the grass, however, a breeze blew across the field, whipping flames up to our knees. We tore off our jackets and rushed about trying to beat down the flames, but there was little we could do. The fire jumped the infield at second base and, burning through the high outfield grass, raced toward St. Mary's. Just, though, as the flames reached a reedy thicket of bamboolike weeds bordering the orphanage, the wind changed and two fire trucks and a red chief's car roared into sight, lights flashing, sirens wailing. "Who is the jackass who started the fire?" the chief said, turning to Coach Matlock once the blaze was out.

"In the years to come," the valedictorian of my class predicted, we will remember "most vividly our class," the boys in whose company we spent four years learning and playing. In the late 1950s distractions from school were comparatively few, and students made strong friendships. Today when I visit Nashville and meet a classmate, I feel warm affection, spontaneous and uncritical. Almost like a relative come to town from the country, I want to hear about his family. At a larger school, one which girls attended, emotion perhaps would not have bound friends quite so solidly. My friends and I dated a great deal, usually girls from Harpeth Hall, a private country day school for girls and something of a sister school. In my school years, though, relationships with girls were insignificant when compared to those with boys. Despite fond dreams of endless fondling, I did not lay a hand on a girl in high school. Actually, a good many more years would pass before I dared to move beyond hand holding to groping. Amid the male friendships, however, was no homo-sexuality. Like an exotic custom practiced on a South Sea Island, its existence was known but foreign, something not to be taken seriously, or condemned, but to be giggled about.

Unlike the valedictorian's prediction, my memories of classmates are more general than vivid. Perhaps that is why I am fond of them. No classmate is associated with searing unpleasantness or disappointment. In fact, my particular memories are slight and humorous. In the back of the room, for example, in which Spanish was taught was a large closet, one big enough for a small armchair desk. One morning shortly after a new Spanish teacher appeared at MBA, Chuck Chumbley secreted him-self in the closet before class. After the class had been underway for ten or so minutes, I knocked at the door. "Miss Smith, I am sorry to inter-rupt," I said, "but I have a message for Chuck Chumbley from the office." "You must be mistaken," Miss Smith answered, "he is not in this class." "Are you sure?" I said. "The office told me he would be here." After she assured me Chuck was not in the room, I apologized for the interruption and left. Five minutes later I was back, saying the office insisted Chuck was in the room. Once more we went through the con-versation. Eventually Miss Smith showed me her roll and I left. Another five minutes passed, and I returned. This time I did not knock; instead I opened the door and said loudly, "Chuck Chumbley, are you here? I have a message for you to go to the office." With that Chuck threw open the closet door and striding out with an armful of books said, "Here I am. Let's go to the office." On the way out he turned to Miss Smith and said, "I don't like sunlight, so I always study in the closet. Everybody knows that." "That's right," I said, and we ran down the stairs.

During my last two years at MBA I paid Jeffrey Buntin a dollar or two a week to pick me up on his way to school in the morning. Jeffrey drove a green Henry J. Because the gas pedal stuck to the floor, Jeffrey attached a string to the pedal and drove with the string in his right hand, the car bucking about in traffic, shooting rapidly forward then suddenly dying. Other drivers gave Jeffrey a wide berth, seeing the car moving in what must have appeared to be an arbitrary manner. That's the way I like to think of my education at MBA, an old Henry J., held together by string and sputtering along in an arbitrary fashion, but nonetheless running through years.

Things, as I told Edward, though, change. Thirty years and a generation have passed since I entered MBA. Instead of being the stuff of inspirational story, Sam Davis is now material for fund raising. Recently I received a letter from the Alumni Association, soliciting contributions for MBA. Depending on the amount I gave, I would become a member in decreasing order and prestige of the Trustees Circle, Ironmaster's Club, MBA Cabinet, Headmaster's Club, MBA Fellows, Sam Davis Society, Monogram Club, and lastly Contributors. Instead of being an intriguing and irritating hodgepodge of gesture and sentiment, academics and athletics, the school is now, I am told, "a recognized educational leader in the Southeast." "Take stock again of what MBA has meant to you and to many of your associates," the fund raisers urged. To my little associates, MBA means a place where they can run up and down hills and build bridges. To me, the contemporary school matters little, about as much as the school of the 1950s matters to present-day students. Still, that school of the 1950s means something to me.

The last time I was in Nashville I found my old letter jacket in the attic. I brought it back to Connecticut, explaining to Vicki that Edward might want to wear it someday. "How many people in Connecticut," I said, "have an MBA jacket?" Having been awarded two or three jackets, some classmates gave them to girlfriends. I struggled to get my single jacket and was not about to give it away then or throw it away now. "She's not getting my jacket" was printed in italics under my picture in the yearbook. MBA and I have aged and are different from what we once were; yet I can't quite let go.

At Cambridge

"WE TAKE Americans for many reasons. Either they are scholars, which you are not," Tom Henn began after I had been in Cambridge four weeks. Tom was right. I had not come to Britain to study. I had been a student at Sewanee, so disciplined that classmates called me "Machine" and sometimes made whirring or clanking sounds when I entered a room. Tom did not explain clearly why St. Catharine's admitted me. The college's reasons were probably as vague as my reasons for applying. In part I applied because I did not receive a Rhodes scholarship to Oxford. Although I never expected to win a scholarship, I didn't think I would be rejected either, and until December of my senior year, when I was interviewed by the Rhodes Committee, thoughts of green quadrangles, madrigals at dawn, and strawberries and cream for tea occasionally drifted through my dreams. Unfortunately, I bored easily and interviewed poorly in those days. Bromides did not bubble naturally and smoothly from my lips, and when asked a hackneyed or ponderous question I had trouble keeping my tongue in check. When asked about the mission of the United Nations, I tried to liven up the interview and said, "On the radio the other night, I heard a preacher say 'U.N. or U.S.—what's it going to be? We have to choose.' That struck me as interesting." That, alas, did not interest the committee, and drawing wit and wisdom from a highland preacher, I must have appeared remarkably provincial.

In truth, I was provincial, not, however, because of preachers. Only rarely did I hear preachers on the radio, and, when I did, I paid little attention to idea, listening instead for colorful language. In part I applied to Cambridge because I suspected that I had received a narrow education. At Sewanee I was a bookworm, studying seven days a week, thinking little, and observing less. Moreover, at that time Sewanee itself was provincial. Ten thousand acres atop the spur of a mountain, the college was contained both physically and intellectually. Among students cults of the South and the Christian gentleman flourished, and form often seemed more important than substance. "Our glorious mother ever be," students sang in the alma mater. Sewanee was a kind of mother, nurturing and protecting but also smothering. Much as first- and second-year courses in English were restricted to "great writers"—Homer, Sophocles, Aeschylus, Dante, Lucretius—so the whole university seemed turned toward the past, not a past of butchery and injustice, a past to anger and quicken, but a past of tradition empurpled by sentiment, a past so superior to the present that it sapped vital curiosity and led to cool satisfaction.

Even when problems beyond the mountain touched the college, Sewanee transformed them into the quaintly anecdotal and thus reduced their significance. Until my last year Clara's, the lone restaurant at Sewanee, was segregated. Then some people from Chattanooga staged a sit-in that coincided with the annual meeting of a secret college society. During the meeting students drank heavily, after which they roamed about waving lanterns and singing songs about George Washington. More raucous than melodious, the singing disturbed the early evening nap of an ancient relic of a bishop of Arkansas. "Jerry, what's that noise?" she asked a student who rented a room in her house. "Oh, it's nothing, Miss Amy," he said. "It's just a bunch of men from Grundy County, going down to Clara's to hang the sit-iners." "Dear me," Miss Amy replied. "I don't mind the men hanging those people, but I do wish they would give them a trial first."

I didn't know to which college to apply at Cambridge, and since no one at Sewanee seemed able to advise me, I chose St. Catharine's on a whim. Because my mother was named Katharine and once went to St. Catherine's School in Richmond, Virginia, and because a girl named Catherine was on my mind, I picked St. Catharine's. Realizing that the deadline for formal applications had long passed, I wrote a letter to Tom Henn, who supervised English studies at the college. I decided to read English at Cambridge because I had majored in English at Sewanee and didn't want to study hard for examinations. Tom agreed with me. "If you wanted to be a student," he told me shortly after my arrival, "you should have stayed in the United States." My letter to Tom was honest. I said that academic matters played no role in my wish to attend St. Catharine's. I explained that I wanted to travel and learn more about life. I also mentioned that I was over six feet tall and weighed about one hundred and ninety pounds. More than anything else, I said, I wanted to row. Although I didn't know it at the time, Tom was a fervent rowing

man. Two and a half weeks after I mailed my letter, I received a note
from the senior tutor. Although the application period had expired, he
explained, the college might have a place for someone like me and he
asked me to send testimonials and a transcript. I attended Cambridge
on the "Pickering Fellowship," not one my parents had expected to
fund. Recently I had won a three-year scholarship to law school at Virginia. Winning the scholarship gratified me, but I wasn't ready for law
school. At Sewanee I made only one B. Even father called me a drudge,
and when Virginia agreed to hold the scholarship for me while I studied
at Cambridge, my parents underwrote the Pickering Fellowship.

When I went to Cambridge, becoming a teacher was far from my
mind. Some of my teachers at Sewanee had been cranks, appealingly
eccentric but wildly irresponsible. During the sit-in at Clara's, Abbo, my
favorite teacher, brought a copy of the *National Geographic* to class.
Opening the magazine, he held up a picture of bare natives gamboling
along the banks of some dark African stream, and then, snorting and
shaking his head, said scornfully, "These people want to go to school
with you." No one spoke; Abbo's prejudices were legendary and so all-
inclusive that most students shared at least one of his dislikes: Germans,
Yankees, ignoramuses, pushy females, the newly rich, Catholics, and
teetotalers. Also, we didn't take his pronouncements seriously, knowing
that they flowed more from bottle than heart. Abbo drank heavily, and,
one afternoon before an examination, he saw me in the hall and called
me into his office. "Pickering, I am indisposed. Take this," he said, handing me the examination, "and go and write it on the blackboard." I
wrote the examination on the board and when I finished took the copy
back to Abbo. "Thank you, Pickering," he said. "Here is fifty cents. Go to
Clara's and have a beer." Not wanting to take the money, I told Abbo I
didn't drink. "I must do something for you, poor Pickering," he said.
"Just take half the examination." I did as he instructed. The next week
Abbo stopped me on campus. "Pickering," he said, "do you know you
took only half the examination? I gave you an A because I am kind.
But you must learn to follow directions or else there will be no hope
for you."

The more outrageous Abbo's behavior, the deeper the impression he
and his classes made upon me. Against what I then thought was my
better nature, I grew almost to love the man and have not forgotten the
authors read in his classes. While the matter of other, more respectable,
courses soon fell like tired leaves into the brown mulch of college days,

Abbo's Wordsworth, Byron, Carlyle, Ruskin, and Bagehot have remained green. Seeing, however, that successful teaching depended not upon the platitudinous virtues in which I wanted to believe—tolerance, sensitivity, even rectitude—but instead upon that lower thing personality, I decided that I would not teach.

Along with the knowledge that I would not be a teacher, I arrived in Cambridge believing literary criticism was mostly trivial, if not silly. As far back as I can remember, I have distrusted words, written or spoken. As a teenager at Sewanee sitting in classes often taught by men, I had been told, with national reputations, I suspended distrust, and until my junior year accepted the ingenious, buttressed by learning, for the actual and the true. Then one day a distinguished teacher called attention to some mistletoe appearing in a short story. "What," he asked, "is mistletoe?" "A parasite, probably in the same family as Spanish moss," answered a boy from Louisiana. "No, no, a hundred times no," the teacher answered. "Mistletoe is the sperm of the gods." Normally I wrote down everything the teacher said in class, but this time I paused. Before Christmas each year I went to my Aunt Lula's farm in Williamson County, Tennessee, and shot mistletoe down from the tops of trees. The plant I hung in the front hallway at home had little to do with gods or sperm. "If I kiss anybody under the mistletoe this year," I whispered to the boy next to me, "I am going to wear a rubber." Thinking myself wonderfully witty, I paused before I added "hat." From that moment on I suspended belief, and lectures which earlier I would have thought heavy with fertile learning struck me as barren.

Despite disenchantment with literary discourse, I attended class and took thorough notes. I liked making *A*s, not because they were signs of learning or because they were necessary to winning scholarships, but for themselves. I liked to add them up, much as I did the baseball cards I owned as a child, and one semester in which I made seven *A*s pleased me immensely. Out of habit and because I lived in a boarding house outside college and didn't know what else to do, I attended lectures my first year at Cambridge. Under no pressure to make a grade and suspicious of literary criticism, however, my attendance was spotty. Although Raymond Williams and George Steiner tried to bind literary criticism to moral choice, I was unconvinced, and the only course of lectures I attended regularly was a twice-weekly series given by a prominent female don. Although the lectures were informative, I attended more on compassionate than on intellectual grounds. Over three hundred students appeared at the first lecture. The don's delivery was dull, however, and despite her learning, the audience dropped off rapidly, so rapidly that by the time I wanted to stop attending myself the number of students was so low that I would have been missed. Rather than risk hurting the don's feelings, I stayed in the course. Only three students, including me, were present at the final lecture. Living in college my second year, I was closer to the lecture halls and might have attended more often had I not come down with a terrible cough. For weeks at a time, I heaved up blood at night. I tried all sorts of remedies, finally settling on milk, keeping a quart by the bed and sipping some whenever I began coughing. During the day I rarely coughed, except in lecture halls where the heat made me retch. Not only did the cough prevent me from attending lectures but for a while it made me think myself a second John Keats. Sensitive and doomed, I wrote a sheaf of fleshly poetry, adorned with wraiths, grapes, urns, breasts, and autumnal sighs.

More stimulating than lectures were the weekly tutorials with Tom Henn. Tom impressed me because along with critical studies he had written about fly fishing. During the Second World War, he had been a brigadier and wrote a manual describing German small arms. Tom was a character and institution like Abbo. Instead of dislikes which led Abbo away from literature and toward politics, Tom's enthusiasm for myth and Irish politics pulled him toward literature. Anglo-Irish, Tom told tales about the troubles of 1916. Three of the five boys he traveled home with from school that year, he said, were killed. The night his family's estate was slated to be burned, the raiders destroyed a house across the valley, not before, however, cleaning out the wine cellar and rendering themselves unfit for further mischief. With the exception of a paper considering whether or not a novel could be tragic, I recall nothing about the essays I wrote for Tom. Whatever I did, however, was undistinguished, and after the first term Tom passed me on to another supervisor.

Although my paper on the novel did not impress Tom, it affected me. Knowing my argument had to focus on specific books, I began reading Faulkner. Although I soon saw that his books contained the traditional elements of tragedy, I did not understand Faulkner until one afternoon in Bowes and Bowes I ran across Cleanth Brooks's *The Yoknapatawpha County*. I looked at Brooks's book because Father once mentioned being at Vanderbilt with him. Brooks wanted, Father told me, to be a good trackman and most afternoons could be found circling endlessly around the football field. *The Yoknapatawpha County* was a model of elegance and good sense, and reading it raised my opinion of literary criticism. The book did not lead me to make large claims for criticism, however; in fact, I thought debate over whether or not a novel could be a tragedy was silly. Interest in the form of a work seemed to me to ignore vital content and like an emphasis upon manners focused on the inessential.

That aside, though, Faulkner bewitched me, and I started writing a southern novel. Not restrained by courses, I wrote rapidly. Speed and skill, though, are very different, and after finishing the novel, I threw it away. The tale began with a young Confederate officer returning to wife and home in Mississippi at the end of the Civil War. Although the man had lost his money, he had his wife and looked forward optimistically to building a new and better life. His wife was little more than a girl. He had married her in 1864 during the lull which followed Forrest's victory at Brice's Crossroads. The day he arrived home was hot and dusty. No one ran out to greet him, and only cicadas answered when he called his wife's name. Seeing the door pushed out of the frame, he hurried across the porch and into the front hall. There at the foot of the grand staircase lay his young bride, clothes torn away and body broken and swollen in decay. A long black line of ants streamed across the floor, and climbing across the girl's left leg, dipped down and entered her body through her private parts, making them quiver lasciviously. As the soldier paused, the name "Maryellen" dying on his lips, an opossum stuck his face up through her belly and, seeing the man, thrust himself up and out of the body and scurried heavily down the back hall leaving clotted brown footprints behind. Such a sight would have broken a lesser man but not my hero. He had ridden with "that Devil Forrest" and was made of sterner stuff. Pulling a long knife out of his belt, he strode across the room and sliced a lock of golden hair from his beloved's brow. Then he set the house afire, burning not simply his bride but the past and all hopes for the future. With smoke billowing like night behind him, he rode down the lane, jaws set, eyes frozen, on the trail of the marauders who savaged his world. From this point on, the novel really became violent and graphic, as my hero tracked his men across the South and West, catching them one by one and subjecting them to fiendishly imaginative deaths.

At Cambridge I read a great deal. During my second year, when I lived in college, I went to the student lounge each morning after breakfast and read the daily newspapers and weekly and monthly magazines:

Times, Guardian, Listener, Spectator, New Society, Field, and *Country Life* among others. After finishing the papers, I walked to a bakery across Trumpington Street and bought a chocolate cake. Then returning to my room, I brewed tea, ate cake, and read. I went through mountains of books, most of them novels. At Sewanee I took many English courses, more than most majors, but I never read a novel. Translations of Greek literature, the poetry and drama of the Renaissance, and the Romantic poets of the nineteenth century were the core of the Sewanee curriculum. Tainting the novel must have been remnants of nineteenth-century moral criticism which condemned novels for intoxicating the imagination and leading young people astray. Although Faulkner certainly intoxicated me, the regimen of reading I pursued sobered me. I read through the eighteenth and nineteenth centuries from Fielding to Henry James. Not only did I read famous authors, but I read shelves of Marryat, Bulwer-Lytton, and Lever. Dickens became my favorite writer, and I read his novels twice. In reading novels I got the sort of literary education which suited me. Dickens's novels were too richly involved for an eighteen-year-old student, forced to cut his days into classes and life into courses. To appreciate the three-decker novel takes hours, the sort of expanse of time usually only available to adults in the evening and now to me at Cambridge. Much more suited to the American college curriculum are the lesser forms: essay, short story, and lyric poem.

Whatever the case, however, my reading roamed far from the texts set for the examinations, and before the last six weeks of my second year, Dick Gooderson, my tutor, called me into his office and said, "Sam, don't you think it's time you read some of the books on the Tripos?" I had not been quite so lax as Dick thought. One of my papers was on Dickens, and for another I had reread Greek tragedy. What I had not looked at and what I never prepared were the texts for the required French paper. Studying for the French paper would not have taken much time, and I didn't prepare it, most probably because I had lost interest in grades and knew that I could do well enough on the other papers to receive a degree. Additionally, having to study something because it was required, not because it appealed to me, may have stuck in my craw. I am quietly willful. Happily, my willfulness manifests itself only rarely, and then it is usually because I have balked at some requirement. When I taught in Jordan years later, an official told me that I could not receive wages until I provided the university with a stool sample. The government had to know, the official explained, if I had parasites. "I wouldn't shit in a pan for the president of the United States, much less for pay," I said, getting up and leaving the office. It being unlikely that I brought dangerous parasites with me from America, my salary was paid two days later without further ado.

Toward the end of my second year at Cambridge I decided against going to law school. Before leaving Tennessee I visited Wilna, an old woman who had worked for my parents for many years. Wilna was ill, and, when I pulled a chair close to her bed, I saw my picture on the bedside table. As we talked, she asked me what I planned doing when I came home from England. "Oh, Mr. Sammy," Wilna exclaimed, half raising herself from the bed when I told her I was going to law school, "Mr. Sammy, don't you be a lawyer. Lawyers don't do right." In my first term at Cambridge I met an American lawyer on sabbatical. During the struggle over equal access to public accommodation, he had originated the argument that requiring the owner of a restaurant, for example, to sell food to people whom he didn't want to serve was a form of involuntary servitude, or slavery. The argument was clever and had received much publicity, but it wasn't right, and when Wilna died, I decided law was not for me.

Still bewitched by Faulkner, I wrote the University of Mississippi, requesting an application for graduate school. Initially all went smoothly. After reading my preliminary statement, the head of graduate studies wrote, promising me a fellowship. All I had to do, he explained, was complete the required forms. Dutifully I filled them out until I reached the health form. On one side was a sketch of a mouth; I was instructed to draw an X through my missing teeth. On the other side were questions about my physical and mental states. I did not mind revealing that I had had the measles and that my tonsils had been removed, but I balked at saying whether or not I got car sick or wet my bed. When I posted the application back to Mississippi, I did not include the health form. In a letter to the director of graduate studies, I explained that the form was in poor taste. He answered sensibly, agreeing that the form was intrusive but stating that the law required it and urging me to fill the form out, "creatively" if necessary. Dickens and Faulkner were never far from my mind at Cambridge, and I wrote back, willfully quoting *A Tale of Two Cities* with its "age of foolishness," saying I would never complete such a form. Thus my scholarly studies of Faulkner ended before they began.

While at St. Catharine's, I attended a few meetings of the college literary group, the Shirley Society, named after the seventeenth-century playright James Shirley. One evening Norman Mailer spoke and much to most people's dismay comported himself with dignity. A poet was better value, tearing off his shirt, urinating out an open window, and ending the evening by asking me to sleep with him. He is the only poet, male or female, to issue me such an invitation. Of course, I have not known many poets. In any case, with a day on the river ahead of me, I didn't have time for such foolishness. My appearance at Shirley Society gatherings was, I am afraid, as occasional as my attendance at lectures.

In contrast, I never missed rowing. Six afternoons a week I was on the Cam. Above Cambridge, the Cam was sweet and cool and muskrats lived among the reeds lining the banks. Below Cambridge near our boathouse, the water was brown and clotted, thick with duck feathers, newspapers, tin cans, and bicycle tires. Farther down, past the gasworks and near the lock, the countryside opened and the river broadened out, sweeping under willows and alongside flat fields, on the borders of which swans nested. Here, when the going was good, one could slip through time almost as easily as through the water and imagine days of Beauty and Certainty. For my friends, the golden days were not medieval or gothic, but the Georgian autumn before World War I, the age of Rupert Brooke and Grantchester with the old mill and "church clock at ten to three." A boatmate organized the St. Simeon Stylites Society, named after a man who supposedly spent thirty-three years sitting on top of a pole. Although our patron was benighted, the society was romantic, rather than bitingly satiric as might be expected. Once a term we donned dinner jackets and punted up to the Red Lion at Grantchester, where we drank and ate and for the moment probably saw ourselves like Brooke, unsuited for "the long littleness of life."

Sentiment played only a small part in the rowing day. After the first term callouses so covered my hands that they looked and felt like feet. Because I often jerked the oar into my chest, all my T-shirts were bloodstained. Despite the rich low country and the green willows, tipped with silver in the spring, the lock was not romantic. Just above it, treated sewerage from Cambridge poured down a sluice into the Cam in a thick brown broth. One wintry day a friend and I rowed down to the lock in a double scull. We drew alongside the bank and stretched the oars out over the towpath, thinking they would hold the shell while we walked about. The current, though, was stronger than we imagined and it spun the shell off the bank and swept it toward the lock. As the shell hung on the lip of the lock, I stripped and, diving through the sewerage, grabbed the shell. I had not noticed anyone about other than my friend until just before I dived into the river. On the other bank of the Cam, black against the green grass and blue sky, stood a young nun. She watched me swim to the boat and pull it back to shore. She even watched as I climbed out of the water and slipped back into my shorts and shirt. Over the years I have not forgotten that nun, and occasionally I imagine lifting the mantle off her head and her hair slipping like waves through my hands and over my arms.

Life may be composed more of images linked by association than by events bound by cause and effect. Nuns have appeared throughout my schooling. When I was five, my parents sent me to a kindergarten run by nuns. I shrank before their black habits and hard discipline and begged to go elsewhere, to a place of light and laughter. My parents listened, and soon I was in Miss Little's kindergarten, playing the tambourine. Not until Sewanee did I cross paths with nuns again; then one night while I sat in an empty classroom studying, a group of friends rushed in and grabbed me. Stripping me to my underpants, they bundled me off to a car and drove eight or so miles across the mountain where they dropped me halfway up a drive leading to a nunnery. Much to their surprise, I didn't turn around and start back to Sewanee but walked up the drive and knocked on the door. When a nun opened the door, I explained why I was in my shorts and asked to use the telephone. The nun invited me in and led me to a sitting room. As I sat there waiting to use the phone, two nuns came in and chatted with me, and a woman who worked there volunteered to take me back to Sewanee. She wasn't needed. When I went into the nunnery, my friends became frightened, thinking the dean would frown on their prank. Saying that they had followed the boys who had torn me away from my studies, they appeared at the nunnery, posing as saints to take me back to Sewanee. After urging my friends to turn the car heater on while driving me back, the nuns sent me off. In class the next Monday Abbo looked at me and then said, "Pickering, I understand that you lost your trousers at a nunnery. In Papist states, there is a long tradition of such things, leading, so I have been told, to the origin of the Foundling Home." "I do hope, poor Pickering," he concluded, "that you are not thinking of going over to Rome."

In Cambridge I lost my trousers on several occasions, usually near the college on King's Parade, though, and never at a nunnery or in the company of poets. Contrary, perhaps, to expectations, being debagged was a sign of affection, not dislike. The danger of such affection, however, was not that it led to a cold and pneumonia but that it could warm up considerably. Standing around a bonfire feeling particularly good-natured after a boat club dinner, several members of my boat decided to broil me. Chanting "burn the American," they tossed me into the flames. Fortunately youth does not know its strength, and I flew over the top of the fire and rolled down and out the far side, singeing a shoe and burning holes in my dinner jacket. Drink flowed at boat club dinners, and by dessert most of my friends were smoldering, just on the edge of spontaneous combustion. Nowadays drink disagrees with me. In restaurants I sip water, not wine, and the only time I have beer is at home when Vicki cooks tacos. Age has diminished my exuberance, and, aware of the frailty of everything, I shun dislocating drink. Years ago at Cambridge when mortality was a word I confused with morality, drinking was fun. Too young to think bright promise could be washed away, my friends and I wandered along Trumpington Street and across the Silver Street bridge, faces aglow, cups in hand, singing and laughing. The occasional tailor's bill was but a small price to pay for such gaiety.

After a beery evening, several of us returned to the college late one night. After stumbling across an unlocked bicycle propped against the front gate, I began cycling around the main courtyard, singing "Daisy, Daisy" and making a fine hullabaloo. Lights came on around the courtyard, and the porter ran out of the lodge and tried to catch me. Since only fellows were allowed to walk on the grass in the courtyard, the porter had to chase me around the sidewalks. Around and around we spun, me ahead, weaving and singing on the bicycle and the porter behind puffing and shouting "stop." My friends stood by the gate and watched until I ran out of song and crashed into a rose bush beside them. Only a torn trouser leg for the worse, I ran through them toward the old Bull Hotel, by then part of the college, yelling, "Run, run, or you will be caught." Even among the innocent, guilt spreads rapidly, and my friends followed me into the Bull. Making a thundering noise like buffalo on the plain, they ran up the steps and down a corridor to one boy's room. I stopped almost at the door, turning aside into a washroom where I crouched under a sink. As could be expected, the porter followed his ears and missed me. The next morning the dean fined my companions five shillings apiece. Later that afternoon when I went into the lodge to check my mail, the porter asked, "Didn't I see you last night, sir?" "Most probably," I answered. "There was a scandalous commotion in main

court and I came out to investigate." "I assume drunken louts were misbehaving," I continued, shaking my head and walking out the door,
"rugby players, most likely; such things should not be allowed. I came
here because I thought this was a scholarly community."

Fond of a glass of sherry himself, the dean was not hard on students
who drank too much. At twelve o'clock the gates of the college were
locked. If a student was outside the gates and wanted to return to his
room without having to pay a fine, he climbed in. A protocol was attached to climbing in. The easiest place to climb in was over the fence
around the Master's Garden, but the master asked students not to come
in through the garden because his flowers might be destroyed. The students respected the master's wishes and climbed in over the old wall
bordering King's Lane, an alley running between King's College and St.
Catharine's. Sometimes, most probably when one glass of sherry after
another led to thoughts of adventure, the dean tried to catch students
climbing in. He enjoyed the sport and bought a powerful sealed beam
light for the purpose. The wall was ten feet high, and, as soon as a student was dangling down into the college with no place to go but the
ground, the dean sprang out of the shadows, shined his light in the student's face, and shouted, "Don't run away from me; I've got you. If you
have been drinking, it's all right, but if you have been to a brothel, you
are in trouble."

On moving into the college, I obtained a room on E-staircase, facing
the Walnut-tree Court. E-staircase was out of the way and inconvenient.
The toilet was across the courtyard in the basement of another building
while the nearest tub was two courtyards away. Inconvenience mattered
little to me, for E-staircase was the oldest part of the college. First occupied in 1634, the building was weather- and history-worn. I liked the
staircase for being narrow and crooked. Above fireplaces in the rooms
dark oak was carved in the shape of Catherine wheels. I had just settled in
when college authorities decided to remove everyone from E-staircase.
There had been little rain in Cambridge for several summers, and the
thick heavy mud on which E-staircase rested had dried, shifting the
building and making it unsafe. While the other inhabitants of the staircase happily moved into the ceramic world of sinks and tubs, I stayed
put. I have always liked old things, not because they teach truth, but
because they endured. For me history is a battered trunk bulging not
with the slate and chalk of instruction, but with the patchwork of story,
beginnings and endings side by side like scraps of cloth stitched on a

quilt. I liked climbing the cramped, narrow stairwell and running my hands along the old newel posts. The staircase resembled an attic, dusty and cluttered but alive with story.

I petitioned the fellows of the college, asking permission to remain in my rooms, declaring that if the building tumbled into Queen's Lane, I would ride it down like a cowboy breaking a mustang. The fellows agreed to my request, and I was the last student ever to live on E-staircase. To celebrate I bought a case of brandy and invited friends over to my rooms after dinner. The labels on the brandy were covered with stars, and soon most of us had blasted off dull ground. For some reason there were tall, thick stacks of newspapers and magazines in the hall outside my room. These we took inside and began to shred, with the result that the paper in the room was eventually waist-high. Over the course of the night some of us found the fuel too rich and crashed back to earth, slipping heavily under the paper like meteors falling into desert sands. Not high flyers by nature, others dug down like moles, and burrowing across the room tossed up paper and assorted snorts and howls. My celebration was just the sort of volatile, high-octane affair the dean enjoyed, and I was ready when he knocked at the door at one-thirty. While my friends dropped down and tossed paper over their heads like hermit crabs escaping the sunlight, I poured a big glass of brandy. Then, opening the door, I handed the dean the glass before he could speak. "Here is a little something for you, old horse," I said. "We have been waiting for you." Then, putting my arm over his shoulders and kicking paper aside, I pulled him into the room and began singing "Should Old Acquaintances be Left Out." The dean looked around, blinked, took a belt of brandy, and was right at home.

My friends at Cambridge had gone to grammar schools or minor public schools. St. Catharine's did not attract many students from prestigious public schools, and the few about were clubby. My rumbustiousness, at best hardy and at worst insensitive and vulgar, did not appeal to clubmen. Toward the end of my stay at Cambridge, I started a rumor that led to my being approached by several clubmen, most not from St. Catharine's. When days became too routine, I often tried to spice them up, much as I had tried to liven up the Rhodes scholarship interview, by saying or doing something to provoke a reaction. What I did was harmless, arising out of playfulness rather than the chilly desire to reduce individuals to dissectable reactions. Some mornings I walked down King's Parade greeting strangers by saying things like "I prayed for your soul last night." Other mornings I hopped about in the shadows of the church at the corner of Trumpington Street and Botolph Lane, cackling like a hatchery full of Orpingtons or Wyandottes. My chicken imitation has always been good, and, after passing by, often on the other side of the road, people stopped and listened. Once a man began to crow like a rooster; I answered him, and together we sounded like poultry house at the Tennessee state fair. The rumor hatched during my last year, however, was a different sort of bird. When an inquisitive, gossipy friend asked how I could afford to attend Cambridge, I responded that although I hesitated to talk about such things the fact was that my father was the Coca-Cola Company's third largest shareholder. Four days later I received an invitation to dinner from a clubman who had never spoken to me before.

Not being a good oarsman contributed to my enjoyment of rowing. If I had been better, I would have probably taken the sport and myself more seriously, and, amid technique and triumph, fun would have disappeared. Giving me almost as much pleasure as rowing itself was the bicycle ride from the college to the boathouse. Weaving in and out of cars, three or four of us would race down King's Parade, Trinity Street, St. John's Street, then across Bridge Street in front of the Round Church to Park Street, and finally across Jesus Green and Midsummer Common. We rowed hard during our outings; afterward, though, all was laughter and song. Every day for a month in the shower until number seven threatened to quit the boat, a friend and I sang, "There are no flies on us. / There are no flies on us. / There may be flies on some of you guys. / But there ain't no flies on us." Repeating the ridiculous has always appealed to me, particularly when the repetition irritates someone. Every morning for three years at Sewanee I began my day by singing, "Open up your mind and let the knowledge shine in. / Face it with a grin. / Bookmen never lose; students always win." Nowadays when Vicki comes outside while I am working, I break into "I'm my own yardman. / I rake the leaves when I can." Although she often goes back inside, Vicki has not threatened to quit the crew, yet.

The summer bumping races were the highlight of the rowing year. All the colleges filled boats, some of the larger colleges filling eight or nine. The boats raced in divisions, and a boat's position within a division depended upon the previous year's finish. Thus the second St. Catharine's boat would start where St. Catharine's number two had finished the summer before, although the boat was composed of an entirely different crew. For a race itself a division rowed down to the lock where the boats turned about and lined up along the bank with slightly over a length of water between each shell. When a cannon was fired, each crew tried to overtake and bump the boat ahead before being bumped by the boat behind. If the two boats immediately ahead were involved in a bump, the following boat rowed by in pursuit of boats still farther ahead. Once a crew picked up a rhythm, the races were great fun. The banks were lined with spectators, drinking, eating, and yelling. Coaches cycled along the towpath beside the Cam, shouting encouragement and firing pistols loaded with blanks as a crew pulled closer to the boat before them.

The start was tense, though, and to loosen us up, I always told the story of P. M. Coatsworth Wallingford, who rose to glory behind his oar, stroking Cat's to Head of the River. Although Coats died at Haling Way, just before the Long Reach, he didn't stop rowing. All heart, he even raised the tempo to thirty-eight strokes per minute near Ditton Meadows, eventually pushing into a sprint so that Cat's bumped 1st and 3rd Trinity opposite Stourbridge Common and went Head of the River. When the crew pulled to the bank to celebrate, Coats refused to release his oar. Not even the big men in the middle of the boat could pry his hands loose, and when the crew lifted Coats out of the shell and stretched him out on the grass for the celebration, bow and number two unlocked the oar and carrying the blade gingerly and reverently put it on a flat, bare spot so Coats could row comfortably. Cat's had never gone Head of the River before, and cigars were passed around, and champagne flowed. While the crew danced about, boozing and thumping each other on the back, Coats lay on his side in the grass, thrusting and grunting, and puffing on a cigar the cox had stuffed in his mouth. The crew knew they could not have succeeded without Coats, and they wanted him to enjoy the celebration. When the ambulance came to tote him away, they gathered around him, taking care of course not to be hit by his oar, and sang "For He's a Jolly Good Fellow." Not until rigor mortis set in eight hours later did Coats stop rowing, and the undertaker, a St. Cat's and rowing man himself, said that just before Coats let his oar go forever, he raised the rhythm to a magnificent fifty-four strokes a minute.

"Mr. Pickering, if ever you have an overnight visitor," my bedmaker told me when I moved on to E-staircase, "just put a flower in the door and I won't disturb you." On the walls of my room I had hung Hogarth's

"The Rake's Progress." The prints gave the bedmaker the wrong impression. Rowing and reading took most of my time, and I did not entertain overnight visitors. Rarely did I go to parties, and, even though I bought a ticket or two, I did not attend a May Ball. Perhaps because I was an only child, I have always been self-sufficient. Instead of enriching, girls complicated experience at that time of my life. Four years earlier, like an anchorite seeking the calm of the desert, I left Vanderbilt and coeducation for Sewanee. Girls, however, are born trackers, and despite my monkish leanings and the out-of-the-way location of my cave on E-staircase, I had occasional visitors. During my first term at Cambridge several Swedish girls found my boardinghouse. For many days running two of them came to my room and ate peanut butter, almost half a jar each visit. At the time I wasn't imaginative enough to think of anything that I could do with two girls and peanut butter, other than make sandwiches, and eventually the girls left me alone. At Cambridge my mind rarely even strolled, much less ran, to things sexual. During one Christmas vacation I met an American student in a cafe in Amsterdam. After I told her about the trip I planned, she asked to come to my hotel room and see the map I had drawn up. Thinking that she was curious about places to visit, I showed her the map. She glanced at it then suggested that we travel together. At the time I did not realize that she meant our trip to include some crunchy doings with peanut butter, and I refused to travel with her, saying I could see more if I went by myself.

Lovers are very different from readers, especially a reader like me. No overnight visitor could brighten E-staircase like a Victorian novel. An ardent reader ambles, toying with interpretation and rolling motive through his mind like a rich sauce on the palate. In love quickness is all, and he who pauses to ponder motive loses the girl. By the time a reader realizes that the soft calls ringing on the breeze were for him, spring and love have flown off to warmer climes. During the summer after my first year at Cambridge I worked for a travel company and for eight weeks conducted twenty-four American girls through nine countries. I was twenty-two, and the girls ranged in age from nineteen to twenty-three. Since I was the only boy on the trip, a couple of girls became infatuated with me. I was so conditioned by reading, however, that when awareness poured over me like a hot shower, the time for action had turned cold. Late one night toward the end of the tour I was awakened by knocking at my door. "Good Lord," I thought, "something terrible has happened to one of the girls." My pajamas having disappeared in Berlin,

I snatched a pillow and, sticking one end between my legs while holding the other over my navel, I hobbled across the room and opened the door. There stood Elena. "Elena, what is it?" I said when she didn't say anything. "What has happened?" "Nothing has happened," she answered. "I just wanted to see if you were in." "Obviously, I'm in," I replied, irritated at being awakened. "Well," she said, pausing, "is there anything you want?" "At one thirty in the morning, sleep, that's all I want," I exclaimed. "Good night," I added, then shut the door. "What was that about?" I thought to myself as I wiggled back under the covers. Sixty seconds later I was out of bed, pillow forgotten, breathing hard, and opening the door. Alas, Elena had disappeared.

Blaming Sewanee for my provinciality is unfair. Education has little effect upon character—at least education doesn't seem to have had much influence upon me. As a child, I always stood apart in a kind of provincial state of mind, refusing to become deeply involved in anything. At Sewanee contemporary history passed me by, not, however, because I consciously avoided it. I had been on the edge of things so long that I was incapable of recognizing important events. When the sit-in took place at Clara's, I ignored it. Instead I tromped about, waving a lantern and singing silly songs. Naively I thought that by going to Cambridge and changing place I could change myself. That didn't happen and while history rolled by, wet and uncomfortable, I remained a sometime observer, high and dry on E-staircase, surrounded by books. When John Kennedy was killed, the other American at St. Catharine's wept. I remained untouched, and when curious friends came by the room to observe my reaction, I didn't react. "Look," I said, "no matter who the president, I am going to brush my teeth before I go to sleep tonight, and tomorrow I am going to eat a big breakfast." While at Cambridge I attended some meetings sponsored by the Campaign for Nuclear Disarmament. Completely unconcerned about nuclear war and not having the slightest interest in world peace, I went to the meetings for the spectacle. Clownish characters appeared, and the atmosphere was entertainingly circuslike. Nowadays I look back on that unconcerned boy with a kind of fond and horrified awe. I have three small children, and when I think about what may lie ahead of them, I am frightened. I wish I could do something, but I have never been a political activist. The closest I ever came to political action occurred in London some years after I left Cambridge. I attended the hundredth anniversary celebration of Gilbert and Sullivan's Savoy operas. During intermission I found myself standing in the bar next to Harold Wilson, the former prime minister. Suddenly an overpowering urge to goose him swept over me. All I had ever wanted to say to a politician seemed to force its way into my thumb, and Bunthorne's and Jane's duet from *Patience* ran through my head. "Bah to you—Ha! ha! to you," I would say as I goosed him. Luckily one Gilbert and Sullivan always leads to another, and *The Mikado* popped into mind. Not wanting to be put on "a little list" of scholarly offenders who "never would be missed," I balled my hands, crammed them into my trousers, and putting political action behind me ran out of the bar.

After graduating from Cambridge I returned to Tennessee and taught high school for a year. Through the British Council, I had obtained a post in Sierra Leone; my parents, however, objected so strongly that I gave it up. Over the telephone Father said, "They must have turned you into some kind of liberal over there." After Father finished his say, Mother told me not to pay attention to him. "He is so upset about this Africa thing," she explained, "that he doesn't know what he is saying. He is almost crazy with worry, and it is making him sick." Behind the desire to go to Africa lay childhood reading, not political consciousness. When I was a boy, my favorite author was Edgar Rice Burroughs, and in elementary school I swung out from many a drab civics or health class into an Africa of the imagination, a green viny place of blooming adventure, a place where I was free to drop myself and the close world of textbooks, chalk, and blackboards.

I left Cambridge with a bang. The day before sailing from Southampton I rowed in a regatta at Marlowe. That night so I could catch the boat train the next morning a friend drove me to London in his old Austin. On the way we almost had a wreck. As we started up a long incline, we saw a car at the top pull out from behind a line of traffic. Speeding toward us in our lane and passing all the cars on his side of the road, he did not turn aside. Just before the collision which would have sent me to a place rather colder than Africa or Tennessee, my friend swerved off the road and we bounced over the shoulder into a field. The driver of the other car did the same thing at almost the same time. Both cars ended in the field, his down a slope behind us. The other driver was drunk; he retained enough presence of mind, however, to lock his doors. Almost before we stopped moving, I was running toward his car. Once there I battered it, kicking in the sides and smashing the hood and trunk with my forearm. By the next morning when the boat train left Victoria Station, all traces of my anger had vanished except for an abrasion and a couple of bruises. Although battering the car satisfied me then and the memory still satisfies me, the incident was a warning. Instead of traveling down main roads, I was better off, uninvolved on the physical and cultural edge of things.

In Tennessee I spent a slow happy year living at home. I applied for a Woodrow Wilson fellowship in order to study English in graduate school. At the interview I talked about Dickens and didn't quote any preachers. After winning the fellowship, I applied to Princeton and, being careful to complete the health form, was admitted. I went to graduate school not because I wanted to teach or because I believed the study of literature benefited society, somehow broadening people and making them more humane. I went because I enjoyed books and thought four years reading at Princeton would be pleasant. Before leaving Tennessee I drove to Sewanee to see Abbo. He had slipped. Although I introduced myself, he did not remember me. He looked absently off into the distance and said, "I have just been singing with the church choir." Then he walked away.

I did not keep up with my Cambridge friends. Only people immediately successful keep up, measuring themselves against and competing with contemporaries. The pressure to be a notable success often makes the person who lives an ordinary life feel guilty. Reading about the triumphs of former classmates, he thinks he has squandered his talents, be they real or imaginary. For such a person, keeping up disturbs and dissatisfies; for him, anonymity is far more comfortable. I was almost forty when I started writing, and by the time I achieved a small success, I was aware of the mortality of words and self, and rivalries seemed beside the point.

Despite knowing little about the doings of my contemporaries at Cambridge, I still wear my college scarf. Claret with two pink stripes running its length, the scarf is practical, not stylish. Thick and warm, it goes well with stocking caps, baggy down coats, and Connecticut winters. On the wall above my desk are two prints of "Catherine Hall." Both are views of the main court, the larger taken from the *Cambridge University Almanack* of 1814 and the smaller produced and colored by R. Harraden and Son in 1809. When I notice the prints, which I rarely do because I have grown accustomed to them, I find it difficult to believe I went to Cambridge. Somebody who spent two years there ought to gleam with polished civility. He ought to revere things British, dreaming of trekking by blue lakes in Cumbria or living in a deeply red eighteenth-century Georgian row house. Unpolished, I often seem foolish and abrasive; last week Vicki called me an "arsoon," the offspring, she explained, of an illicit coupling between a buffoon and an arse. When colleagues in the English Department wax sentimental after reading about places they visited in Britain, I become exasperated. "Britain," I want to say. "That's not your life. Windham, Willimantic, and Danielson are."

Yet despite the years and lack of contact, I sent announcements to the *St. Catharine's Society Magazine* when my children were born. I am on leave this spring and for a while thought about taking my family to Cambridge and living there. I imagined riding a bicycle through the streets and coaching a crew. I saw myself thoughtless and full of fun, a younger me not burdened with worries about the future. I stayed in Connecticut and did not return to Cambridge, however, because my mother and father who are old and ill need me in this country. I did go back once though. Ten years ago I attended an old boy dinner and stayed overnight in the college. At the dinner I drank too much. The next morning I could not find the pants to my suit. Although the pants had to be in my room, searching for them was beyond me. Putting on the gray flannels which I had worn up from London the day before and which I had hung in the closet was all I could manage. On my way out of the college I stopped at the porter's lodge and, giving the porter my address in London, asked him to have the pants mailed to me when they turned up. Having been at St. Catharine's for many years, the porter recognized me. In fact he was on duty the night I bicycled around the main court, singing and shouting. "Lost your trousers again, sir?" he said as he took down my address. "Things don't change much, do they?" "No, they don't," I said, tipping him and walking out of the lodge. When I reached the street, I turned around toward the college. Wondering if the rose bush into which I crashed was still there, I stepped back and leaned to my left in order to see around the gate. In doing so, I tripped and, stumbling to the side, fell heavily into a nun.

Office Hours

T APED TO the door of my office in the English Department is a sign reading "Sam Pickering Office Hours MWF 12–1:30, TuTh 3:30–4:30." Not many of my colleagues have office hours five days a week, and when I walk past their doors and see that they are in only on Tuesdays and Thursdays, I feel a little smug and superior and then, if truth will out, a little resentful. Why should they, I think, receive salaries like mine when they are never around? The resentment does not last long, however, and has usually vanished by the time I have checked the mail. Shortly afterward I, too, have vanished, for the sign on my door smacks of time past not present. I have aged and don't keep the office hours I once did. In second grade my favorite game was Red Rover. At recess our teacher, Miss Courtney Hollins, split the class in half and arranged us in two lines, ten yards apart and facing each other. Once we joined hands, Miss Courtney asked someone, usually me, to begin the game. "Red Rover, Red Rover," I shouted, "let Linda come over." With that Linda, who was in the line opposite, released the hands she held and running at me tried to break through our line. If she failed, she joined our side; if she succeeded, she chose one of us to go back and join her line. When Miss Courtney did not ask me to start the game, and Linda got to call "Red Rover" before I did, she always called me to "come over." When she called, I ran at her as hard as I could, for in those days knowing someone down was a sign of true affection. Years ago when I began teaching, life was still Red Roverish, and I held long office hours in hopes that some afternoon wild exuberance, freckled and brown-eyed like Linda, would burst through the door and bowl me out of my chair and across the desk into romance.

Actually, I did not dream so much about Linda as I did her older cousins, naked beach girls bronze and pink with sand between their toes. Such dreams, though, have gone the way of long office hours. I have reached the stage of life in which bare youth seems dull. This fall I hurt my back and for therapy began swimming in the university pool. The gymnasium is old, and quarters are cramped. There is no faculty locker room and students and faculty shower together. After I became accustomed to communal bathing, something that had disappeared from my life with high school football, I looked about me. Youth, straight and slender with elastic muscles, I discovered, was boringly similar, and my eyes slid across the students much as one's vision slides over a long smooth expanse of gray stones on a beach. Only once did I pause. Tattooed in the hollow of a boy's hip was a purple panther. The panther, though, did not hold my attention long. Like the boy, it was sleek and young, too perfect to be interesting. In contrast to the students, faculty members did not shed individuality with their clothes. While some were dry and crumpled, others looked like yellow pears, round and softly juicy. While some were bald, others were as hairy as tumbleweeds. When I saw withered arms and legs and scars running across backs and chests, I wondered about the lives the faculty led. Unlike the panther, they had roamed and been marked. If they were lucky or thoughtful, they crept forward, pushed not by bulging muscles, but by wisdom, scarring and withering, but forever shaping.

When I started teaching I kept office hours in part because I anticipated savoring the lies I thought students would ladle out to delay tests or raise grades. I was disappointed; all I have sipped is thin gruel, not the rich, intoxicating and wonderfully satisfying stew which my friends and I brewed for professors twenty-five years ago. The old boy who taught philosophy in my college was long past the paper-reading age, and the only way to get an *A* was by a thorough application of flattery, thick, buttery flattery. "I am so pleased that you are going to major in philosophy," he told me as I sat in his office early one morning before class. Declaring a major in philosophy, something that could easily be changed once the semester ended and grades were recorded, got one a *B+*. To get an *A*, however, required a pound or two more of oil. I wasn't sure what I was going to say next until he remarked, "And by the by, what do you think of Aristotle?" Butter be damned, suddenly inspiration sprang to hand like a bottle of Durkee's sauce, and I spread it on warm and creamy. "Oh, I liked Aristotle just fine," I answered, "but Socrates has changed my life. You know Doug Parini, don't you?" "Yes, indeed," he answered, "a most perceptive student and another major. I see a great deal of him." Doug lived in my dormitory and although not much of a student, he was perceptive. In fact, he advised me that books did not matter in philosophy. "If you want to be a philosopher-king, flatter," he said. "I flatter; therefore, I am an A student."

"Doug and I, Dr. Ballard," I said, "are roommates. At the beginning of the semester we didn't room together. We met in your course and became so interested in philosophy that we decided to room together in order to discuss your lectures." "Every evening," I continued, seeing old Ballard puff and swell like an English muffin soaked with margarine, "every evening we choose some controversial topic and debate it according to the Socratic method. To you, sir, we owe all our intellectual growth." "Oh, my, Pickering," Ballard began, "your story overwhelms me. It makes me glad I am a teacher. Sometimes, you know, teaching can be lonely and dispiriting." "Sir," I said, leaning forward and laying my hand like a butter knife on Ballard's knee, "don't be dispirited. When you get down in the dumps, think of Doug and me and the hundreds of other students for whom you have made the difference." "Bless you, Pickering, bless you," the old man answered. In class later that day Ballard repeated my tale, leaving out, thank the Lord, Doug's and my name. He said that in all his years of teaching no tribute had so touched him. At the end of the course I received an A. The next semester I became an English major and never again set foot in a philosophy class.

Occasionally I feel responsible and visit my office during office hours. Not all my time there is boring. Once this fall something odd came through the door. In college I belonged to a fraternity, all recollections of which like those of philosophy I suppressed. In November as the man with whom I share the office and I sat speculating about when the first snowfall would occur, a student came in. "Which of you is Professor Pickering?" he asked. "I am," I said, whereupon the student strode across the room, bent over, and whispered, "Are you a Brother in the Bond?" "A what?" I exclaimed and leaned back in my chair. "A Brother in the Bond," he said, stooping closer and sticking out his arm to shake hands. In defense I stuck my hand up before my face and he grabbed it. "Are you a Brother in the Bond?" he repeated a little louder than before, and then with his little and ring fingers gave my hand two quick squeezes, squeezes so fleshly that I was about to tumble backward out of my chair until I realized the handshake was the secret grip of my old fraternity and the mysterious bond was the Bond of Phi Delta Theta. There being no chapter of Phi Delta Theta on campus, the student, I learned, wanted to start one, and he wanted me to be its advisor. My enthusiasm for things fraternal like my dreams of beach girls had long since washed away, and I refused. Not all my old acquaintances, however, have given up surf and spray, striped umbrellas, and suntan lotion. Doug Parini is still a hardy fraternity man. Sometime ago at the funeral of a mutual friend and member of the fraternity, a pause occurred in the burial service while the undertaker and his crew lowered the casket into the grave. Doug, so I heard, then stepped forward and turning to the mourners said, "Ladies and gentlemen, during this brief intermission I would like to say something about a subject near to the heart of our departed brother. I want to say a few words about Phi Delta Theta."

The man with whom I share the office lectures on modern literature. In modern literature nothing is what it seems. Everything is sex. The lightbulb, the calendar, the chair, my shoes and socks, all have to do with sex, and as soon as the student left the office, my colleague turned and said, "A secret handshake, a secret life. What does this portend?" All it portended, I am afraid, was that for the rest of the semester I avoided being near the English Department during my office hours. Sometime when I was alone in the office, I thought, the student might reappear and, slipping me the secret grip, ask me again to become an advisor.

In avoiding office hours, I have not shut the door to life. It's just that my interests have changed. Instead of to youth and the future, I am drawn to age and the past. While younger teachers sit behind desks, thinking fondly about Red Rover, I am rummaging through trunks and chests, anywhere curiosities lie dusty and neglected. In Nashville this past Christmas I found two late nineteenth century mourning fans in an old cherry wood chest. The sticks of both fans were bone and the leaves satin. Unlike that of the full mourning fan, the leaf of the half mourning fan was gray. Painted on it a grieving woman stood before a tomb in a country graveyard at dusk. Atop the tomb was an urn; behind were dark green trees, probably yews. In the same drawer I found an album of old songs and sheet music. Typically entitled "Darling Little Blue Eyed Nell," "I'd Choose to Be a Daisy," and "Let Me Kiss Him for His Mother," many of the songs were sentimental, smacking of shady arbors, trellises, old lace, and thwarted love.

A good number of the others were southern patriotic songs published during the Civil War: "Bonnie Blue Flag," "The Stars of Our Banner," and "The Boy Defender of Kentucky's Honor." "You can never win us back, / Never! Never! / Though we perish on the track / Of your endeavor!" the "Southrons' Chaunt of Defiance" proclaimed. The oddest

song in the book was "We're Coming Fodder Abraham. We're Coming-
in a Horn," published just after the Emancipation Proclamation in 1863
in Nashville, Tennessee, when the city was occupied by Union forces.
On the cover of the song was a drawing of a powder horn. Through it
and out to an army camp on the other side marched scores of black
troops. Instead of celebrating freeing the slaves and increasing the size
of the northern armies, the song was comic. Written by "An Intelligent
Contraband," it made both blacks and Lincoln appear ridiculous. "De
Conscript bill passed de house," the second verse began: "From de top,
to bottom, / To send us down to Dixie Land, / To Confisticate de Cotton,
/ We're coming Fodder Abraham, / To make de army bigger, / Come
white folks behave yourself's, / And be good, as any Nigger."

The album belonged to Nannie Brown, my great-grandmother. In
turning from the future toward the past, I am drawn toward things familial. In rummaging through a folder of old papers, I discovered that
my mother's grandfather had been named after John Hampden, the
seventeenth-century English patriot. Killed on Chalgrove Field in 1643,
Hampden was a Parliamentarian and one of the leaders of the forces op-
posed to King Charles I. Thoughts about the future of the United States
make me gloomy. Americans have forgotten not their roots but the dirt
out of which all people grow and which binds man to equal man. In
accumulating wealth and power, people seem intent upon building
dynasties: royalist, glittering, and self-important. Maybe, just maybe,
knowledge of a Hampden in their past will keep my children close to
the earth, far from burning wealth and pride.

My father grew up in Carthage, Tennessee, a small town on the Cumberland River, some fifty miles east of Nashville. In the days when I kept
office hours big and grand places of the world attracted me: Paris, London, Vienna, their shop windows shining with silver and gold. Now I
am drawn to small towns, particularly those in the hills around Carthage: Maggart, Stonewall, Hickman, Grant, Pleasant Shade, Sykes,
Rawl's Creek, Kempville, Donoho, Barrett's Camp Ground, Lancaster
Hill, Riddleton, Pigeon Roost, and Doweltown. Instead of burning with
buying and selling, they seem aglow with story, often more tale than
truth but always warm. For years the heaviest drinker in Maggart was
Albert Hennard. Almost since the day of their marriage, his wife Amanda
Leigh had pleaded with him to stop. Sixteen wet years passed, and then,
on Amanda Leigh's fortieth birthday, Albert gave up drink. That night
there was a meeting at the Methodist Church in Carthage, and Amanda

Leigh begged Albert to take her as a birthday present. At the meeting Amanda Leigh felt the waters of glory rising and testified. "Oh, brothers and sisters," she said, "today is my birthday and there is sunshine in my soul. I have achieved the greatest triumph of my life. For sixteen long, dark years, I have striven to induce my Albert to board the Gospel Ship and stop drinking filthy liquor, and today, Praise the Lord"—she shouted—"he plucked out the demon's dart and pledged his word that he would never touch a drop of alcohol again." "When he told me that," she continued, her eyes, it was said, shining like the bright hills of glory, "he made me the happiest woman in Smith County and I threw my arms around his neck and kissed him." When Amanda Leigh finished there was a moment of respectful silence, then from the back of the room a deep voice rolled forward saying, "Served him right."

According to rumor, the voice was that of Levi Crowell, editor of the local paper, the *Carthage Courier,* and a stout tippler in his own right. Be the rumor true or false, however, Levi himself was not immune to domestic pressure. His wife Chloris was the starch and whalebone behind the School Board, the Carthage Reform Society, and the Ladies of the Christian Church. When the Ladies met to organize a meeting of the Sons of Temperance, Chloris volunteered Levi for the customary toast to Water, "the purest and best of all God's Creation." When Chloris ordered, Levi generally marched. As editor of the paper, Levi was good with words. For this skirmish, though, he filled his canteen with something other than the purest and the best, so, he was later heard to say, he could speak with a "tongue of flame." "Smith Countians," he began his toast, "I have seen water twinkling like little jewels on the sleeping lids of infancy. I have seen the pearly rill of a damsel's tears running past lips of ripest cherry. I have seen it glide down the wrinkled valleys beside the woodland hill under the hoary brow of age. I have seen the morning dew make the earth sparkle emerald green as the sun burst forth resplendent from her bed of night. I have heard the merry laughter of the purling spring, the thunder of the ocean, and the gladsome music of the plashing brook. I have laughed as it bubbled through the pebbly vale and wept with joy as its daughter the rainbow curved radiant like a smile across the blue canopy of heaven. And yes, oh, yes I have lifted my arms in thanks and dreamed of the crystal streams and sparkling fountains of fair Canaan. But dear Smith Countians, I must now say to you, in all honesty, that water, as a beverage, is a dismal failure."

Like those folks, as the spiritual put it, sitting at the welcome table, feasting on milk and honey, singing and not growing weary, I never tire of listening to stories, no matter how ridiculous they are. Even jokes appeal to me, and when I hear one I like I shut my office, rush home, and tell it to Vicki. "Three anthropologists from New Jersey," I began recently, went to the Amazon to search for the lost tribe. Unfortunately, the tribe found them before they found it and, binding their hands and tying them together neck to neck, led them back to the village. Each of the anthropologists was then bound to a stake and sticks were piled around his feet, after which the village chief, dressed in toucan feathers and assorted bones, approached. Stopping before the first anthropologist, the chief said, "Which do you prefer: death or bunga, bunga?" Understandably, the anthropologist answered, "Bunga, bunga." This caused great joy in the village, and the natives began to dance shouting "bunga, bunga" and shaking huge orange gourds. When the initial enthusiasm died down, two natives came forward, untied the anthropologist, and led him to the riverbank, where they chopped off his tits and testicles and put caterpillars in his ears, ants up his nose, and leeches on his navel. They then dragged him back to the stake and amid peals of good-natured laughter burned him alive.

After the commotion subsided and the smoke blew away, the chief approached the second anthropologist and said, "Which do you prefer: death or bunga, bunga?" The anthropologist didn't know what to say. For a moment he thought about choosing death, but hope springs eternal, even near the Amazon, and deciding that the chief must have misunderstood his colleague when he asked for "bunga, bunga" instead of death, he said in a loud, clear voice, "Bunga, bunga." Almost immediately the two natives ran forward, tore him from the stake, and dragged him to the river, where they served him much as they did his companion, after which they reduced him to charcoal. Having seen what happened to his friends, the third anthropologist was ready for the chief and when asked whether he preferred death or bunga, bunga, he said, "Death." For a moment a pall fell over the village; the natives dropped their gourds, and the chief turned away from the anthropologist. His shoulders sagged, and his toucan feathers drooped. The gloom did not last long, however; suddenly the chief squared his shoulders and turning back to the anthropologist said, "Death you have asked for, death you shall have." Then raising his voice and waving his gourd, he added, "But first a little bunga, bunga."

"What do you think?" I said after Vicki didn't react. "That's it?" she said. "I don't get it. Why would they give him 'bunga, bunga' when he asked for death? They are the same. That's a silly story." I want people to enjoy the stories I tell, so I said, "You are right. The tale is silly. Let me try this on you. It is a Carthage story." Albert Hennard and Hiram Povey had long been drinking companions, and when Albert set his foot on the path of righteousness, he left poor Hiram to wander alone in the wilderness around Maggart. One night Hiram disappeared. Since he had spent the afternoon drinking bootleg whiskey in Enos Mayfield's backyard and since he had last been seen staggering along the banks of the Cumberland River, people assumed that Hiram fell in and drowned. The volunteer fire department dragged the river under the bridge and just below Carthage but couldn't find the body. Since the Cumberland flowed swiftly past Carthage until it reached a shoal at Nashville, the head of the fire department, Captain O. P. Rash, advised the grieving widow, Bevie Povey, to go to Nashville and ask police to keep watch for Hiram. In Nashville the chief of police asked Bevie if there was anything peculiar about Hiram that would help identify the body. "You see," the chief said, "a lot of people jump off the bridge down here, and you'd be surprised how difficult they are to identify after spending ten or fifteen days in the water." Hiram was nondescript and ne'er-do-well, and for a moment Bevie didn't know what to say. But then relief spread like a napkin across her face, and she said, "Why yes, there is something. Hiram's deaf."

At the end of the story Vicki smiled, and I decided to spring three new things on her that I picked up while rummaging around in the library during office hours. "Where there's a will," I said, "there are relatives." Not getting a reaction, I pushed on, saying, "You can teach a monkey to multiply but only a snake can be an adder." "Sam," Vicki began in an all too familiar voice. "No, no," I interrupted, "let me tell you this last one. It's about Carthage." Sometime before his unfortunate demise, Hiram came home late. He was unsteady on his feet, and when Bevie tried to shore him up she smelled his breath. "You and that no account Albert Hennard have been over at Enos Mayfield's again, drinking homemade beer, haven't you?" "No, ma'am," Hiram answered, grabbing the back of the sofa for support, "not a drop. I've been eating frogs' legs. What you smell are the hops."

Vicki left the room without saying anything. That was all right though. I didn't have time to tell any more stories because something about my best friend Garth had just come to mind, and I wanted to go to the library and rummage around for a bit. In addition to enabling me to collect stories, not keeping office hours gives me more time to speculate about people's oddities. Before I hurt my back, Garth and I ran almost every day. Having run together for years, our conversation like that of real friends had long ago forsaken the abstract and the intellectual for the personal and the familial. One day the subject of control came up, and we discussed the various things we did to control our lives. Our run took us through the university farm, over Horsebarn Hill, around by the piggery, by the sheep and cattle barns, and then in front of the stables. I am suspicious when great claims are made for the influence of environment upon behavior. Still, whenever Garth and I ran, the rich brown aroma of animals was always on the breeze, and as we went down Horsebarn Hill toward the piggery, our conversation usually dipped into the earthy.

"All this talk about controlling appetite and converting the imaginative into the practical is well and good," I said one day, "but what about other sorts, more personal kinds of control? That's what interests me." "What do you mean?" Garth said. "Well," I said, "take these sheep, for example. Have you ever seen them mate? Vicki and I were down here last weekend with the children and saw a pair going at it." "In and out, just like that," I said, snapping my fingers, "faster than a speeding bullet." "Of course," I went on, "sheep can't delay things like people by doing multiplication tables or repeating the Gettysburg Address." "Frogs," Garth said. "What?" I said. "Frogs," Garth answered, "that's what I think about when I want to slow things down. Frogs, lots of them."

Garth's statement intrigued me. I had never met a person who thought about frogs at such moments. Once I met a woman who said she tried to name all of Anthony Trollope's novels in the order in which they were published. She was an English professor, though, and her answer was in character. Garth, however, was a chemist, and so far as I knew chemists didn't have much to do with frogs in the twentieth century. When I asked him, Garth said he wasn't sure what kind of frogs he thought about. Frogs were frogs, he said, and so I decided that after the run and a shower, I would go to the library and read about frogs to see if I could figure out what kind of frog Garth had in mind. Once back at the domestic lily pad, however, things familial appeared, and all thoughts of frogs splashed into the subconscious, only to surface at the word "hops." The first two candidates I came up with in the library for Garth's frog were the hermit spadefoot toad and the Florida gopher frog. The spadefoot was a possibility because he lived underground and only left his burrow at night. For people like Garth and me, with little tadpoles in our ponds, night is the only time available for thinking about frogs. Outside of the breeding season, the Florida gopher frog for his part lives alone in a highland turtle's burrow, popularly known as a gopher hole. The gopher frog was a candidate because the lots of males Garth's and my age often resemble that of the gopher frog. Once their eggs are laid, our females don't have much use for us, and, banished from the pond, we spend solitary lives at our gopher holes: over a desk in an office or swimming back and forth in the university pool.

Instead of waiting passively for the door to open, bringing what it will, the person who avoids office hours and becomes a rummager can control mood. When murky thoughts like those about the gopher frog's life surface, the rummager can dive to clear water. There he can always find just the right frog. No, I decided, Garth did not think about loners like the gopher frog or the hermit spadefoot toad. Garth is bright and cheery, and his thoughts turned to lots of frogs in the spring, that time of pussy willows, redwing blackbirds, and spring peepers. From the marsh just under the hill behind the graveyard, the low wet fields where Angus graze in late summer, and the pond behind the piggery, the shore black with alders, comes the thin, sweet call of the spring peeper. Piping happy promise, the peeper is just the frog for the lover of life, and in Garth's case that may include more than wife. In my rummaging I discovered that until recently the technical name of the peeper was *Hyla pickeringi,* in plain words Pickering's frog.

"That," I told Vicki later in the kitchen, "is the kind of thing a chemist might know." "And in saying he thought about lots of frogs, that dear boy," I went on, "was delivering a coded message full of affection for me, the sort of thing a man just can't come out and say to another man." "Coded message," Vicki said widening her eyes, "poppycock." Then reaching over to the counter by the sink, she picked up a bag of meat scraps and, handing them to me, told me to take them out to the wood-pile for the crows. Much of the time I once would have spent in my office I now spend outdoors. I particularly like feeding crows. Several roost near us, and I have learned to recognize four. I have named them after places in Hanover County, Virginia, where I spent summers as a child: Morris, Cold Harbor, Beaver Dam, and Ash Cake. The next two I recognize I will name Langfoot and Old Polly. Morris now recognizes me and, sometimes when he sees me in the backyard, he lights on the woodpile, preens, and struts back and forth, hoping for a bite to eat.

Vicki knows I enjoy feeding the crows, and she keeps a bag of scraps handy to give me when I grow long of tongue in the kitchen. Actually, I rummage around outdoors quite a bit.

The university plans to build a new gymnasium. So far, though, the only thing up is a sign, saying how much the building will cost. To put the sign up, the university bulldozed part of an old stone wall. In the process a small rhododendron was uprooted. Some ten days after the sign was erected, I found the rhododendron. Although it had lost most of its leaves and its roots were battered, I carried it home and planted it in a small dell beside my house. The dell is filled with plants I have found abandoned, so many that Vicki calls it "Sam's Shelter for Homeless Plants" and tells friends that she expects I'll soon write the government and demand aid to expand the shelter. Plants, of course, are not the only thing I collect outdoors. Not long ago a honeybee stung my little girl Eliza on her stomach. I pulled the stinger out of Eliza and, pressing it between two pieces of Scotch tape, stuck it in her scrapbook with a note attached saying, "The stinger of the first bee that stung Eliza, September 16, 1986."

Rummagers are collectors, usually of things which have more anecdotal than monetary value. Money defines and in the process limits; the worth of something valuable has a way of excluding other considerations and becoming the central fact about an object. Like a mote a price tag can so blind a beholder that he never appreciates an object for itself. The things which I store away are conversation pieces, at best arousing curiosity and loosening tongues but rarely stirring envy or greed. Vicki and I and the children spend summers on a farm in Nova Scotia. Once there, we rarely leave except to go to the grocery, and I spend most days roaming field and beach with the children, hunting for flowers and bugs and collecting rocks and seashells. The desire to rummage through the past, though, is in my blood, and, like Linda in Red Rover, old barns in Nova Scotia seem to call my name, and I long to burst into their lofts and stalls, cluttered, I imagine, with ancient tools and trunks filled with tokens of an earlier generation's family life: bee stingers and watermarked sheet music.

Two years ago I discovered a way to control my longings. I decided to limit my search to a single conversation piece each summer. Once the piece was mine, I behaved much like Garth with his peepers. Whenever I looked at a barn, I thought about tractors and combines, whole back forties of them, and mastered the urge to rummage. This past June I found what I was looking for in the first loft I explored. Wrapped in a piece of oilcloth and mounted and framed was what seemed a bouquet of dried flowers. Initially the frame attracted me. The flowers were in the center of the frame under glass on a raised oval, backed by blue velvet. The sides of the frame fluted down and out like a mansard roof, covered in gold leaf. At first I ran my fingers over the frame, paying little attention to the flowers, but since my children and I had already spent many hours learning the names of wildflowers, I looked closely at the flowers to see if I could identify them. Although some resembled phlox while others appeared to be buttercups and lady's slippers, they were not simple wildflowers. They were woven out of hair, all shades of hair: yellow, brown, black, gray, and red. Binding the flowers together, thin vines of white hair twisted through the bouquet. Maybe, I thought, the flowers had been woven by a young invalid, a girl slowly dying of tuberculosis. At her death her parents framed them and hung them in the parlor as remembrance and maybe, too, as an encouraging emblem of that better land of corn and wine, of flowers which never wilt, and of youth bright and robust in white robes and golden slippers.

No matter who made the flowers, though, I had found my conversation piece and the bouquet now hangs inside the front door of my house in Connecticut. I am less sympathetic now than I was years ago to cultural high seriousness, and the odd appeals to me more than the arty. Some months back I ate dinner with the owner of a Matisse, a dancer sketched in black on a white background. The Matisse was for sale, and while we ate the owner discussed prospective buyers, occasioning laughter by describing one man who after seeing the sketch lost interest, explaining the dancer had the ugliest nose he had ever seen. "Imagine," my host declared, "judging a Matisse by its nose." After dinner I looked carefully at the sketch; the buyer, I decided, had been kind. Not only the nose but the entire face was ugly, resembling the beaked, heavy-jowled head of a condor. Out of place in the living room, the sketch belonged, I thought, in a bathroom, a green and gold bathroom, hung with paper depicting an iridescent jungle of blue snakes, scarlet monkeys and orange elephants.

What bothers me, I suppose, is the blinding and numbing pretentiousness which often accrues to the cultural. Once I would have accepted most claims made for things cultural and would probably even have repeated them uncritically. Rummaging, however, changes a person. As I have drifted from office hours and schedule, finding pleasure in the odd, the neglected, and the out-of-the-way, so I have grown less inclined to accept conventional judgments about art. Although suspicious of most things labeled intellectual, I don't think I have become less thoughtful. I read as much now as I ever did. Some changes have occurred in the way I read, though. Instead of reading for idea, I read for story. Moreover, since I rarely leave home, I read more travel books. Although getting to Nova Scotia is a bit of a journey, Vicki and I stay put once we arrive. Going anywhere with small children is difficult. Last year we made only one day trip, driving fifty miles to Cape Sable Island, an island of fishermen and long, empty beaches not far from Yarmouth. The afternoon before we left I picked blueberries for our breakfast, and we got an early start. Unfortunately, we had to stop halfway and clean the car. The roads were curvy, and Francis, our five-year-old and champion blueberry eater, got sick and sprayed blue all over his brother Edward and the back seat.

After scrubbing the inside of the car, I drove slowly, and we arrived at Cape Sable Island at lunch time. Cape Sable Island is a working island, and finding a place to eat is not easy. After driving through all the villages on the island, we finally stopped at Pop's Hamburgers, a small grill next to a fish-processing plant and across the street from a boat manufacturer. Men and women in high-topped rubber boots filled Pop's. When Vicki and I and the children entered, everybody looked at us, not out of ill feeling but out of curiosity because we were strangers. Rummagers are usually retiring if not shy people. Alone in a barn, the rummager imagines himself a world-renowned explorer. At his desk with time on his hands, he dreams and may even write letters so odd they call attention to him. But when facing a crowd, he shrinks. In Pop's I found an empty corner table where I hoped to pass quickly and silently through mayonnaise and mustard, burger and bun. Alas, Francis ordered a big glass of milk. When it arrived, he leaned back so far in his chair that it flipped over, throwing milk on the floor and down the neck of a woman sitting behind him.

Vicki and I should have carried a picnic lunch, and instead of hurrying to Cape Sable Island we ought to have poked along, pulling over whenever we saw an interesting shop or barn. Stopping with small children can be tiring, but the reason we didn't stop and the reason why I no longer travel much is that travel like office hours seems mostly a matter of rigorous schedule, hurdling from one place to another along a big road or in a fast plane. A great deal is passed but little is remembered.

Resisting the urge to get somewhere fast is hard, and so I stay home. Travel was not always such a matter of schedule and speed. Sometimes it was a matter of flowers and leisure, even dream. Once people could sing "I Will Meet You at the Station," as the old hymn put it, and imagine fields robed in beauty and valleys green and fair. In 1905 the passenger division of the Boston and Albany Railroad published "A Railroad Beautiful," a brochure "Containing Illustrations and Descriptions of Its Work in Landscape Gardening at Railroad Stations." With its double-track system, the Boston and Albany, the passenger division claimed, "gives the finest train service out of New England, and the route lies through the PICTURESQUE BERKSHIRE HILLS, the MOHAWK VALLEY, thence via NIAGARA FALLS."

Vicki was right in thinking I might ask the government for aid to expand my shelter for homeless plants. Not keeping office hours has given me more time to write. Of course, my writing like my reading has changed. Ten years ago I wrote scholarly articles; now I write letters. Recently the powers who control the university gymnasium decided to increase the size of the weight room. By right of eminent domain, they seized half the locker room and, blocking it off, pushed all the lockers into the space which was left. With aisles between lockers smaller than galleyways on a submarine, the locker room is very fleshly. Not even a frog could hop to the shower without brushing against someone's bare ankle. Now whenever I undress in the locker room, thoughts of secret handshakes and primitive fraternity rituals come to mind, and so I wrote a letter to the head of Recreation and Intramurals. "Although the familiarity into which the faculty has been thrust," I said, "is likely to lead to increased collegiality over the short haul, in the long run serious damage could be done to the reputation of our university." "Already," I noted, "two members of the Classics Department, who, it is rumored, are inclined toward 'the Greek way,' have taken to lurking in the locker room. What lies ahead for those of us who continue to frequent the locker room I dare not say, but at the very least, someone is certain to get eczema. Indeed, I will go so far as to predict that it won't be long before a goosing occurs."

I spend a goodly portion of my office hours at home writing at my desk. Much I write is in response to what I receive. After the Executive Committee of the English Department meets, it sends each member of the department a copy of the minutes. The eighth item in the minutes for October 8, 1986, stated, "Mr. Rollins announced that the Annual

Equipment Competition is currently in progress." "Dear Bill," I responded the next day, "where can I line up for the Competition?" "I could win this thing," I wrote, "pants down." Unfortunately, most of the mail I receive is not so odd as the Executive Committee's minutes. Much, I am afraid, smacks of the busy world of office hours, doing and accomplishing. "One of the members from the financial community gave us your name. We would like to help you," began a letter one Gary sent me last week, urging me to take out a second mortgage. Money is the subject of practically every letter I receive. "Dear Sam," the class agent for my school's alumni fund wrote, our school "is on another roll, one that will add strength to existing strength and assure students yet to come the excellence of education, of faculty, of facilities, and of associates we found." My classmate's letter was so garbled that, if I were not certain that he spent last year in Tennessee, I would suspect that he came to Connecticut and while visiting the university wandered into the locker room and was whacked over the head with a gourd and goosed.

A mailbox resembles an office door. Through it as through a door stride the unwanted, and that person who does not keep office hours in order to avoid what might come through the door had better avoid reading his mail as well. In December I received a letter from a former college chum. Although someone told me he was a successful real estate developer, I had not heard from him in twenty-five years. When I saw his name and return address on the envelope, I was eager to read the letter. What sort of family, I wondered, did he have? Perhaps he had read my latest book and was writing to tell me he liked it. Woe is me, the letter concerned "the Phi House" at my undergraduate college, and Bones, as my chum signed himself, was extending the fraternal hand to squeeze money out of me. Some alumni were raising money in order to repair the house. "We're shooting," Bones wrote, "for cash gifts of $250 to $500 per man now, plus equal annual pledges for three years." Realizing that shaking out that kind of money might be difficult, Bones ended by urging me to give, writing, "I'll just have to bug you about it, if you don't." Insects fascinate me, and I wondered what sort of bug Bones had in mind. Although some assassin bugs suck blood, I ruled them out. Bones was a nice guy and despite being after money was not the assassin sort. To discover the right bug, I started for the library. Along the way I ran through all the bugs I knew, stink bug, tumblebug, bessie bug, chinch bug, and then toad bug. When toad bug sprang to mind, I stopped. The word "toad" made me think about spring peepers. Suppose that in the library I discovered there was a Pickering's bedbug, just like there was a Pickering's frog. Then Bones's letter, I realized, would have nothing to do with the Phi House but would be another coded message full of long-suppressed affection for me. If that were so, it probably meant that my hormones were out of order and had been out of order for decades. Hormones are not something I rummage around with, and I turned around and went home. That afternoon I didn't even go to the gymnasium to swim; instead I wrote a note to the head of the English Department asking why he had not answered my query about the Equipment Competition.

I have closed my door to bare students and brothers in the bond, not because I dislike them but because my interests have changed. About other groups which I have shut out of my life, I feel stronger. I dislike people who become jobs or ideologies, professional professions. As far as feelings go, though, mine are mild, growing more out of distaste than dislike. Strong feelings are for people who keep office hours. Pollinated by sharp convictions of rectitude and staked to the little rod of principle, zeal thrives in the closed hothouse of narrow responsibility. Still, I do have feelings and whenever politely possible I avoid lawyers and judges, spokespersons, brokers, creative accountants, people who cheat on their taxes with the help of creative accountants, and anyone driving a Mercedes. Of course, success in avoiding such people depends about as much on them as it does on me, and frankly they have not been as conscientious as I have. The occasional Mercedes will turn around in my driveway, and almost every time I bend over in the locker room to pull up my shorts, I seem to brush against a lawyer.

This past July an old buddy and his wife and her dog dropped in to eat lunch with us in Nova Scotia and stayed for eleven days and thirty-four meals. A friend from piney days gone by when I spent summers as a camp counselor in Maine, Jake coached junior football and taught algebra, world history, and vocabulary to ninth graders in a private school outside Princeton, New Jersey. Almost immediately Jake became part of our Nova Scotia family. He insisted upon cooking breakfast, after which he took the children exploring. When it rained, he played Monster, Dark, and Treasure Hunt with them in the barn. Mim, his wife, did not fit in quite so well. If Jake soon seemed a kindly great-uncle from the country, Mim was a cousin I wanted removed. She had a long nose and no earlobes, and at Jake's wedding some friends who had known her longer than I said, rather unkindly I thought at the time, that once she got her nose into Jake there was nothing he could do. Besides having a nose for Jake, Mim had a nose for money. After graduating from Walnut Hill School and Vassar, she became an accountant, a very creative one who just two years after setting up business in Trenton bought a house in Princeton and moved her practice into Princeton's Palmer Square. She and Jake had driven to Nova Scotia in her white Mercedes; at home Jake drove a Dodge Dart. Although she preferred a black car, she bought a white one, Mim explained, because it made a greater impression on her clients, "many of whom were new to Princeton and new to money."

The interior of the Mercedes was blue, a color chosen, I decided, to match the ribbons which Mim tied on the head of her dog Dolli to make a fall. Spelled with an *i*, not an *ie* or *y*, Dolli's name had been chosen with care. Dolli was a Lhasa Apso and, if she could have talked, she would not have spoken to Vicki or me, or even Jake. Untainted by mongrel blood, she was descended from a long line of pedigreed bitches, until this century kept only by Tibetan nobility. According to Jake, she was named Dolli for two reasons. Firstly she was "Mim's Little Dolli"; secondly and more importantly, Mim believed Dolli's ancestry could be traced directly to the household of a sixteenth-century Dalai Lama, thriving at least fifty years, she insisted, before the Puritans landed at Plymouth. Despite the regal pedigree, I didn't care for Dolli.

Two years ago Vicki and I spent an afternoon with Mim and Jake in Princeton. Not having hit it off with Mim at the wedding, I was surprised when Jake invited us over. After accepting his invitation, I was apprehensive. Their yard was fenced, and when we arrived Dolli was outside. Having learned from Jake that Dolli was Mim's great love, I walked over to the fence to pet her. By making a lot over Dolli I thought I would endear myself to Mim and grease the way for me to slip smoothly through the afternoon. Stretched on the grass near the fence, Dolli was chewing what I assumed was a dog biscuit. I was wrong; the biscuit turned out to be something less appetizing, to my palate at least and I hope to the palates of right-behaving dogs. I realize I risk being judged provincial for disliking Dolli solely on the basis of her choice of munchies. Until a breed becomes Americanized, perhaps allowances should be made for the tastes of exotic dogs, particularly those raised inside the Potala on a diet of dough rolls and yak butter. Be that as it may, however, I was not pleased when Dolli appeared in Nova Scotia, and I forbade the children to pet her. The children obeyed, and in truth, despite her culinary preferences, Dolli was not a nuisance, choosing to spend much time out of the house and in the barn chasing mice. Unfortunately, her mistress showed little interest in wild life, preferring instead to curry away mornings in the bathroom. Mim's grooming would not have irritated me if our house had had more than one bathroom. Not only did she lock herself in the only bathroom for an hour immediately after breakfast, but she used all the hot water.

After she spent seventy-four minutes in the bathroom one morning and then appeared dressed like a British officer in the Crimean War, wearing a jacket with two rows of gold buttons running down the front and with her hair stuffed under a pink Balaklava helmet, I felt like telling her to kiss my behind. Happily, I controlled myself, and four mornings later with Dolli's assistance life went me crudely better. With the bathroom door locked, I was caught short and forced to hightail it over to a grove of spruce trees some two hundred yards from the house. After doing what had to be done, I walked through the spruce into the back field to see if any berries were ripe. I poked about in the field looking for blueberries, then wild strawberries, and, I suppose, lost track of time until I heard Mim call Dolli. From the spruce trees came a yap, and then Dolli appeared running to the house. "Dolli couldn't have," I thought. But, of course, she had and, like Jack Sprat and his wife, had licked the platter clean. Worried that the children might pet Dolli, I ran to the house. I was too late. Mim sat in the rocking chair in the kitchen, holding Dolli in her lap and kissing her on the mouth. "What is it, Sam?" she asked. "You look like you have been running." "Just getting my exercise," I answered, then added, "What a sweet picture you two make. Kiss that dear dog once for me, will you?" I then went outside, sat on the porch, and looking up at the peacock blue sky thought about how fine the morning was.

The story is a little raw, but for a rummager life is occasionally raw. In an office with its white, sheltering walls, thoughts can be kept high, neat, and straight like books on a shelf, and days themselves can be dusted and polished. In Nannie Brown's album was the music to the Virginia reel "Billy in the Low Ground." Not for me now the high and the straight; I want to rummage the fertile low ground, thinking about yak butter and, then, Smith County doings.

After Hiram Povey's disappearance, Sheriff Baughman advised Enos Mayfield to stop selling liquor and homemade beer. For his part, Enos was loath to quit. His wife Claudine, however, was tired of being looked down upon as the better half of a disreputable whole. Wanting respect like that Amanda Leigh Hennard received when Albert stopped drinking, she joined forces with Sheriff Baughman and begged Enos to change his ways. She also, according to Levi Crowell, deprived him of her presence in the evening. Although a hardy reprobate, Enos was not strong enough to stand against the combined forces of law and love. Claudine knew Enos was addicted to low company. So that his friends would not hang around her house after he went out of the wholesale liquor business, she pestered him into opening an eatery across the river near the railway station in South Carthage. Brewing being different from baking, the food at the Railroad Inn, as Claudine called the place, did not attract the leading citizens of Smith County. The Inn's only steady customers were drummers waiting for trains and Enos's drinking companions, booze'em friends, as Levi Crowell dubbed them, who spent more time in the shed behind the eatery than inside the eatery itself.

Since the Inn was out of his jurisdiction, Sheriff Baughman paid no attention to the goings-on in the shed, and Claudine, having duly gotten a share of respect, joined the Methodist Church. Busy climbing Zion's Hill, she put the dark shades of this dismal shore, Enos's friends, behind her, and dreamed of meeting the shining ones, golden harps ringing in their hands. Occasionally, however, the pathway to heaven took her near and once even into the eatery. For an all-day meeting at the Cedar Point Methodist Church, an evangelist traveled up from Nashville. That afternoon snow began to fall, and the train on which he was to return to Nashville was delayed. Not thinking it proper to let a man of God wait alone at the station, the elders of the Cedar Point Church and several parishioners and their guests, among them Claudine, accompanied the evangelist to South Carthage. When the telegraph operator learned the train was way behind schedule, Claudine suggested eating dinner at the Inn. Making a greater profit from the sale of liquid rather than solid nourishment, Enos had allowed the Inn to become shabby. The coal dust on the tables did not bother the elders so much as the flies stuck to the butter. Seeing that the elders were annoyed, Claudine was embarrassed, and, Levi Crowell recounted, taking her husband aside, she asked him to put the butter on one plate and the flies on another, saying, "Let the brethren mix them to suit themselves."

Despite editing the *Courier,* Levi was not a completely reliable chronicler of Smith County life. But that's all right with me. I'm not so reliable myself, as anyone who looks for me in the English Department during my office hours will quickly learn. Moreover, I have come to believe that reliability isn't much virtue. In fact, reliability may be another name for inflexibility. Since I began rummaging, few of the virtues which reliable people say are important have held up well. High in the office where life can be discussed as an abstraction, honesty, for example, seems noble. Down in the low ground, where, as the spiritual puts it, there is a "wheel in the middle of a wheel," life is fleshly and fly-specked, and truth often appears abrasive and cruel. Honesty may not be the coin of that other realm, and the person who wants to board the Gospel Train, before Gabriel blows his horn and pulls out of the station, had better spend some time sowing seeds of kindness, telling tales which turn the low ground green.

Two months or so after Bevie Povey went to Nashville and asked the police to be on the lookout for Hiram, the chief telephoned her. He said that in the past six weeks a roomful of bodies had been fished out of the Cumberland. Although he had looked, he said, and couldn't tell if any of them were deaf, there was a good chance that one of the men was Hiram, and he asked Bevie to come down and try to make an identification. The next Saturday Bevie put on her Sunday hat and dress and rode the train to Nashville. The chief himself took her into the morgue. All the drowning victims were in one room. They had been stripped, washed, had the mud pumped out of them, and then laid on long thin tables and covered with sheets. So that the bodies wouldn't be "offensive" the room was icy. Sheriff Baughman having warned Bevie the room would be cold, she took her winter coat and scarf and did not catch a chill. When she came to the first table, Bevie lifted the sheet, looked, and then said, "This ain't Hiram." At the second table, she again lifted the sheet and after looking said, "This ain't Hiram." At the third and fourth tables she did the same, always saying, "This ain't Hiram." After lifting the sheet on the fifth table, however, she paused, bent over, studied the body carefully, then, after shaking her head long and seriously, said, "This ain't Hiram. But somebody sure has lost a lovely friend."

The account of Bevie at the morgue is an old story. Unlike that "old, old story of unseen things above," it is a tale of the low ground. But as earthly things often resemble heavenly, so it may be a type of that great story, not grave or earnest, but gently humorous and comforting. I came upon it one afternoon during my office hours. When I returned to Connecticut after spending Christmas with my parents in Tennessee this year, I brought a box of family papers and pictures back with me. Stuck in an envelope between the obituary of Hampden Francis Ratcliffe and a picture of his wife Alice Garthright were two pages of Carthage tales.

Copied out by my grandfather in longhand, they were attributed to Levi Crowell. Once I found them, I spent the afternoon reading then thinking about them. "What use did you make of your time?" Vicki asked when she fetched me for dinner. "You didn't waste the day reading about frogs again, did you?" "No, I have lost interest in frogs, bad for the hormones," I said. "To tell the truth I have just been rummaging around." "You really ought to be more responsible and keep office hours," she said, "or someday you're going to get busted right out of the university. All this rummaging and letter writing will get you in trouble." "Busted" sounded familiar, I thought, and then I remembered the word "bust" appeared in one of Levi Crowell's stories. "I might be fired," I said, "but let's eat dinner first." "By the by," I added, "I hope we are going to have more blueberry pie tonight." "Of course," I said, after a pause, "pie can be dangerous." "What do you mean?" Vicki said. "Well," I began, "do you remember my telling you that after Hiram's death Bevie spoiled their boy, Little B. H.? Feeling sorry for B. H. because his daddy was dead, Bevie let him eat whatever he wanted, and since he wanted a lot, he grew big around as a cannonball." "It seems," I went on before Vicki could interrupt, "that one night he ate almost two-thirds of a pie, though I'm not sure if it was a blueberry pie." "Anyway," I continued, "Bevie was worried. 'Little B. H.,' she said apprehensively, 'if you eat any more pie you are going to bust.' 'All right, Mamma,' he said, loading up his fork and speaking like somebody who had heard it all before, 'you just slice me another piece and get out of the way.'"

Family Scrapbook

T HIS PAST SUMMER I explored the back house on our farm in Nova Scotia. Beneath a pile of lawn chairs, fish boxes, and a clothes wringer, an Eastonia wringer with "Improved Sure Grip Clamps," I found an old trunk. Because the trunk was locked I was immediately curious and pushing the chairs and boxes aside made an open space and set about springing the lock. When I opened the trunk, the first thing I saw was a small book, a diary Vicki's grandmother wrote in 1903. A friend gave it to her that Christmas, and Vicki's grandmother kept it up for two months, January and February. The diary recorded the comings and goings of a bright, lively young girl, a senior in high school from a prominent but only moderately well-to-do family in Columbus, Ohio. Margaret Fuller Jones, or Maggie as her friends called her, enjoyed dancing and boys and for a short time loved writing about them.

On New Year's Day at a friend's house, Wen, she wrote, "kissed and kissed me and I *liked* it all. He is perfectly adorable, ten dances is all we had!" Boys and girls walked home from school together, sometimes gathering at the girls' houses, where they stole kisses. Once when Margaret visited Lucy and Lucy's parents were out for half an hour, Wen appeared. That night Margaret wrote, "There was no one there but us! It was bliss! To be in his dear arms and to feel his breath on my face! O!" Wen was not Margaret's only beau. After Lefty gave her some pictures of himself, she wrote, "One of him is the most *devilishly divine* thing you ever saw! I'm in love with him!" Early in January, when Charles left for Princeton, she wrote, "Chas goes today-O-O how it hurts! He came out in the afternoon to say goodbye. Someday (if that sweet someday ever comes) we won't ever have to say goodbye. We both cryed a little I think—and it was all so dear and as heavenly that I can't put it down in words! He's gone!" Smacking not of kisses so much as the joyous delight of a young girl before whom life lay open and promising, the diary was appealingly romantic and optimistic. As I read it, the narrow gray world of the back house began to glow. Stuck in the diary were the words of a song, cut from a newspaper. The tone of the song and the spirit of the diary were the same, gaily loving and brightly innocent: "If You Lak-a-Me, Lak I Lak-a-You, / And We Lak-a-Both the Same, / I Lak-a Say, This Very Day, / I Lak-a Change Your Name; / 'Cause I Love-a-You and Love-a-You True. / And If You-a Love-a-Me / One Live as Two, Two Live as One, / Under the Bamboo Tree."

Outside the back house the sun was shining. Years ago I would not have been inside on such a day. When I was small, sunny days were invitations to roam field and wood. Discovery was immediate and fertility everywhere. Rolling in the grass about the roots of a boxwood was a ball of green June bugs. Down in a low field Guernseys grazed swollen with extravagant promises of strength and health. During that dawn brightness burst through the dark. When I found a dead goose in the woods and poked it with a stick, clumps of orange and black carrion beetles tumbled out, falling over each other like clowns at a circus. Gone are those days now, and instead of playing lightly across the ribs and bringing laughter to the brow, the painted faces of clowns chill the breast, appearing as grotesque emblems of ravaging disease. Nowadays a clear sky brings clouds to my heart. On the brightest day I imagine dark mortality, and my children staring at me, pale and questioning. Wherever she goes, my little girl Eliza carries Kitty, a small stuffed, yellow kitten with blue eyes. On clear days when one can see through the horizon, I wonder what life holds for Eliza, and imagine a hard world of broken hopes in which Kitty lies dusty and forgotten. And so, instead of broad open places, I prefer the closed in and cluttered, places which do not invite the imagination to paint large canvases but which turn thought away from the future and channel it into the past. There with old books and letters about me, I smile and see Eliza with Margaret her great-grandmother, and Kitty, too, laughing and talking about boys under the bamboo tree.

In the shadows of the back house, I imagined Margaret's dancing happily through a carefree childhood. Reality was harder and sadder. When Margaret was thirteen, her mother died from stomach cancer. She suffered for two years, and, on her death, a Columbus newspaper paid tribute to the quiet fortitude with which she endured "long pain." "The hands that wrought so patiently and well, are lying on her breast. The feet that carried her along the pathway of life to the summit of all the joys and sad anxieties of motherhood, are at rest," the obituary concluded. "The flaxen hair of other days, now tinged with the gray maturity of years, rests like a crown and halo upon the ashy brow that shall know no pain again. How poor and impertinent all words seem beside the ashes of those we love! How narrow life appears when viewed from the edge of Eternity!"

After her mother's death, Margaret was lonely. Although her maternal grandmother lived with the family, Margaret found it difficult to share everything with her. As a result she wrote long letters to her older sister Grace, who was attending Bryn Mawr. In some she said simply that she was "very lonesome." In others she wrote about the things she would have shared with a mother: the pleasure she found in a new belt ribbon, the secret "trademarks" school friends fashioned out of their initials, and the tunes she had learned to play on her guitar, songs like "Romeo and Juliet" and "The Prettiest Girl I Ever Saw." In other letters she was playful; in 1899 she wrote a letter to Santa Claus, sending it by way of Bryn Mawr. "Dear Santa Claus," she wrote, "I am a very good girl, least I think I am; I want a pretty silver seal, and a book and lots of candy." Because her winter coat was getting shabby, she asked for a "gold cape." If Santa wasn't able to come up with the cape, "a nice pretty set of yellow fox furs" would do, she added. Thinking that Santa would not know much about them, at the end of the letter she asked Grace to send her "any pretty Gibson pictures," explaining that she was building a collection and already had eight or so she cut from old copies of *McClure's* magazine.

Grace was both confidante and ally. When Margaret decided she needed a new party dress and her grandmother thought her old organdy one would do, Margaret wrote Grace, drawing a picture on which she marked the soiled parts of the dress. Then she quoted a friend, Belle Bradford, who remarked after looking at the dress, "What a shame it is that your pretty dress is so dirty." In the middle of November 1899 she wrote Grace that recently six friends called upon her, two girls and four boys. She didn't ask them into the house, she said, because she "was afraid papa wouldn't like it." Consequently, they all stood outside on the curb and talked for an hour. The boys, she wrote, were "fishing for an invitation to come and see me." "Would you ask them in?" she wrote Grace. "You see I ask you because it makes grandma mad if I even say 'boy' to her and papa don't know nearly as well as *you* do. It will be so nice when you get home for now I have nobody to ask such questions." "You may think me silly," she concluded, "but I don't know what to do. I wouldn't dare to ask a boy in for it might make dad hopping."

More playful than hopping, Margaret's father George Dudley Jones was not the sort to get angry or stay angry. One of eleven children, "born poor," as he recounted, he was a lawyer and sometime politician, serving Columbus in various capacities, as city solicitor, for example, and occasionally as acting mayor. His hobby and greatest intellectual interest was philosophy. A leader of the local theosophic society, he made speeches ranging across the practical and the social, from trade policies to race, and newspapers referred to him as "scholar of the Franklin county bar." On vacations he often attended Chautauquas and although not religious went to churches to hear prominent divines and guest speakers. For Jones, philosophy was more than talk. Not only did he name Margaret after Margaret Fuller, whom he called "the most truly intellectual of all women," but he named his only son, who died at three, Emerson after Ralph Waldo Emerson. Although he was not wealthy and had trouble coming up with tuition, he believed strongly in the education of women and sent Grace to Bryn Mawr and Margaret to Wellesley. While Margaret was at Wellesley, he wrote her at least once a week. Margaret kept the letters and I found them in the trunk. Almost an emblem of the clarity with which he thought, Jones wrote a clean strong hand. Individual letters were almost always tall and bold and rarely flowed confusingly one into another. Full of practical advice, home truths, and good humor, his correspondence read like the conversation of a man at ease with himself and, if not completely comfortable with the world and its doings, at least assured enough to believe that thought, like the rod and the staff that aided the pilgrim, provided an adequate guide for right living.

Over and over he stressed the importance of thinking and urged Margaret to study diligently. "Observe and listen as you go about and reason upon all things," he wrote. "It is a sin to be stupid and there is no need for it." "One of the chief uses of a collegiate training is to get control of the mind," he declared. "This is perhaps of as much value to the student as the facts which he may acquire. Unless you acquire the true scholarly spirit the *facts* you learn will not be of any great value." He believed that women and men should be educated similarly. "The old time distinctions and discrimination which were made against the education of women" were based, he explained, "on a sort of savage ignorance and prejudice." A "trained mind" brought independence, contentment, and simplicity, itself closely bound to contentment. Once Margaret disciplined her mind, not only would she be able to obtain work but she would be immune to idleness and envy. Margaret was a good student, but she was also a popular, sociable girl, and occasionally Jones felt obliged to write things like "more thinking and less football will be better for you." In letter after letter, he urged her to visit Concord and Lexington and discover Boston, not the "tony hotels" but Faneuil Hall, Old South Church, and the Statehouse. "To be familiar with New England, topographically and historically," he said, "is to have a competent education in the birth and growth of democracy on the western continent and of the philosophy of self-government by a nation of free men." Once at Wellesley Margaret immediately became involved in college social life, and Jones despaired, writing, "I am afraid you don't attach as much importance to historical scenes and situations as you do to dry goods stores and ribbon shops."

Fashion, Jones believed, seduced people from thought and honest simplicity and fostered envy and corroding idleness. "Do you wear tight corsets or drink poisons to reduce your size? I am told," he remarked of an acquaintance in Columbus, that she "is lacing her idiotic self to death. The sooner she succeeds the better—for it will save time and trouble if it is done soon. You can see in her case what idleness can do. It is said idleness is the Devil's Workshop and nothing was ever more true. A young woman who puts aside all honest work of every kind and devotes herself to the merest vanity at the age of 18 or 19 years is certainly lost."

In Jones's mind, physical and mental health were linked, and he urged Margaret to live naturally, warning her against low shoes and late hours and entreating her to gain weight and to exercise regularly by walking or riding. At the end of her first year he offered her twenty-five dollars if she would get her weight up to a hundred and forty pounds. Not only would the weight provide strength and a bulwark against the grippe, but plumpness itself was a sign of superiority to fashion. As plumpness was natural and not artificial, it also revealed honesty, "the great hobby," Jones wrote Margaret, "of your grandfather Jones." "There is nothing like honesty and truthfulness in thought not less than in word and deed," he wrote. "Always be sincere. You can't afford for temporary advantage to be anything less than true and candid." Unlike fashion, which diverted attention from the actual and thus complicated life, honesty led to simple living. "The *simple life* is the best kind," Jones wrote in making suggestions about Margaret's courses, "things like the natural sciences, chemistry, biology, etc. will bring you down to simple things—that is *primary things.*" Belief in primary things led him to prefer comedy to tragedy. After seeing a play at the Southern Theatre in Columbus, he wrote Margaret that he had "gotten too old for tragedy" and would have preferred seeing *The Bachelor's Courtship, Rip Van Winkle,* or "something of the serio-comic plays in which there is a true, strong flavor of actual life and not so much imaginary and artificial life with fine clothing etc." "As you get older you will learn," he added, "that there is something better in sincere human nature than in all the garish frippery of pretence."

Despite the advice, Jones rarely took himself too seriously. Moreover, as a good speaker, he liked the sound of words and instead of preaching often played. Of a fancy wedding, he wrote lightly, "It was just *a dream.* The bride was beautiful and the groom was magnificent. The costumes of the ladies were all that heart could wish—the decorations of the church were charming and Cecil Fanning's singing *just set me wild.* As usual the organ played, 'Here comes the bride etc.' It seems to me I have heard that played before in the dim, indistinct past. The gowns were all *effective.* I don't know where the contracting parties went for their trip but I presume to *Niagara Falls* or *Mammoth Cave.*"

Jones wanted Margaret to become self-reliant, and his advice rarely cloyed because its source was earthy common sense rather than abstract theory. In suggesting that Margaret attend church, he said he went himself, explaining that "while I often hear things I don't approve and don't believe on the whole I think it best to make it a habit to attend church once a week. You can do that and yet do your own thinking. I would not wish you to allow anyone to think for you." In his letters, he commented freely on foolish behavior. In lamenting that no country or climate was free from the pestiferous grippe, he advised Margaret to "turn christian scientist and then you *can't* be sick." An illness which could be avoided was alcoholism, and if Jones was ardent about anything, it was the dangers of drink, writing Margaret that he "would rather bury a daughter than have her marry a drunken man." Yet when a friend of his "began drinking whiskey in a wholesale way and finally killed himself at it," Jones did not criticize alcohol. Instead he noted, "it is strange how big a fool a man can make of himself sometimes." Pondering the nature of man was typical of Jones and undermined idealism and any tendencies he might have had toward zeal. "I know enough of men," he declared, "to know that the ordinary man is not a very *high animal.*" In itself alcohol was neither good nor bad, and occasionally it afforded Jones merriment. "The weather," he once wrote Margaret, "is dry enough to suit the most extreme antisaloon league man." When he and his second wife, whom he married in 1900 and whom he called "your mother" in letters to Margaret, attended a dinner at which strong cider was served, he wrote lightly, "They had some beautiful cider of which your mother and I both drank generously. Your mother spoke frequently of the elegance of the flavor and the *effect* of the aforesaid cider. The elderly ladies always appear to like cider—it must be something in the apples that makes the cider so attractive."

Although common sense kept Jones out of the temperance movement, it led to a temperate life in which the rational handling of money was a certain sign of rational thinking. On many occasions, Jones warned Margaret, "*Money dont grow on trees.*" In part Jones felt obliged to warn Margaret because his finances were never strong. A goodly portion of his income came from small properties in Columbus. The people who rented them were poor and often unable to pay rent on time. Although Jones's second wife had some means and once took him to Cuba for a vacation, she had two daughters of her own in college and could not pay Margaret's bills as well. In struggling to be economical, Jones was his usual thoughtful self. Ponderings about economy often led him on to other things. "Your mother," he wrote Margaret in 1904, "gave me a beautiful pocketbook which I very much need. But badly as I need a pocketbook I need something to put in it much worse." "But I believe in having a pocketbook and in the orderly care of money," he continued. "To see a man without a pocketbook and stuffing his money away in his vestcoat pockets or in his trousers is a bad sign." Jones forever urged Margaret to watch her finances, noting in December 1904 that her expenses were so great that, instead of four hundred and fifty dollars, a year at Wellesley was liable to cost eight hundred. Despite worrying about money, Jones wanted his daughter to get about and grow independent, and at the end of her first year he wrote her, playfully saying that she had seen so much of "Boston and New York and the other big places" that on her return home Columbus "will not seem like more than a *flea-bite.*"

Despite being pleased by her traveling, he worried that life at Wellesley had given Margaret a taste for luxurious living. "I am afraid that you are getting used to so much grandeur that our plain place and plain living will not suit you any more." On learning that Margaret had spent a holiday with a wealthy family in Rhode Island, he urged her not to forget that her family did not have great means. Money, he explained, "is a very very hard thing to get but powerful easy to get *rid of.* I am afraid college life is getting entirely too extravagant and luxurious. I think it would be better if the girls had to do some of their own washing, ironing, and sewing. It would rest their minds when they study too hard and would help them to save their money." Concerned about more than being able to keep Margaret at Wellesley, Jones worried that money would become too important in Margaret's life and she would lose sight of his "primary things." When a fashionable girl became engaged to the son of a wealthy brewer in Columbus, he observed that young women "who make pretensions of being *tony*" were often in a hurry to marry for money. Outside of their wealth, he wrote, the brewer's sons had little to recommend them. Money, he added, "is a very nice and convenient thing to have about one's person at times but it may be gotten at too great a cost. I would rather both my girls should stay unmarried than that they should marry a man who is of no account." "There is a world of difference between a man and a mere pretence of a man," he concluded. "I hope as you go along that you will not be unmindful of the distinctions which I make respecting men."

"I am afraid my letter this time," Jones wrote in 1905, "will be a good deal like a wash-day dinner in the country used to be, sort of scrappy, made up of odds and ends." Although he lectured quite a bit, all Jones's letters resembled wash-day meals. Gossip, advice, and doings about the house spun through the pages like condiments on a lazy Susan. In November 1904 he wrote that Snowball, the family horse, had been sent to the country for the winter. Boarding a horse in town, he explained, cost sixteen dollars a month while the charge in the country was four dollars. Before Christmas 1904 Matt, a black servant, invited Grace to speak at his church. Handbills were printed, and Matt gave Grace "a flaming send off," saying "how long he had known her and how good housekeepers her mother and grandmother had been." Typically, Jones used the occasion to write about equality and decency, lamenting "there are many people who never learn the lesson of justice but are guided all through life by prejudice and considerations of selfishness." In another letter, after noting that a Mr. Howard had said "I greatly resemble Christopher Columbus," Jones asked Margaret, "Do you know how Columbus looked?" When a woman he knew tried to get rid of her worthless husband Tricksy, Jones wrote, "*Tricksy won't go.*" Although offered a settlement of twelve hundred dollars a year for life, Tricksy wanted a lump payment of fifty thousand dollars and refused to budge. "What do you think?" Jones asked, adding, "I believe if I were he I would hold on to my job until I got my price." In his letters, Jones often moved from small events to large conclusions. When Grace went to Europe, he noted that he would never go to Europe unless they sent him "*the price.*" "It may be they dont one *half of them* over there know me at all," he wrote. "I tell you when one gets away from home one finds that the folks haven't been studying much about one. Travel has a powerful tendency to take self conceit out of one's mind. Down in Cuba I found quite a lot of people who didn't know either me or your mother, never heard of us in fact."

Several letters were occasional. On February 12, 1905, he observed that had Lincoln been alive he would have been ninety-six years old. "It is doubtful if his equal has lived among us since his death," he wrote; Lincoln "was a plain homely man but he was honest and patriotic. Your grandfather Jones was in many respects like him. There are few such people any more. Men in politics are there for what they can make in many cases." In April 1905 he noted that Margaret's mother had been dead for six years and wondered if she thought about her. "No more faithful, devoted spirit ever lived," he wrote. "There was nothing she could do for you which she did not do." Telling Margaret that "you are today where she would have liked you to be," he urged her to "cherish a devoted reverence for her character," adding "her mind was vigorous and practical. Her nature was honest, fervent, and candid. She was pure in thought and most affectionate."

Often the qualities we admire in another are those we think most valuable in ourselves, and Jones described himself as accurately as he did Margaret's mother. In reading his letters, I came to admire, even envy, Jones's practical mind and candid, honest nature. His vision was clear, and muddling self-doubt never weakened him. Instead of digging through the distant past, Jones wrote affectionate letters for the present, guides for a daughter entering a world sunny with promise. Jones said things to Margaret which I believe good and true, things which I will probably never say to my children but which I want them to read. I don't have Jones's certainty. Years spent in classrooms turning and twisting matters have made me a doubter, sometimes even of purity and decency. Above all, it is the calm rectitude of the ordinary man which shines through Jones's letters and which I want my children to appreciate. Great acts are not possible for the ordinary person, but decency and niceness are, and they can make a difference, not to an age or epoch, but to a day or an hour.

Two Sundays ago Vicki and I and the children went for a walk at the university farm. Near a gully along the edge of a cornfield on the farm's western border is a large patch of milkweed. By this time of year, late October, pods are dry and beginning to split. Each fall we search out the milkweed and all of us, the children, Vicki, and I, break off the plants and, shaking the pods over our heads, fill the air with silky white seeds. They blow about then fall to the ground in drifts, and the children kick them into the air again and toss armfuls over their heads. To reach the milkweed we walked along a farm road, on one side of which were gardens planted by townspeople. By October the gardens as well as most of the gardeners had gone to seed. In one garden, though, an older couple was hard at work. We waved to them as we passed, and they waved back. While we were tossing the milkweed about, the couple finished working, and the husband walked over and handed me five carrots. The two biggest, he said, were "Mama Carrot and Daddy Carrot." The others were "the three little carrots." A handful of carrots won't make a bowl of vegetable soup, and when looked at in terms of the great scope of things what the man did was insignificant. My family and I don't live in a world of big perspectives, however. We live amid little particulars. That night we ate the carrots, and afterward Vicki and I held hands, feeling affection not simply for each other but for life itself, days white with soft milkweed and warmed by strangers bearing carrots.

To my mind, Jones was a man like the gardener. Sure of himself and openly loving, he sent gifts to Margaret, letters which I hope will someday appeal to my children, making them feel good about life and those who stumble through it. Of course, I am naive. Jones's letters probably had little influence upon Margaret. My hunch is that no weight of advice can deter a person from doing what he wants to do. As this essay will affect me more than my children, so the letters probably had more influence upon Jones than Margaret. Always reasonable and content to be satisfied with lesser things, Jones knew this, and often, after ranging long and thoughtfully over several topics, he ended simply saying, "Be a good girl and you will be a happy one." Margaret was a good girl, and her years at Wellesley were remarkably happy. In the trunk along with her father's letters was a scrapbook she kept while at college. Water having seeped into the trunk, the green cover of the book had split and the pages had swollen. Bound firmly into a wooden spine, however, none of the pages or their contents had pulled loose, and the book along with a bundle of letters which she wrote her grandmother provides a rich picture of Margaret's years at Wellesley.

In late September 1904 the Joneses left Columbus for Wellesley. They stopped in New York, staying at the Albemarle Hotel, Madison Square West. Margaret wrote her grandmother that New York was "the grandest place" she had ever seen. In part she was pleased because she did a lot of shopping, buying a suit, a coat, and "a very pretty brown velvet and silk hat." She was also pleased because Charles, one of the boys from her diary, came up from Princeton and took her sightseeing, to Grant's Tomb and around Columbus and Barnard, and then out to dinner and the theater. The first item pasted in the scrapbook itself was a notice from Wellesley apologizing for not having enough room to accommodate all freshmen in college dormitories. Reassuringly, college authorities noted that the town itself was "almost entirely a place of residence," having "no factories or workshops of any size within its limits." The streets were "supplied with electric lights"; snow was removed "with all possible promptness"; and "village houses for students" were "carefully inspected by a member of the board of health of the College." In some homes, however, "greatly to our regret," college officials stated, rooms for two students were not supplied with single beds, adding almost as an afterthought that "the point of facilities for bathing is also one upon which careful parents will wish to inform themselves."

By the end of September Margaret was happy with a Mrs. Stevens at 12 Abbott Street, sharing a small bed sitting room with a tall, fat, "fine looking" German girl from Duluth. Twelve girls ate meals in the house while six lived with Mrs. Stevens. Besides Margaret and her roommate there were girls from Kansas, Illinois, Rhode Island, and Massachusetts. A snapshot shows Margaret and a group of girls together in a corner of a room. Agreeable clutter is everywhere; pillows and blankets are on the floor. An oriental rug hangs over a stool while another tumbles off a bed. Two score pictures and cards, each on its own string, hang from the ceiling, twisting and seemingly falling like large pieces of confetti. Almost immediately Margaret bubbled over with enthusiasm. "This place," she wrote her grandmother, "is the most ideal place for a college that a person could imagine! Honestly Granny the campus is perfect! Such a beautiful lake and such hills, I wish you could see it all! The girls have all been lovely to me."

In 1904 colleges were responsible for students' behavior and welfare. Village houses remained open until ten o'clock. When a student left Wellesley, she filled out a white card detailing where and when she was going and when she would return. When she got back, she turned in a blue card, again saying where she had been and giving the exact time of her return. A student had to be back by seven-thirty in the evening unless she had "registered to be away under a chaperon." "Without a chaperon approved by the Faculty," the rules stated, "undergraduates shall not travel in the evening, nor drive with men in the evening; shall not attend public evening entertainments outside of Wellesley; and shall not enter the precincts of any men's college or building used as dormitory for the student of such college." Dormitories were kept quiet. Students who wanted to play musical instruments had to "conform to certain hours."

Sunday was not so much a day of rest as it was a day of little play. Students were forbidden to drive, bicycle, or go boating on Sunday, and without permission from a house president could not travel "in either railway or electric cars." In 1904, as now, appearance was reality. Unlike today, however, acknowledging the importance of appearance and then making rules for the sake of propriety did not make college officials uncomfortable. "Students," Wellesley regulations stated, "shall not solicit advertisements for student publications." Furthermore, payment for such advertisements had "to be collected by correspondence" or by an agent who was "not a member of the College."

Practical matters filled Margaret's first days, paying tuition—one hundred and sixty five dollars for the academic year—and taking placement tests. The tests, particularly the language tests, made her nervous. She wanted badly to please her father and do as well as Grace had done at Bryn Mawr. Happily, she did just that, offering English, history, mathematics, Latin, German, and French and being admitted to the freshman class "without conditions." Her success in languages was a matter of pride both to herself and to her teachers in Columbus. "I believe also," one of them wrote in congratulating her on her performance in French, "that a noble woman has more claim than an honest man to be called the noblest work of God and when I see a girl who has such promise of becoming one I cannot but feel interested." Although the sentiment was good, the teacher probably pitched his congratulations too high for Margaret or any of the Joneses. Just when Margaret received the congratulatory letter, she was writing a good, down-to-earth letter to her grandmother, saying, "What do you think Granny! I have two caterpillars on the table in a glass jar! We have to keep all sorts of bugs in our rooms for Zoology! I don't mind it much though." "I've lots of studying to do today," she continued merrily, "and worst of all I have to *darn my stockings!* It's nearly making me shed tears to think about it— But it 'has to be did.'"

During her first semester Margaret probably raised an army of bugs, for zoology was her most time-consuming class, meeting Tuesday through Friday from ten-fifty to twelve-thirty. There were no Monday classes, and first class of Margaret's week was Hygiene, which met at nine o'clock every Tuesday for forty-five minutes. Margaret's German and solid geometry classes each met four times a week, while her English course met twice. With Mondays free, Margaret's schedule wasn't rigorous. On most days she attended class three hours a day for a total of fifteen hours a week. She was disappointed, however, that her English course met on Saturday afternoon at one-thirty. "My work is pretty stiff," she wrote her grandmother, "but as Pop says I'm in college to work. It's sort of horrid though to have such a schedule as I have; so many of the girls have Saturday afternoon off." "Still," she added, "I don't mind so much." Probably she did not mind because courses were not rigorous.

Margaret was not one of those sad people who kept bundles of tests and term papers, thinking they constituted a record of college days and marked growth. Instead the litter of life outside the classroom fills her scrapbook. Still, she kept copies of a few examinations, none of which were difficult. Despite the caterpillars, Margaret's zoology class spent much of its time dissecting frogs, as three of the six questions on the semester examination focused on the frog's anatomy. Seven questions appeared on the English examination. Students were asked to "state and illustrate two important rules for the use of the comma, the semi-colon, the colon, and the dash." "Write a letter to a friend," another question instructed, "discussing the merits and defects of one of the books that you have read in connection with English I." A good student, Margaret did not disappoint Pop, but she never worked as hard perhaps as he would have liked. In part this was because the courses don't seem to have required strenuous work. On the examination in English given in June 1905, students were told among other things to rewrite four sentences giving "definite reasons" for their revisions. "I lived out West," the first sentence stated, "where the Indians were supposed to be, but in my estimation there was a great lack of the fiery redskins, so I would take much delight in attiring myself in all sorts of gay colors and by robbing the nearest chicken-coop of its feathers, I was able to deck my hair with a long line of gaudy tail-pieces." In another question, students were asked to choose one from three subjects—a woman baking a cake, a boy fishing, or May Day—and were then instructed to write three 150-word themes, the first to be an exposition, the second a description, and the last a narrative. The course in Hygiene ran for the entire first year; during the second semester classes concentrated on plumbing. On the examination one question asked students to define sewer, drain pipe, soil pipe, trap, and cesspool while another asked, "What are the essentials of a good trap?" Still another instructed students to sketch "a plumbing system for a dwelling house." Tests for advanced courses were more challenging, but they too were not especially difficult. In 1906 in English 2 students were told first to arrange some twenty-one "topics" pertaining to Woman Suffrage "in logical, brief form" and then comment on "reasons for changing the printed order or for rejecting any of the material." Among the topics were: woman is more moral than man; the only other disenfranchised classes are idiots, criminals, and children; very many women now in business; and according to the Declaration of Independence, all persons are born free and equal.

Despite this particular question and the controversy to which it pointed, political matters rarely appeared in Margaret's scrapbook. Only once did she seem interested in politics, and then the political was mixed with the social. In the scrapbook was a campaign button, an inch and a quarter in diameter and manufactured by the Baltimore Badge and Novelty Company for the presidential election of 1904. On the front of the button was a picture of Alton B. Parker and Henry G. Davis, nominees of the Democratic party for president and vice-president. Margaret enjoyed music and took her guitar to Wellesley, and although her father was a strong Democrat, she probably supported Parker more for musical than political reasons. In the scrapbook are three pages of campaign songs which Margaret copied in longhand. "We're coming, we're coming, a choice little band," girls sang. "Of good Parker Prophets we now take our stand / We didn't vote for Teddy, for this is what we think / He's too much inclined at the big trusts to wink." "Good-bye Teddy," another song began, "We must leave you / Exiled from the White House door / Something tells us it will grieve you / And will make you mighty sore / Parker's name is on the ballot / Good-bye! Hard luck to Ted!"

When Margaret wrote her father that she was supporting Parker, Jones replied that he was pleased but added that Parker would not be elected. He was "a Wall Street man," Jones noted, and "not much of a Democrat according to my ideas." Still, he was glad Margaret supported the Democratic candidate rather than the Republican. Typically, though, toward the end of his letter he wrote, "I don't wish you to think as I do however." "Do your own thinking," he urged, "whether it be of politics or religion or any other thing." If after study "you find yourself in another party than that of your father," he advised, "go into it freely. When I began to understand something of politics I separated politically from my father, who was a most sensible and sincere man. So in all ways learn to investigate and think for yourself and thus be somebody."

Margaret was more interested in things social than things political, and when she separated from her father, it was not from his politics but from his view of what an ideal student should be. Soon after arriving at Wellesley, she began writing Charles. Their correspondence was innocently dreamy and sweet. "Our ideas of fun and a good time on rainy days as expressed in our letters didn't seem to agree," Charles wrote. "I do like to paddle around in the wet and get drenched but on a stormy day a big log fire and just you with me to love and be loved, Margaret, that seems too much like heaven to be had on this earth." "Do you remember discussing with Burt ideal places for a proposal?" Charles continued. "His was much that picture only he had a cold snowy night instead of a rainy one. I always thought that so much better than the one you suggested of the ocean, moonlight, sail boat, and dancing pavilion. That always makes me think of circumstances as just a summer affair while in winter, it seems so much more serious."

In the middle of October Charles invited Margaret to Princeton for the senior prom and the Yale game. "It's the last football game I'll ever see on the varsity field as an undergraduate, and it's the Senior Dance given by my class," he wrote. "There are a lot of sentimental things attached to the doings this fall and I want you here with me to enjoy what is to be enjoyed and should the day bear sorrow into the camp of the tigers I want you to comfort me." As soon as he learned about the invitation, Jones wrote Margaret, saying he disapproved of her going. "You are just fairly in College and to break loose now and go 500 or 600 miles to a dance looks to me very foolish," he said. "It will break up your study habits, make you sick, and be expensive." After noting that he regarded such a "jaunt" as unreasonable, he then asked reasonable questions about chaperons and transportation, after which he concluded, writing, "If you do go which I hope you will not you must not go on any trip at Thanksgiving but must stay at college and make up for *lost time* and *lost money.*"

Margaret went to Princeton, and the scrapbook contains all sorts of memorabilia from the trip: a railway schedule and tickets for the New York, New Haven, and Hartford Railway; telegrams from Charles asking about the time of her arrival; a cigarette with Tower Club printed on it; program and ticket stubs for a concert given by Princeton's glee, banjo, and mandolin clubs at Alexander Hall at eight-fifteen on November 11; ticket stubs for the Yale game the next day at two o'clock; pictures of Charles and his friends, the parade before the game, the game itself; and lastly Margaret's card for the senior dance. Before the weekend Margaret and Charles wrote several letters. "How does West Point 6 Princeton 12 sound when coupled with West Point 11 Yale 6?" he wrote early in November. "Our stock is rising but I dare not hope for too much. It ought to be enough for me to know that I am to have you with me for a couple of days and not go hoping for a football championship along with that." Margaret's chaperon was a Mrs. Kellogg, a good-natured woman from Morristown who wrote Margaret, "I guess I'll take a paper of pins to stick into myself as I sit on the side lines at the Prom along about 4 A.M., but I don't suppose you'll mind if the old lady dozes a bit will you?" Mrs. Kellogg's girth was as expansive as her sense of humor, and this caused Charles some concern. "I'm sorry Mrs. Kellogg is so large," he wrote, "for we are going to the concert and dance with 'Brie' Ogden, Miss *Sou* Mix, and Mrs. Ogden all in one carriage. Brie and I can ride with the driver."

The day Margaret left Princeton to return to Wellesley, Charles wrote her a gloomy letter. He said he had been reading Kipling. "Permit me to quote a little," he wrote. "The fire upon your altar dies, / The flowers decay, / The goddess of your sacrifice / *Has flown away.* / What profit then, to sing or slay / The sacrifice from day to day?" "I could also very appropriately quote," he wrote, "the whole of 'The Vampire' but I shall not because 'Two things greater than all things are, / The first is love and the second war / And since we know not how war may prove, / Heart of my hearts, let us talk of love.'" "Kipling is good," Charles continued, "but he is a little sourballed. He makes good reading when a fellow has the blues." "Dear," he wrote, "next time you write please make it a love letter."

Alas, Charles may have had to wait some time for his love letter. If he was melancholy, Margaret was gay and so busy that she neglected her correspondence, even that to her parents, so much so that on November 24, her father sent a telegram. "What is the matter?" he asked. "We have received no letter. Answer at once." Nothing was the matter; Margaret was simply whirling about in a wash of invitations and had been ever since she arrived at Wellesley. Not only were there numerous receptions sponsored by college officials and undergraduate associations but girls in the upper classes held luncheons for and invited freshmen to dances, plays, and concerts at "the Barn," the college's gathering place. Life at Wellesley was festive. Despite the restrictions on playing instruments, music was everywhere. Students sang a great deal, and among the first items in the scrapbook were five pages of college songs and cheers. To the tune of "Yale Boolah," freshmen sang: "I've heard about the Wellesley girls / And all their cunning ways / About their freshmen working hard / For days and days and days. / And then their reputation / Of which they may be proud / And each girl thank her lucky stars / That she's one of the Wellesley crowd." "We are, we are, we are great, *Yell I* began, "Sure as, sure as, sure as fate. / Wellesley, Wellesley 1908 / 1-9-0-8 / Wellesley."

In her second year Margaret became a member of the Mandolin Club. Musical clubs, particularly glee, banjo, and mandolin clubs, were important parts of campus life at the turn of the century, and Margaret's scrapbook contains programs of concerts put on by clubs from Princeton, Amherst, and Wellesley among others. On New Year's Day, 1906, the Yale glee, banjo, and mandolin clubs performed at the Odeon Music Hall in Columbus. Margaret attended the performance and a dinner and dance given in the clubs' honor. On her program she put a check by the names of the boys she knew. The Banjo Club began the evening by playing "Down the Field." The Glee Club then sang "Brave Mother Yale," "Going a-Dreaming," "Peter Piper," and "Tutti Frutti," this last performed with the Banjo Club. The program was divided into three parts; the second began with the Mandolin Club's playing "Dream of the Violets." The evening ended with the Glee Club's singing "Bright College Years," the last stanza of which concluded, "Oh, let us strive that ever we / May let these words our watch-cry be, / Where'er upon life's sea we sail, / 'For God, for Country and for Yale.'"

Wellesley had its own music-filled festivals, Tree Day and Float Day in particular. Wellesley students rowed a great deal. Float Day, 1908, began with a "Parade of Class Crews," led by the 1908 Crew in crimson and followed by the 1909 Crew in cornflower blue, the 1910 Crew in violet, and the 1911 Crew in yellow and white. After the crews formed a *W,* a "procession of decorated skiffs representing an Elizabethan Pageant" appeared. In the first skiff were Neptune and Amphitrite; in the second Queen Elizabeth and her Court. Behind the Queen came Nereus, Tritons, and Nereids, and in the last skiff were Merrymakers and Musicians. Next on the program were eleven songs, the last being the alma mater. After the songs the College Crew in blue rowed past, and the celebration ended with a band concert and fireworks.

On Tree Day there was more dance than song, and the festivities appear to have been more romantic. On Tree Day, 1905, "The Flower and the Leafe," a fifteenth-century poem, provided the "Argument" for the dance. "A Gentlewoman, shielded by an Arbour," the program explained, "looketh out upon a meadow where presently a Troupe of other Ladies, being led by Diana, learn from her a Measure. Knights yclad in Armour follow and joust upon the Sward until nine Victors are crowned with Laurel Leaves, which are the Symbol of the Tree that they all worship. Then other Ladies and other Knights come forth to dance. But they, following their Queen, the Ladie Flora, do Honour to the Flowers until which Time the Wind it casts them down and they are succoured by Diana's Troupe. Then being cheered, they too regard the Tree. 'Afterwards this Gentlewoman learneth by one of these Ladies the Meaning hereof, which is this: They which Honour the Flower, a Thing fading with every Blast, are such as look after Beauty and Wordly Pleasure. But they that Honour the Leaf, which abideth with the Root, notwithstanding the Frosts and Winter Storms, are they which follow virtue and during qualities without Regard of Wordly Respect.'" On Tree Day, 1908, dancers put on the story of Pluto's abduction of Persephone and dramatized Demeter's grief and final happiness at her daughter's reappearance in spring. Margaret was one of six main performers. She danced the part of "many colored" Iris who along with Apollo pleaded Demeter's case to Jove.

Along with song, dance filled many of Margaret's days at Wellesley, and her scrapbook bulges with dance cards, several with small, brightly colored pencils still attached. Margaret's enjoyment of dancing came naturally. For her father, simplicity was a virtue, not one, however, which narrowed life and shaped the ascetic but a virtue which so guided a person that he could remain content amid temptation and foolishness.

For George Jones, a relatively simple life brought self-assurance and freed him to enjoy "gaiety," particularly dancing, of which, he wrote Margaret, he was "very fond." At a college prom or hop, as they were sometimes called, twenty-four dances were usually scheduled; on the back of a dance card, six "extras" were occasionally listed. Most proms began with a two-step; a waltz followed; and for the rest of the evening, the two dances usually alternated. Before the dancing began there was a concert program, most often composed of light classical pieces. At the senior hop at Amherst in 1908, for example, the "Concert Programme" consisted of the overture to *The Barber of Seville* and selections from *The Merry Widow.*

For me, the cards from the proms Margaret attended have much charm. Only the sentimentalist romanticizes the past at the expense of the present; yet the titles of the dances promise gaiety and lighten the day. Whirling lightly through the songs were a chorus of girls: Starlight Maid, Ramona, My Lady of the North, Madcap Princess, Sergeant Kitty, Molly O, Daddy's Little Girl, and Queen of Hearts. Holding them tightly were Bill Simmons, Gingerbread Man, Mayor of Tokio, My Diabolo Beau, Brown of Harvard, Tattooed Man, and Gipsy Baron. Indians, orientals, and all sorts of colorful exotics appeared in song titles: Powhatan's Daughter, Princess Pocahontas, Red Feather, Omar Khayyam, the King of Pomeru, and the Mullah of Miasmia. As couples spun around the floor, so did the globe, and bands played "Forty-five Minutes from Broadway," "Topeka," "The Isle of Spice," "Lilliputia," "Toyland," and "Robinson Crusoe's Isle." Titles of many tunes smacked vaguely of things military: "Gingerbread Cadets," "Mascot of the Troop," "Beat of the Drum," "Officer of the Day," "Spirit of Loyalty," and "Captain in Command." At times the titles reduced college to football and romance: "The Pigskin," "The Triple Cheer," "Down the Field," "Summer Evening," "Sylvan Reveries," "Rose Dreams," "Golden Sunset," "North Star," "Moonlight," and "Eternelle Ivresse."

Now a matter of beer, money, new cars, and artificial turf, football is rarely associated with smoky fall days, the hidden thermos, hands clasped secretly together under a plaid blanket, and an embarrassing friend forever blowing a bugle and urging the tiger to rise up and roar down the field. Such thoughts are, of course, as one song title put it, "A Bit of Blarney." Romance, alas, may have fared worse than football, and "Heart Throbs" and "The School Girl" seem to have gone the way of all flesh. Still, how much fun it must have been to spend an evening dancing to tunes like "Dill Pickles"; "Piff, Paff, Poof"; "Pearl and Pumpkin"; "How'd You Like to Spoon with Me"; "Everybody Works But Father"; and "Just a Little Rocking Chair and You."

In March 1905 Margaret wrote her grandmother that she was going to be "in a little play at the College Settlement house in Boston." Put on by six freshmen, the "little social comedy," she wrote, "ought to be quite a bit of fun." The play was *The Kleptomaniac,* a one-act comedy. Margaret played one of the two major roles, a Mrs. John Burton (Peggy) who at a recital given by Miss Farquhar lost a purse containing one hundred dollars and her engagement ring. Ending with Peggy's recovering the purse and "kissing it rapturously," *The Kleptomaniac* was fun. Throughout college, drama gave Margaret quite a bit of pleasure, almost as much as song and dance, and the scrapbook contains many theater programs. Not only did she see numerous college productions, *The Rivals* at Amherst and *Much Ado About Nothing* at Wellesley for example, but she saw plays in Boston and New York. Like her father, she preferred light drama, for the most part seeing forgotten comedies and musical entertainments like *The Duke of Killicranke, Brother Jacques, The Vanderbilt Cup, Mlle. Modeste, The Embassy Ball, The Man in the Box,* and *Strongheart.* On front of the program for this last play was a picture of the leading man dressed in a football uniform. The play was about college life and football in particular. The first act took place in the "Rooms of Frank Nelson and Dick Livingston at Columbia," while the second, on Thanksgiving two days later, took place in the "Dressing-room of the Columbia football team at the polo grounds."

When college societies staged plays, programs were often more interesting than the dramas themselves. In spring 1905 Margaret attended a production of Ben Jonson's *The Silent Woman,* the "Annual Theatricals" of Delta Upsilon at Harvard. Delta Upsilon performed in Cambridge, Boston, and Wellesley. In 1906 Pi Eta of Harvard staged performances of *The Girl and the Chauffeur,* a musical comedy written by members of the society, in Malden, Boston, Lowell, and Cambridge. Unlike those for commercial theater, the programs for these productions were impressively full. Their covers were colored; and printed on thick, weighty paper, the programs contained numerous pictures, long lists of patronesses, and pages thick with advertisements. Pi Eta listed thirty-six patronesses in Boston, forty-six in Cambridge, sixty-five in Lowell, and twenty-six in Malden. Not only were the numbers large, but many of the names sound familiar or at least sound as if they ought to be familiar today. Among Delta Upsilon's patronesses were Mrs. John Quincy Adams, Mrs. Thomas Bailey Aldrich, Mrs. Willian Endicott, Jr., Mrs. Charles W. Elliott, Mrs. Francis Lee Higginson, Mrs. Julia Ward Howe, Miss Alice Longfellow, Mrs. Sarah Orne Jewett, Mrs. Fogg Osgood, and, to echo things familial but far removed, Mrs. Edward C. Pickering.

The cultural and social aristocracies of Massachusetts have not disappeared, but standards of living have leveled up, and aristocracies count for less than they once did. Ours is an age of commerce, and the passing of time is not marked so much by the passing of tone-setting families as it is by the passing of products. Unlike the poet, we do not lament lost ages by wondering what happened to the snows of yesteryear. Instead we, or at least I, wonder about stores that have vanished and those products which they once sold and which have also disappeared. Amid brisk talk of electronic gadgetry, I am uncomfortable and long for the slow patter of a portable Smith Corona. For a person like me, the theater programs are reassuring, for many of the advertisements are for products and establishments still in existence. As a child I ate Necco sweets, or at least I think I did, and when Christmas drew near eagerly waited for the F. A. O. Schwartz catalogue of toys. Later I occasionally wore clothes from Brooks Brothers and Rogers, Peet, ready-made, however, and not too much more expensive than the woolen "Sack Suits" which the Harvard Co-operative Society advertised for twenty-eight dollars. Once during a trip to Boston, I ate at Durgin Park, somewhat later, I think, than the seven P.M. closing time advertised in 1905. In Boston the age of the car was well underway. In March 1905 Margaret attended the "Third Annual Automobile Show" held in Symphony Hall, and theater programs contained advertisements for cars. The "Silent Speedy Sporty" Haynes Model O Touring Car with a four-cylinder motor capable of producing thirty to thirty-five horsepower cost $2,250. Four models of the Franklin were available, costing from $1,400 to $4,000. If these prices were too high, a person could pick up a ten-horsepower Cadillac Runabout for $750. "We have many instances," Alvin T. Fuller of the Motor Mart on Park Square declared, "in which these cars have run an entire season without the necessary outlay of a single dollar for repairs or operating, beyond the cost of gasolene and oil."

Not every community embraced the car so fervently as Boston; some were still behind the sway of the horse. In 1906 four livery stables and no automobiles were advertised in the program of the Amherst College Dramatics Association. On Amity Street, T. L. Page said he always had

single and double teams on hand. Social things at Amherst were on a
more informal level than at Harvard; in 1906 the Dramatics Association listed only six patronesses. "Terpsy" advised students, "Keep your
clothes well pressed during Prom week," while "Peanut John" urged students not to forget him. "Most of the boys are getting wise," James F.
Page stated: "Paying $6.00 to $8.00 for $5.00 shoes is on the wane. Buy
your shoes in town, get a good fit, and save from $1.00 to $3.00 on
every pair."

In March 1907, when the Triangle Club of Princeton came to Columbus, Margaret attended their *The Mummy Monarch,* a blend of the music
hall and Gilbert and Sullivan. "The action of the play centers around the
return to life of two mummies, King and Queen of Egypt 2000 B.C.," the
synopsis began. "They are blown out of the Pyramids by an enterprising
American college professor who is assisted by Nitro Bomski, a Russian."
During Margaret's college days, light entertainments like that of the Triangle Club appear to have been more widespread than they are today. In
1905, for example, Margaret saw the "Seventh Annual Tech Show,"
MIT's *The Chemical Maid,* the story of the love between an American
sailor and Maud, the chemical maid who was the product of a "mar-
velous experiment" by Sir Explode, a famous Dutch chemist. With
twenty-six songs and at least five dances, the play bubbled frivolously.
Much attention was paid to costumes, and among other pictures in the
program was one of the Daisy and Bee Ballet, three "women" dressed as
daisies and three men dressed as bees. The women wore large floppy
blossoms on their heads and what appear to be green dresses with white
petals around the shoulders and waists. Over their legs the bees wore
dark tights, topped off at the waist by crinkly velvet shorts. Above the
waist they wore vests, sticking out of the backs of which were wings,
each three feet long, thus giving them a wingspan of six feet. On their
heads were caps with comically long, wavy feelers.

At times Margaret's Wellesley years seem long, green summers. Like a
bee gathering nectar from flowers, she flew from experience to experience, carrying away bits and pieces of brightness, the stuff of gentle
memory, nourishing not simply her recollections but my affection and
admiration. Somehow out of the clutter of the scrapbook, amid things
which have no important meaning, shine solidity and strength. Margaret was happy, and her happiness grew out of enjoyment of the ordinary and the inessential, about all most of us will ever have and about
the best things we can ever dream about. Pasted, and sometimes sewed,

into the book were banquet and dessert forks, bus schedules, packing slips from boxes of candy, dried flowers, and the heavy, colored foil with which flowers were wrapped. Margaret often attached the foil to the book with shiny hat pins, the heads of which almost glowed in turquoise, violet, blue, silver, and pearl. On May 20, 1905, she watched the sixteenth meeting of the New England Intercollegiate Athletic Association at Worcester, Massachusetts. The following October she saw the Harvard-Brown football game. Along with ticket stubs for track, football, and baseball, she pasted a sticker for the "Amherst College Basketball Association 1905" into the scrapbook. Not only did she attend a lot of athletic events, but Margaret herself liked the out-of-doors. Besides riding horses and ice skating, she watched birds, and in 1905 on the Massachusetts Audubon Society Check-List noted that she saw sixty species including the screech owl, belted kingfisher, phoebe, bobolink, snowflake, indigo bunting, bluebird, scarlet tanager, and yellow palm warbler.

Life was very social within Wellesley itself. Throughout the year classes and various societies sponsored dances and teas and put on entertainments. Students invited one another to dances at the Barn, and Margaret kept many of the dance cards. Cards for these dances were not the ornate chapbooks, complete with crest or seal, colored pencil, and decorated cover, which accompanied proms at men's colleges. The dances, though, did seem to offer more variety. Instead of alternating between waltzes and two-steps, the occasional caprice or schottische appeared. Not only did the students enjoy the dances, but they put thought into them. "The Juniors of the Shakespeare Societie at the Barn, the XXVII° daye of March MDCCCCV from 3 o'clock until 6 i' the afternoon," an invitation read, "you shall be welcome, Ladye. Pray you come. And Ladies, we will every one bee mask'd. The musicke playes: will you not dance?" Margaret wore a white Zorro-type mask and seems to have danced twenty-three out of the twenty-four dances.

Besides entertainments at the Barn students asked each other to tea and to meals, usually sending invitations. They also entertained friends and guests, often male, at the Wellesley Inn. Accounts were paid monthly at the Inn, and during February 1905 Margaret ran up a bill of twelve dollars and forty cents. For three dollars on the twelfth she and three guests ate dinner; the next day she paid for four luncheons at fifty cents each. On the fifteenth she was charged forty cents, probably for tea. On the twenty-second she paid for two luncheons, each costing a dollar, and two dinners at a dollar and twenty cents each. On the twenty-sixth she bought two dinners at a dollar and twenty-five cents each. For the month there was a ten-cent error in the bill, but she did not catch it. Occasionally Margaret kept a napkin for a meal. Instead of being functionally white, the napkins were decorated, with, for example, ox-eyed daisies and black-eyed Susans bursting through pillows of grass, or purple, green, and red tea sets, complete with pots, cups, saucers, sugar containers, dessert plates, almost everything except ladyfingers.

Midway through her second year, in December 1905, Margaret agreed to join Zeta Alpha Society, and on her return to school in January she and fourteen other girls became members. There were five societies at Wellesley: the Agora, Phi Sigma Fraternity, the Shakespeare Society, Society Tau Zeta Epsilon, and Margaret's Zeta Alpha. "We are bound together by a strong tie of good fellowship," the president of Zeta Alpha wrote Margaret. "I do not want to give you an idealized account, nor to represent things as more than they are, yet I feel that I can say with perfect sincerity that the ideals which Zeta Alpha holds before us are ideals which we hope will in the end make us truer and nobler women. I do not need to tell you that the sharing of such inspiration is conducive to a friendship which is closer than most." In addition to dances like the one sponsored by the Shakespeare Society, societies also undertook cultural projects. "Our work for this year consists of a detailed study of the period of the Italian Renaissance, and is designed to complement our more general study of the same period last year," the president explained to Margaret. "The open meeting in May will be a dramatic representation of some characteristic product of the period, as was our masque 'Orfeo.' We spend some time on the minor writers, but devote most of our attention to the lives and works of such representative men such as Dante, Petrarch, and Boccaccio."

After Margaret agreed to join Zeta Alpha, she immediately received a bundle of congratulatory letters. "The society," one member wrote, "has meant more to me than any thing else in college." "How happy we all are at the prospect of welcoming you into the very dearest, closest fellowship of the college," another member wrote enthusiastically. "It is a great thing to know that whatever you do, whatever you say, there will be thirty girls to back you up," still another girl wrote. "Of course this makes you all the more careful for you live for the society's sake and don't wish to shame it in any way, but that restraining influence is the finest thing, and you grow to be proud of it." Each society owned a house, and although membership brought "delightful comradeship," it could also narrow one's interests and restrict acquaintances. The societies themselves were aware of the dangers of exclusiveness and in "Intersociety Rules and Regulations" urged members both to make and keep "friendships with girls who are outside of the society."

Margaret was popular and, although she was most certainly pleased at being invited to join Zeta Alpha, she enjoyed the diversity of college doings too much to generate any kind of exclusive enthusiasm for a society. When looked at from the perspective of her scrapbook, Margaret's interests did not shrink when she joined a society. In fact, Zeta Alpha seems simply one among the many things remembered in the scrapbook. During the summer after her first year at Wellesley the Joneses spent three weeks at Hotel del Otero at Spring Park on Lake Minnetonka, not far from Minneapolis. In the scrapbook are more items related to this vacation than to Zeta Alpha. Margaret and her family traveled from Columbus to Chicago, then from Chicago to Minneapolis, where they took the Great Northern Railway to Minnetonka, round trip between Minneapolis and Minnetonka costing fifty cents or two dollars and twenty-five cents for a book containing tickets for ten trips.

For Margaret, life at the hotel resembled that at Wellesley. Once off the train she was whirling through things. She went rowing and blistered her hands, went to dances and concerts, and met many boys and girls. On the lake she ran across three Wellesley girls; unfortunately, the four of them were outnumbered by girls from Wells, the college her two stepsisters attended in Ithaca, New York. "This will have to be a case of quality not quantity," Margaret wrote her grandmother. As usual a number of boys were attracted by Margaret's energy and high spirits, and among the souvenirs of the summer are cryptic notes, Turkish cigarettes, and a half page of shirt labels from, for example, Whipple and Malmstedt in Minneapolis, Brokaw Brothers in New York, L. G. Hoffman in St. Paul, and F. B. Boyd in St. Louis. Margaret and Lila MacDonald, one of her stepsisters, seem to have been the life of the hotel. "Monday afternoon," a reporter wrote in his account of news from Minnetonka, "the guests were given a pretty Japanese tea in the dainty tearoom and a congenial gathering of men and women spent the dreary afternoon in pleasant sociability. Miss MacDonald and Miss Jones of Columbus, Ohio, assisted in entertaining delightfully. They both appeared dressed as babies, and both sang and danced prettily." Impromptu concerts were popular at the hotel. College girls, the reporter said, were responsible for many of them. "Miss Morgan of St. Paul, Miss Jones of Columbus, a Wellesley college girl, Miss MacDonald, Columbus, who comes from Wells, and Miss Lou Palmer of Vermont," the paper stated, "are among the chief entertainers, who sing merry college songs accompanied on the piano, banjo and guitar."

During her second year at Wellesley Margaret was house president of Simpson Cottage, and she and her roommate Frida from New York shared a suite of two rooms. Frida was creative, and she and Margaret spent time decorating their rooms. Margaret told her grandmother that the rooms were "perfectly stunning." "We haven't any foolishness up at all," she explained, "I mean posters and pennants." Frida supplied four "beautiful rugs" and much "dark mission style" furniture. Each room had a fireplace, and the curtains as well as couch covers were made out of dark green burlap. A small vestibule connected the two rooms with the hall; over the outside door the girls hung Bagdad curtains. Assurance marked the rooms. Having successfully completed a year at Wellesley, Margaret felt confident enough to delight in herself. The decorations, she told her grandmother, were "all very artistic, you know." Frida herself was gifted and independent and maybe even unconventional. Rooming with her, rather than a member of Zeta Alpha, might be a sign of Margaret's own independence. Be that as it may, however, in mid-November Frida left college to spend a week in New York. "Nothing," Margaret wrote, "like having enough money to chase all around every where and on top of every thing else brains enough to make up the work." Frida was a budding poet, and one of her poems had been chosen as class song. "Crimson the light that glows," it began, "Deep within the rose / We've chosen for our token; / For while we may live / We'll ever faithful give / Our class a love unbroken. / And we will all declaim / Wellesley's loved name / In reverent accents spoken, / Loyal to her and to our class of nineteen-eight." In 1906 *Harper's Magazine* printed a short poem she wrote entitled "Of Love." "They sing of love who never won his grace," the poem stated. "On harp and lute / They vaunt the glories of his dwelling-place. / They who are in his presence,—face to face / Are stricken mute."

Margaret did not covet Frida's intelligence or poetic gifts. In the ability to make friends, Margaret was herself gifted. What she did envy, though, was Frida's wealth. At times Wellesley was not easy for someone like Margaret who came from a family of comparatively modest means, but who had imagination and who did not want financial circumstance to hinder her enjoyment of college. If there was a worm in the bouquet of Margaret's Wellesley days, it was the lack of money, and George Jones was right in preaching simplicity and warning his daughter against luxury. Even so, not having means like Frida bothered Margaret, and in letters to her grandmother she forever alluded to her need for money, usually humorously. "Except for my pocket books I'm reasonably happy," she wrote in 1906. "I wish my money grew on trees, as Pop reminds me it doesn't about fifteen times every letter." Margaret went to many dances and often wanted money for clothes. After she was asked to the junior prom at Amherst, she wrote her grandmother, saying, "I wish some kind of angel would present me with almost a hundred dollars to get some pretty new clothes to take up there. My clothes are all a perfect mess." "You know," she continued, "it's like pulling hair to convince Pop that I need anything to wear—except my skin!"

The light phrase at the end of the letter was typical of Margaret. Much as the advice her father gave her often began weightily but ended lightly with an anecdote, so Margaret was incapable of sustaining so trivial a plea, and like her father she turned to humor. In truth, Margaret probably needed some clothes. She received and accepted so many invitations that her father accused her of going to college "to play." There was some basis for the accusation. "I have been having a pretty good time lately— people have been so nice to me," she wrote her grandmother in May 1906. "Two weeks ago last Sat. my Rhode Island friend Cheney Cook took me to the theater and luncheon. A week ago last Saturday I went to Woonsocket over Sunday with Gertrude Cook. I had a corking time too. Then last Sunday Charles came to see me, clear from Albany. Wasn't he nice? But I'm not very crazy about him anyway. He went back at midnight Sunday night. Last night a St. Paul friend of mine, Thurston Johnson, came out to see me from Boston Tech., and a Harvard Senior, a New York man, Bobby Woodbridge." "Tonight I am going in to Boston in an automobile to the Cornell Glee Club Concert with another Harvard Senior. Won't it be jolly?" she asked, then tacked another page of engagements onto her social calendar. "Tomorrow Winifred Reed, a Cincinnati girl here in the house, and a peach, and I are going to the Touraine to luncheon with a Harvard and a Yale man, and afterwards we are all going to the big track meet." "There Granny dear," she finally ended, "am I not a gay butterfly? Still I am doing my work just the same. Then you see next Monday I start for Amherst, nothing preventing."

Little prevented Margaret from having fun. Going home for Christmas and spring vacations seems to have been the only thing she wanted to do but didn't accomplish. Her father thought frequent trips to Columbus an unnecessary expense and did not allow her to come home every vacation. "We all missed you here this spring," he wrote her in 1905, "but it is all right. It will cultivate individual force of character for you to be thrown on your own resources. It is an education to be away from home." Indeed, it was an education but primarily a social one. Margaret spent that spring in New York with Frida and her family, attending the theater and going to fashionable spots like the Cafe Lafayette. Gertrude Cook was another of Margaret's close friends, and in 1906 Margaret spent Christmas with the Cooks in Woonsocket, Rhode Island. The Cooks were warm and gracious, and Margaret received a bag of presents: silver sugar tongs, "a package of *very grand* Russian tea," a handkerchief, a "big pink silk bag," and a pair of silk stockings, this last from Gertrude. Although Margaret missed her family, she was not lonely. "I've been having an awfully good time," she wrote; "lots of people" had come to see her and Gertrude. "I went to a dance on Wednesday night, and yesterday afternoon," she added, "Gertrude and I served at a tea given for the wife of the governor of Rhode Island. Weren't we fussy!"

In the catalogue of boys mentioned to her grandmother was Charles. Since appearing in her diary and then inviting her to Princeton for her first college weekend, Charles had lost his high place in Margaret's affections. He never slipped out of the scrapbook, however, and kept reappearing. In June 1905 he graduated from Princeton, and Margaret was his guest for commencement week. The week was full, starting on the ninth with the annual golf match between graduates and undergraduates and ending on the fourteenth, the afternoon of commencement, with a baseball game between Princeton and West Virginia. In between were luncheons, shows, a prom, an oratorical contest, concerts, and a baseball game between Yale and Princeton. Norman Thomas gave the valedictory; Charles incidentally was also a good student, being one of five Senior Honormen in Civil Engineering. His interests went beyond science, however, for he once gave Margaret a set of Thackeray's novels. After graduation Charles went to work for a railway. Pasted in the scrapbook alongside invitations to parties was a pass issued by the Cumberland Valley Railroad Company allowing Charles and his "Corps" unrestricted travel between Harrisburg and Winchester and on all Branch Roads until December 31, 1905.

By spring 1906 Margaret had quarreled with Charles, and that March she sent an angry telegram to him in Chambersburg, Pennsylvania. "Letter received," she wrote. "I wish to simplify matters by withdrawing absolutely and entirely." Having graduated from college, Charles was probably growing serious about love and Margaret. For her part Margaret was only in her second year of college and was not ready to be serious about most things, particularly not about love. She took the quarrel lightly. "Charles and I have had a 'horrible smash up.' Isn't that exciting?" she wrote her grandmother. Whatever the case, the smash did not derail Margaret. Later that week she wrote gaily to her grandmother. "Yesterday," she recounted, "I went in to Boston with a man I met in Rhode Island to the theater. I had an awfully good time but the man bores me to death." "On May day," she wrote later in the letter, "all the girls dressed up like children and we played around the campus. It was more fun!"

In 1906 Margaret was too young for Charles. Playing around the college and dressing up for the theater and promenades, Margaret was not prepared to accept the limitations love put on fun. By spring 1906 Charles was just one among many boys, and Margaret's scrapbook swells with letters and invitations. In January 1908 a boy whom she had once dated at Amherst but who had graduated and gone to work in St. Paul wrote her. "How are all my rivals doing in Providence, West Point, Harvard, Princeton, Yale, and a few others?—a fine chance for Minnesota," he said. "Write and tell me who holds your heart and I shall be the giant and tear it from his grasp (from act 2, Nellie the Beautiful Cloak Model)." By her last year someone was close to holding Margaret's heart, Billy, a senior at Amherst. Margaret's first cousin from Columbus, Gardiner Lattimer, attended Amherst, and when Margaret enrolled at Wellesley, he treated her like a sister. After graduation Gardiner returned to Columbus and worked in wholesale drugs, the family business. "I often wonder what the next five years has in store for you and me," he wrote Margaret in 1907. "I wonder if we will be very differently situated than we are now. One thing here's hoping we will both be safely married. I have often wished that we hadn't gone and been cousins. It would have simplified things in lots of ways. Probably fate however knew what she was doing when she portioned out her clay as she did."

Not long after Margaret settled in at Wellesley, Gardiner invited her to Amherst and introduced her to his friends. Margaret was a great hit, and dance cards for proms at Amherst outnumber those from any other school. Of course, the cards may not reflect Margaret's popularity so much as they reveal that dances at Amherst meant more to her than those elsewhere. In her second year Margaret began to write her grandmother about Billy. "Billy was here a week ago and I had an awfully good time with him," she wrote in October 1905. "He's a nice man granny dear." In December 1906 she described a dance, writing, "I went up to Amherst last Saturday to the Hop and stayed till Monday noon. I had a grand time Granny. It seemed awfully funny not to have Gardiner there, but still Billy was pretty good to me. I like him a lot Granny."

Reading about Billy made me recall my first love. With feelings of glee and sadness, I remember the tentative hints I made about her, hints like those of Margaret, filled with both joy and fear, joy in the knowledge that a girl "liked" me and fear that others would not approve and the little world I colored gaily in my imagination would be rubbed away by the harsh day. By spring of her last year Margaret was in love. What her family might think made her apprehensive. Too young to dissimulate and too full of happiness to remain quiet about her feelings, she wrote her grandmother. "I went up to Amherst ten days ago to the Senior Hop. Chi Psi had a house party on Sunday," she told her in March 1908. "No body at home knows about that and you mustn't tell them for it would make Pop cross! But I had a *perfect* time and Billy is such a dear and I am *so* crazy about him. I guess he'll be here a day or two next week if nothing happens. I wish you knew William, Granny dear, for I am sure you'd like him very much." At the senior hop Margaret danced seven of the twenty dances with Billy. The last dance on Margaret's card was a popular waltz, "Campus Dreams," a fitting tune with which to end the hop and a metaphor for Margaret's love for Billy, itself destined to be a campus dream and the soft stuff of sentimental, perhaps poignant, recollection.

Margaret didn't marry Billy. Family story has it that she was pushed into marrying for money. Family story, though, is usually wrong. Whatever happened, however, for a while in 1908, Billy was a big part of Margaret's life and letters. On Valentine's Day he sent her roses; on Easter, a lily. Pleading financial problems, Margaret's father did not attend her graduation. Margaret was hurt and felt abandoned. Billy was near, though, and in her thoughts Margaret relied upon him as she might have upon her father. Just before commencement, she wrote her grandmother, saying she could not pay her bills and get home on less than a hundred dollars. In the letter she sounded sad and desperate, saying she didn't have the courage to ask her father for money. She wrote that she had been bothered by money "*every second*" during her years at Wellesley, and she ended almost in tears, writing "Billy is so dear to me—he loves me too and he is most concerned about my well fare, too. *You* and *Billy* and *God* love me anyway. Goodnight dearest grandmother that ever lived."

At Wellesley Margaret's affection for Billy was well known. In "an original operetta" performed by her class, Margaret played "an Amherst Prom Girl." "I guess that's pretty cute," she wrote. "Can't you see me much dressed up in purple and white, singing, 'I'm an Amherst girl'?" In Margaret's mind, her love went beyond operetta. Although Margaret remained at Wellesley, Billy visited her family in Columbus in 1908 during the spring break. In July Margaret visited his family in St. Louis and thought them splendid. "I don't know," she wrote her grandmother, "that I have ever liked a family, as a whole and individually any better." In her scrapbook is a picture of what must have been Billy's home at "1756 Missouri Ave. St. Louis." A large three-story building, the house is a Victorian conglomeration of curves and angles and of wood and brick. Three chimneys and two porches are visible; one porch runs across the front of the house and along the right side. Above it on the front, looking Elizabethan, is the second smaller porch. At the left side of the house stands a two-story, rounded silolike structure, topped with a cupola, Islamic in inspiration. At the edge of the cupola, gables begin, and across the front of the house above the porches the roof pitches and slides and turns in abrupt angles.

The house is weighty and formidable, a monument to Victorian success and solidity. From appearances, its owner should have had means enough to lend a son and his bride financial help at the beginning of a marriage. Appearances may deceive, however. Certainly Billy had no monetary expectations; at least Margaret was unaware of any. "I really haven't made any plans for the summer," she wrote her grandmother before commencement. "I judge I'll be home the rest of my days now unless William gets money enough to marry me—and he isn't likely to do that for some little time."

In the scrapbook, Billy is a shadowy figure, hidden behind invitations, dance cards, railway tickets, and Valentines. Only in Margaret's letters does he live. Unlike correspondence from other boys, she didn't put any of Billy's letters in the scrapbook. Maybe they were too personal or meant too much to be crammed in alongside what she thought were only tokens of the fleeting business of college life. Whatever the reason, Billy almost seems more fiction than reality, a love lost to all except sentiment and curiosity. Stitched tightly to a page, the last item in Margaret's scrapbook is a blue necktie. For a while I thought Margaret might have worn it in her role as the Amherst Prom Girl, but then I began to wonder and pulled the tie loose from the page. On the back the label read, "Correct Dress for Men—Radasch-Haberdasher—Springfield, Mass." Margaret must have gotten the tie away from Billy at the end of a dance or banquet. I wish I had left the tie alone. I like imagining Margaret's dancing lightly across life's stage as the Amherst Prom Girl. Disappointment is not something I wanted for Margaret or want for her great-granddaughter, my Eliza.

I am saving Margaret's scrapbook for Eliza. She is only nineteen months old, and, although I know it is silly, I can't help thinking she resembles her great-grandmother. Like Margaret she seems gloriously sunny and as wholesome as buttermilk. Like Margaret she loves to dance. As soon as the clock radio begins to play in the morning, Eliza stands in her crib and cries, "Daddy, dance." I pick her up, and we spin about the bedroom, Daddy and, to draw from the title of a tune popular in Margaret's day, his "School Girl" to be. Since reading George Jones's letters, I have thought a lot about the advice I would give Eliza if she were in college. Like Jones, I would write her about the importance of simplicity and warn her against money and luxury. To his statement "Be a good girl and you will be a happy one," I would only add, "Be nice to people." I would not write about studies or grades. I want Eliza to have fun, play a guitar, go to the theater, wear long dresses, and have boys sign her dance card. And then I want her to be "safely married," as Gardiner Lattimer put it. Like Jones I think men and women usually have happier, better lives if they marry. Not long after Margaret left for Wellesley, Jones wrote her a letter filled with local news. In passing he noted that a wealthy maiden lady in Columbus was still unmarried. "Your mother thinks it strange that I concern myself," he wrote, "but you know I always thought it the duty of women to marry. I should think it would be so terribly lonesome for the poor old soul alone in that big house—where there is room enough for two anyhow." About Eliza's husband I don't have much to say. All I tell friends is that I hope she will marry someone as nice as her mother did. Where Eliza goes to college isn't important. Still, I am sentimental, and if she attended Wellesley, I would be pleased. If her school days slip normally along, she will enter college in the year 2003, ninety-nine years after Margaret entered Wellesley. Lastly, I hope she keeps a scrapbook. A generation or two after she stitches in the last necktie, perhaps someone feeling low and a bit melancholy will discover the book in some back house and opening its pages will smile and find his life brighter as he wanders through the past and a familial world rich with hope and affection.

Eating under the Stars

"HOW DID YOU know you were eating rectum?" I said. "Look," he said, "when you eat rectum, you know it." True enough, I thought and tried to imagine Istanbul, a cafe in a narrow passage filled with laborers, and the smell of sheep's rectum, sliced and simmering in olive oil, garlic, and red peppers. A place, I thought, similar to the restaurant in Damascus where I ate testicles.

Like Istanbul, Damascus can be hot and ugly. In summer dust blows in from the desert, and heat blankets the city while roads made for a slower age swell like aneurysms. In the center of town gray buildings rise from piles of rubble, and people swarm, buying and selling. On every corner ragged children shriek "Marlboro, Marlboro" or "Kent, Kent" as they rush about hawking cigarettes smuggled from Beirut. Not far from the Place of Martyrs, though, is a cool winding street. Halfway down one side is a modest restaurant. Here I often sat undisturbed and drank tea and ate tabbouleh and boiled testicles. The restaurant is not listed in a guide to Damascus, and in truth I have never eaten in a restaurant recommended by a guidebook or with stars after its name. Instead I eat under the stars.

Friends know that I enjoy eating out, and at birthdays and Christmas have given me subscriptions to *Gourmet* and *Cuisine*. I appreciate the gifts and study the magazines—not, though, to learn where and what to eat but what to avoid. Eating out should be a real going out and should risk not merely the palate but the self. Eating should be an adventure unpredictable as life beyond the suburbs. Too often, alas, eating is a decadent form of high church religion attended by perfumes, sauces, censers, and priests. In its preciousness the ritual separates the devotee from life and fosters the illusion that beauty and truth are nurtured by ceremony instead of rising rich and hardy from vulgarity. At its best, good eating is a pentecostal experience, spontaneous and original.

Recently I ate in a Christian restaurant near Greenville, North Carolina. I had gone to Greenville to be considered for a post at a university.

At the end of the first day of interviews, my hosts discussed where we should eat dinner. Several mentioned slow-food restaurants with French-sounding names, and my stomach sank. Then one man laughed and said, "How about the Christian place on the highway?" "Right, that's where I want to go," I burst out and, standing, picked up my overcoat and was through the door before anyone could object. When I saw the "Corner of Dixie" surrounded by big Fords and Chevrolets, I knew I had come to the right place. The floor was linoleum and the tabletops Formica. In the middle of the place mats were the menu and a blessing; religion and business go better together than asparagus and hollandaise sauce and around the border of the mats were advertisements, urging right-thinking people to have their cars repaired at Buck Thompson's Garage, shop at Butler's Supermarket, and buy insurance from "Johnny" Johnson. When the waitress came over to take our orders, she asked, "How are y'all this evening?" "Mighty fine," I answered—whereupon she slowly raised her pad and pencil over her head, looked toward the ceiling, and said, "Praise the Lord." My companions winced but I was in the right pew. Later when the waitress brought our meals, she looked at me as she put them down and said, "The Lord's Supper." "Amen," I answered and settled down to hush puppies, coleslaw, ice tea, scallops, and deviled crabs—a feast that seemed inexhaustible like that of the loaves and fishes. Unfortunately, my companions were not true believers and didn't enjoy themselves. Somebody else got the post at the university.

Restaurants like the Corner of Dixie often serve wonderful appetizers; frequently these are not on the menu and one has to ask for them before they appear. Outside Farmville, Virginia, the Beesleys ran a family-style restaurant, noted for fried chicken, homemade pies, and Mr. Beesley's conversation. One night when I went in, Mrs. Beesley wasn't behind the counter as usual. Mr. Beesley, though, was wiping tables. "Good evening, Mr. Beesley," I said, "how are you?" Then looking around, I added, "Where is Mrs. Beesley? I do hope she's not sick." "Oh, no," he said, putting down his rag, "she's not sick. She's in the bathroom and will be out directly." The seasoning in this hors d'oeuvre might be too strong for some tastes, but I think it makes a fine starter for a meal. Conversational appetizers should be seasoned highly. In two- and three-star restaurants conversation is always bad. Like a heavy tomato sauce, decorum smothers not only the food but life as people treat the food and each other reverently and speak in hushed tones. The better the food the poorer the conversation; never take a talker to a fine restaurant unless you don't want to hear him.

Ever since I can remember I have enjoyed strong food and strong talk. When I was small, we had a cook named Wilna. Wilna dipped snuff. In the morning before she began work, she put snuff behind her lower lip, so much snuff that her lip pouched out and hung down. She always set a blue Maxwell House Coffee can on top of the stove, and when she was busy stirring and mixing and didn't have time to go outside and spit, she'd aim for the can. Wilna's aim was pretty good, but sometimes she missed. Occasionally my father got upset and complained. Mother brooked no nonsense. "It takes a peck of dirt to kill you," she said, "and snuff hardly counts." "God Almighty," she continued, "what do you want to eat? Everything worth eating has got dirt in it."

Mother was right. No one should be sensitive to dirt. Restaurants high in the stars keep people from seeing the ground, and the person who refuses to see food as it is is not going to see life or even himself accurately. The Mediterranean custom of going into the kitchen of a restaurant to see what is cooking should be widely adopted. The first few times a person visits a kitchen, however, can be disturbing, particularly if one is unaccustomed to life. In Jordan a friend invited me and a companion to visit his village near Jerash. A sheep was slaughtered, and we feasted on a mound of mutton piled on rice, nuts, and yogurt. No women appeared during the meal, and afterward I insisted upon meeting my friend's mother, who had cooked the sheep. My friend led me and my companion into the kitchen. The mother came forward, and, as I thanked her, she smiled broadly. She had no teeth, and her gums were whiter than snow. "Oh, Lord," my companion gasped, "hoof and mouth disease. Do you suppose she tasted the food while she cooked it?" On the way home, my companion got sick. I fared better; a touch of snuff early in life does wonders for digestion.

For the eater-outer interested in the marrow of life, rules are helpful. Avoid restaurants that advertise famous views; a good view leads to romanticism and loss of perspective. Never eat in a restaurant on top of a tall building. So long as they lack covered entrances and footmen, restaurants in basements are a better choice. Outside France stay away from restaurants with French-sounding names. In foreign countries shun restaurants that have floor shows or folk dancing. Such restaurants provide a packaged tourist experience. Instead search out a local restaurant and enjoy the authentic tourist experience and get fleeced right.

Twenty years ago in Budapest I wandered into a shabby restaurant. After I sat down and ordered a bottle of wine, a heavyset, bearded man rushed over and, throwing his arms around me, exclaimed, "People to People, America to Hungary—yes?" Being young I did not want to offend a man who thought so highly of America, and I said, "People to People—yes." Whereupon the man turned around and shouted, "Some wine for the band from the American." A waiter went into the kitchen and, coming back with a bottle of wine, carried it to a little table near the platform along the wall. Then the man hugged me, and, turning away, picked up his accordion and became the band.

Restaurants with waitresses are better than those with waiters. Waiters are too formal and their dress is dull. Waitresses are different. In a seafood restaurant near Thunderbolt, Georgia, my waitress wore green-striped hot pants and a yellow shirt. In black letters across the front of the shirt was written "I Give All My Friends Crabs." When you hunger for life, go to Georgia. Better yet, eat in a restaurant there in which you are the only member of your race. I once did this outside Eulonia. The meal was ordinary and disappointing until a big man walked over, leaned on the table while the waitress was taking my order for dessert, and said, "Bessie, I see you are serving more crackers at lunch than usual." Butterflies began to flutter through my system, and I decided to pass up dessert. Of course, eating abroad will stir more than butterflies. The real eater-outer never travels in foreign countries without pills for the butterfly's lowly cousin, the worm. "How will I know if I have them?" I asked an embassy doctor in Egypt. "Oh," he said, "they are jolly little fellows, and you'll see them sporting about in your stool." He was right.

The traveler who wants to experience life under the stars must avoid Intercontinentals, Meridiens, and Sheratons. After a long day in a foreign country, the temptation to eat in one's hotel is almost irresistible. The true eater-outer realizes this and picks a hotel accordingly. In Palmyra Vicki and I avoided the new Meridien and stayed in the Hotel Tadmor. Aside from a dumb boy who cleaned the rooms and a clerk with a withered left arm, we were the only people there. Behind the door of our room, someone had written "this ain't the Hilton." Unlike the Hilton, the Tadmor had character. Hanging from a wall in the lobby was the skin of a hyena. I investigated; it stank. Our room, though, was stronger. Crusts of spittle stuck to the walls. Four feet from our window was the back of another dingy building. Between it and the Tadmor ran an open sewer. When the breeze died during the day, the strong smell of stale urine pervaded the room, and Vicki was convinced that the odor had burned into the walls and stained them yellow. The Tadmor had a small kitchen and rarely served meals. A meal in the Tadmor, I knew, would be memorable, and although the clerk told me tourists usually ate at a restaurant near the ruins, I prevailed upon him to prepare dinner for us. The dumb boy served and we ate heartily.

During the day shysters lurk in the ruins hunting tourists. Like the band in Budapest, a good shyster is worth a bottle of wine and should not be avoided. One spent forty minutes in the hot sun approaching us after he saw us sitting in the shade beneath a Roman column. Pacing studiously back and forth, he pretended to search a plot of ground fifty yards in front of us. Finally he drew near and, putting his hand into his trousers, pulled out eight or nine coins and said, "Have you seen money like this? I collect Roman coins. Yesterday while riding my motorcycle, I lost many and I have spent today looking for them." When we said that we had not seen any coins on the ground, he offered us a piece of hard candy and asked, "Where do you come from?" When we said we were from America, he raised his eyes and said, "Thanks be to God." He was so pleased that he offered to sell us coins from his collection at a special price.

At night shysters vanish and pariah dogs come out of their burrows in the ruins and scavenge on the edge of town. Rabies is common in Syria, and one stays away from wild dogs. Although the dogs disappear by mid-morning, packs lurk near town at dawn, threatening anyone on foot. Eating under the stars, however, broadens a person and enables him to cope with the unexpected. In Palmyra dinner at the Tadmor prepared me for the dogs. In Damascus we heard that sunrise was "splendid" in Palmyra and we determined to get up before dawn and walk out to the ruins. I had no trouble getting up early because I had been up, and down, since midnight. The dinner I ate the night before was moody and kept rising and sinking. When we left the hotel, I was weak and, seeing a walking stick in the lobby, I took it to lean on. Without the meal I would not have needed the stick, and without the stick the dogs would have bitten us. The stick had a heavy knob at one end, and when the dogs came snarling after us outside town, I knocked two over and the rest ran away. Unfortunately, when the sun came up, turning the columns, as Vicki told me, softly tangerine, I was crouched doglike in the sand, spewing tomatoes, cucumbers, and beans over what I hoped

were the ancient remains of a greengrocer's shop. People who try to eat
and live amid the stars are forever nauseated by the discrepancy between life and their expectations. On my knees in the rubble I missed
the sunrise and play of colors over the columns. I saw only gray sand,
but my discomfort was temporary. A romantic view did not dissatisfy
me with the good earth, and soon I was eager for another hotel and restaurant far from the stars and their misleading glitter.

Eating in a hotel of character builds character and antibodies. In
Bukhara I stayed in the Oriental, a small hotel rarely visited by for-
eigners. My room was on the ground floor and was the only room with a
private lavatory. Local people knew this, and when they succumbed to
the ailment I suffered from in Palmyra, they rushed into the hotel and,
taking the key from a rack in the lobby, hurried to my room. "To each
according to his need" seems reasonable to me; nevertheless, when I returned to my room after sightseeing, I was surprised. Water is precious
in Bukhara and during the day it is cut off. Baths have to be scheduled,
dishes pile up, and toilets cannot be flushed. What I found in my room
was breathtaking, and I considered changing hotels. Quickly, though, I
realized the only alternative was the sterile In-Tourist hotel, and I knew
meals there would not be memorable. If a simple room in the Oriental
could be so surprising, what, I wondered, would the food be like, and in
good spirits I began cleaning "things."

Like that of the Tadmor, the Oriental's dining room was in the basement. To reach it one had to go out the front door and around to a side
entrance. There was no menu, only food for the day. Since no restaurants were nearby, the management expected guests would eat in the
hotel, and early in the evening put salads out on a number of tables.
From the doorway the salads looked like raisin custard. When I approached my table, however, the raisins flew away, and I saw the salads
consisted of onions and sliced radishes. Two dumplings were the main
dish. My first dumpling was doughy and, reckoning that the second
wasn't worth three bites, I decided to down it quickly. I opened my
mouth and stuffed it all in. Immediately something jabbed my tongue,
and I reached up and pulled out a feather. I didn't recognize the feather,
but I knew that it did not come from a chicken and that there were more
in my mouth.

When I was a boy, clowns were my favorite circus performers, and
when a small car darted into the arena and clowns began clambering out
of its doors and windows, I was wonderfully happy. An astonishing

number of clowns always climbed out of the car, and just when I was certain the car was empty, another clown would stick up his head. It was a mystery to me how so many clowns could get into a small car, and, as I pulled the feathers out of my mouth, I thought about the circus. Whoever packed my dumpling with feathers should have stuffed small cars with clowns. Just when I thought I had extracted the last feather, another would stick into my gums. Eventually there were enough feathers on my plate to refurbish a small buzzard.

Fifty years ago Woody Ankerrow ran a pool hall and cafe in Carthage, Tennessee. Every day at noon my grandfather walked over from his insurance office and ate a sandwich and a bowl of soup. The food wasn't good, but the loafers bending over the pool tables knew all the county gossip. Soup was served steaming hot in big green bowls, and if a man cocked a quick ear toward the pool tables and sipped deliberately, he could learn who was doing what to whom and where. One day a finely drawn tale of untoward activities at Chestnut Mound so absorbed my grandfather's interest that he was halfway through his soup before he noticed something strange in the bottom of his bowl. Dipping his spoon deep into the soup, he dredged up Woody Ankerrow's false teeth. Old man Ankerrow always took his teeth out when he cooked. On this occasion he dropped them into an empty bowl and, forgetting where they were, poured soup over them. Later when Grandfather described his discovery of the false teeth, he said, "I should have known immediately that something was wrong because the soup had more bite than usual." And that is what I want when I go out to eat. Good taste in food or life matters little to me. When I eat under the stars, I hope my food has more bite than usual.

Patterns

"JOHN," the letter from the dean began, "if you are going to jog during the day, two P.M., 3/8/86, don't do it where you will be seen (Route 72). It presents a very negative view of university to the public." My friend John is a neat, orderly man. Although his running shirts usually have something like "Tony's Pizza" or "The Baker's Dozen" printed on the back, they are always clean, and his shorts are unrevealingly baggy and smack of 1958 and the country club. "The dean's right," I said when John showed me the note, "an old fart like you shouldn't be on the main road. Imagine what people think when the first thing they see at the university is your big behind. Only thin faculty under forty should even be allowed to walk near Seventy-Two."

Although the dean's attempt to control jogging was silly, culture is based upon the general acceptance of patterns of behavior. Rarely are the patterns stated or consciously agreed upon, and often people are aware of them only when they are broken. Even those who imagine themselves outside society and thus untrammeled by convention are usually tightly bound to propriety. I am not one of the faithful, but even now I become upset when I remember what a banker said to me in Sunday School thirty-five years ago. On the day the banker visited the class, the subject of racial segregation arose. I was nine years old and lived in a world filled with black people. Although there were certain things, like attending school, that black and white people did not do together, I was unaware of subtleties and spent little thought on such matters. Black people were in all the places I liked best, out-of-doors in the dairy barn or in the house in the kitchen. They took care of me, picking me up when I fell down and cleaning my knees when I skinned them. I liked nothing better than watching Mealy churn milk or "helping" Bessie or Lizzie make a chocolate pie. And so when the banker said that black people were inferior and should not be allowed to eat in restaurants with whites, I was puzzled. What the man said did not seem right, and raising my hand like a good little boy who had studied his Sunday

School lesson, I said, "Sir, you must be wrong because the bible says 'all men are created equal.'" The man glared at me, obviously angry, and I wondered what I had done. "Do you think," he finally said, "that some nigger in north Nashville is equal to you?"

Most violations of propriety involve manners. Although they do not sear like the banker's words, strangely enough they cling to memory with a tenacity far exceeding their significance. About eight years ago I attended a performance of Noel Coward's *Blithe Spirit* at the National Theater in London. At the time I was writing a book, and life was drab. Except for buying food, I rarely left my room, and two weeks often passed without my speaking to anyone but grocers. A light comedy like *Blithe Spirit,* I decided, was just the thing to pick me up, and on arriving at the theater I settled happily into my seat, gleefully anticipating magical pastels and seltzer bottles. Until the first intermission everything fizzed along frivolously; immediately in front of me, however, sat two young women. During the break between acts they removed brushes and fingernail files from their purses and spent the intermission brushing each other's hair, then cleaning their fingernails. Tweezers appeared at the second intermission, and the girls plucked each other's eyebrows, paying close attention to hairs growing above the bridge of the nose. A curly hair over one girl's nose proved particularly pesky, and I was about to suggest her friend hire a backhoe for the job when suddenly the hair tore loose, bringing with it a long taproot and a ball of skin.

Instead of chuckling over Coward's comedy of manners, I left the theater fuming. Later I realized I should not have been upset. Like the girls' behavior, manners themselves are arbitrary and, if not comic, are often absurd if examined closely. Why, for example, should a man stand when a woman enters a room or give up his seat on a bus? Once upon a time when women were forever pregnant and died by the droves in childbirth, relinquishing a seat was reasonable. The stronger vessel should have sheltered the weaker. Nowadays women are not always enceinte; indeed, my wife Vicki was the first woman on our street to have a baby in ten years. Moreover, other things are different now too. Men are weaker than women. Women live longer and are less likely to commit suicide, become alcoholics, or have nervous breakdowns. If manners were raised upon reason, men would not stand when women entered a room. Women would stand, open doors, and pull out chairs for men.

Manners, of course, are not reasonable. Whenever a woman enters a room and I notice a man remaining seated, I condemn him much as I condemned the girls in the theater. Still, if manners for me are part of a civilizing pattern of behavior and something not to be thought about rationally or tampered with, they frequently strike youth as silly or repressive. Youth is right; patterns of behavior do control and repress. For the most part, however, people don't notice their influence. Indeed, what passes for spontaneity is frequently a manifestation of manners or "upbringing." And in truth, ordinary life would be exhausting if a person had to analyze all his prospective actions. What should be thought about, though, is another's advice, particularly when it suggests behavior that does not seem right. From the twenty or so years I have been teaching, I have few regrets. Only one cloud really darkens memory. One day early in May I walked across the green at Dartmouth College. Spring had come and the lawn was crowded with people. Blue jeans had melted away, and young girls blossomed like crocus, yellow and purple, aglow with smiles and hope. No one seemed in a hurry, and people milled about absorbing the promise of the season. Then suddenly the mood was broken. A student came out of a building and seeing someone he knew yelled, "Fuck you." The cry bounced back and forth off walls, and by the time the echo died, spring had faded. Before realizing it, I crossed the green and stopped the boy. I was too angry to say anything sensible so I told him to be in my office the next morning at eight o'clock.

Walking back to the English Department, I wondered what I would say the next morning. By then a lecture on manners would strike the student, and me, as pompous. At a loss, I went to an older, distinguished, and supposedly shrewd colleague for advice. "This is easily taken care of," he said and then explained what he had once done. Something about what he did jarred, but since he was more experienced and I could think of nothing else to do, I suppressed doubt and followed his suggestions. The next morning when the student appeared in my office, I told him to sit down. Then I turned away and began grading papers. I heard my watch ticking and time passed slowly, each second seeming an age. Finally the student burst out, "Aren't you going to say anything?" I turned around slowly, looked at him, and then said, "Get out." "What?" he said, "Get out," I repeated, "you aren't worth talking to." He got up, started to speak, but then slumped out silently. For a moment I felt exhilarated. The feeling, though, like spring on the green soon passed, and ever since I have felt small and guilty. Never again have I followed a colleague's advice without mulling it over, and over. What I did was cruel. I stripped the boy of dignity and self-respect and, if he resembles me, gave him a recollection which will always make him cringe.

In rebelling against one pattern youth usually falls into another and behaves uninterestingly. Young people play head games. A few dye their hair black and comb it upward into spikes. Some let it grow long and wear it in ponytails, while others shave their heads. Beyond this and like things, revolt rarely goes. Rebellion quickly drains energy and ceases to be fun. As one grows older what brings ever-increasing pleasure is the attempt to fit things into place. Without linen closets, dressers, secretaries, highboys, desks, and tool-chests, life in an acquisitive society would be practically impossible. Much as one generation unconsciously absorbs the manners of the previous generation, so people inherit sideboards, corner cupboards, and sugar chests, pushing in their possessions alongside those of their ancestors. Instead, though, of inhibiting and crowding, the past often excites and invigorates. Digging through inheritance, material or cultural, unearths mysteries. In a small box in a great-aunt's house, I found keys to compartments on the Louisville and Nashville Railroad. The keys were numbered; one was stamped 3516 while the other was D64283. What, I wondered, was their significance? Had an ancestor traveled from Nashville to Louisville on a honeymoon and kept the keys as a memento? Although this at first seemed plausible, I rejected it. On a wedding trip the husband would have the keys. Not only was it unlikely that he would take the railroad's property for sentimental reasons, but it was improbable that a blushing Victorian bride would ask for the keys as remembrance of the journey. Although I was unable to fit them into the experience of people locked in the past, the keys opened my imagination. Soon I was rolling along the rails from Nashville to Louisville, spinning through a starry night, silver with gentle love.

Inherent in the exploration of patterns is also pleasure in discovering variation. In my family is a set of Rose Medallion china, supposedly the first set shipped from China to the United States. Whatever the set's history, though, the workmanship is wondrous. The plates resemble pages torn from rich, imaginary leather-bound novels. On one a dancing master twists daintily about in little green slippers; on another a flower seller holds orange blossoms up to pale, smiling ladies. On a third a deferential teacher reads to a group of girls; behind them a small bird with yellow wings sits with his blue, iridescent head cocked and a black eye fixed on the teacher's scroll. Like gardens the plates burst with life: bushes of pink roses, piles of orange and pink melons, bunches of daisies with yellow centers and blue petals, and mounds of red and black berries. Although each plate is unique, the set is clearly of a pattern. Within the pattern, though, there is variation. On the stem of a flower will cling a grasshopper or a beetle with an orange head and a black ring around its neck. Discovering variations pleased me almost as much, I think, as it pleased the craftsmen to make them.

Patterns form boundaries and provide foundations. Without a pattern to work both with and against, creation or individuality may be impossible. Outside patterns things seem to vanish into a black unknown. Whatever the case, high creativity is beyond my grasp; play, however, comes easily to hand. Always my play depends upon commonly recognized patterns, usually verbal ones. I like to tinker with aphorisms and twist their meanings, writing, for instance, about a man "whose bite is much worse than his bark." Of late, descriptions of wine have caught my eye. Since an extraordinary number of wines seem, according to dinner party goers, to be full-bodied, I serve vintages more interesting to the palate. The wines on my table are "spindle-shanked," "big-breasted," or, as Vicki said the other day, of a Medoc, "gloriously well-hung."

My life does not come from a storybook or a travel brochure. In my house father knows worst. When we go to the beach, somebody steps on a piece of glass, and the car gets stuck in the sand. When I ask Edward to put his bristle blocks up after cleaning behind him and Francis and Eliza all day, he doesn't smile, kiss my hand, and say, "I will do it right now, Daddy, because you do so much for us." No indeed—Edward squares about, sticks out his chin, and shouts, "I hate you." Instead of upsetting me, such exchanges delight. Like insects on the Rose Medallion, they awaken and intrigue because they are unexpected. Since life never spins along in an ideal storybook pattern, the unexpected is often the usual and possibilities of disappointment and unhappiness are forever present. The best antidote against disillusioning disappointment or, what may be more likely, boredom is awareness of and delight in pattern. For fifteen years I have been at home and in bed by ten o'clock on New Year's Eve. Although accounts of high hilarity fill magazines and acquaintances regale me with stories of ripe, juicy foolishness, I have never been dissatisfied. Each New Year's Eve Vicki and I toy with the holiday pattern. This past year we celebrated conventionally enough with champagne, albeit at five-thirty at dinner in the kitchen with the children, feasting on Gorton's all-natural fish sticks, Hellmann's tartar sauce, lima beans, and fudge cake.

Akin to the pleasure of variation is enjoyment of the unfinished. Perhaps because they seem imposed rather than natural, the polished and the highly finished ring false. Suspecting that nothing can ultimately be finished, people often find the highly polished deceptive and superficial. In contrast, the unfinished invites completion by the imagination and thereby lures one into labeling it genuine. Of course, the unfinished may not be genuine but only dirty. When Vicki and I lived in Syria, we went out of our way to eat hummus in a combination cafe and barbershop deep in the Hamadeus Souk in Damascus. The cafe had only one table downstairs, and people who ate there shared it with the barber. Upstairs was more room, but part of the ceiling had fallen and pigeons nested in the rafters. Consequently the floor was covered with feathers and droppings splattered the tables. Yet, unaccountably, the filth did not offend us and, invariably, we ate upstairs and enjoyed it.

Being part of a pattern, on the other hand, not only gives scope for creativity but provides continuity, from which come assurance and meaning. Each year a battered, one-legged Santa Claus hangs at the top of our Christmas tree. Santa's beard is now gray with age, and his jacket has faded, becoming more orange than red. Although we add shiny new ornaments to the tree each year, Santa will not lose his place at the top. He has been there for over forty years; when I was nine and he was four, Winkie the cat tore off his leg. As people think about holidays past and the fallings from life, the long groaning board of friends and family whom they will not see again, Christmas can be melancholy. Somehow old Santa at the top of the tree veils time's passing and softens the hard awareness of mortality.

Along with comforting continuity, patterns can increase the significance of life. A pattern implies structure and meaning. As a result people work hard to discover patterns and thereby escape the terrible feeling that life is meaningless. Universities depend upon the hankering for pattern for their existence, and long classroom hours are spent searching for and explaining patterns. Usually explanations are weighed heavily in favor of the complex and against the simple and the random. The significance for society is great; perhaps the inordinate complexity of the legal system, for example, results from lawyers' having spent seven years in the university. At the same time, however, that belief in pattern creates deceptive complexity, it can also reduce things to false simplicity. After any event, academics are always ready to impose pattern and discover cause and effect. To cure the ills of society, theorists propose methods of instruction. What a theorist predicts will result from a method, however, is not always what occurs. This past fall on *Wonderworks,* a television show for children, my son Francis watched *Booker,* an account of Booker T. Washington's struggle to read. Meant to be inspirational, the show attempted to teach black pride and drive home the lesson that work and diligence brought rewards. Francis's classmates in nursery school come from a globe of countries and in a prism of colors. Yet during his two years at school Francis has seemingly been oblivious to color. At the end of *Booker,* however, he turned to me and, instead of saying something about persistence, he said simply, "I am glad I'm not dark."

A person had better enjoy variation because breaking out of a pattern is almost impossible. Events are bound to repeat themselves throughout life. Like a refrain, following a cluster of deceivingly different stanzas, the same things recur. I first sang "Heartbreak Hotel" in the old gymnasium at Montgomery Bell Academy in Nashville, Tennessee, in 1956. I was a sophomore in high school and stood on splintery bleachers. The moment sticks in memory, in great part because I have sung "Heartbreak Hotel" many times since, despite my now being older than fifteen and the song's being always out of date and place. In spring 1976 at a dinner with businessmen in the Rossiya Hotel in Moscow, I drank too much vodka and joined a small band in the hotel, entertaining people with parts of "Hound Dog," "Don't Be Cruel," and "Heartbreak Hotel." Ten years have passed since I was in Russia, and almost that long has passed since I tasted vodka. Today I rarely go near drink, and my colleagues think me solid, even dull.

Alas, breaking out of a pattern is as hard for a human as it is for a songbird. Occasionally I find myself humming "Heartbreak Hotel," and last month I gave another public performance. A visiting literary luminary was on campus, and I was supposed to have dinner with him. My friend John held a cocktail party in his honor. A committee meeting ran overtime, and I arrived late. Having swallowed a gallon or two of fuel, the luminary was well lit and argumentative. I fancy myself a minor light and, not wanting to be outshone, I quickly forced down some high octane and was soon ablaze. After the pumps ran dry at John's house, those among us who were glowing went to dinner at the Mansfield Depot, a train station now converted into a restaurant. Two hours later John and I stepped outside. The food had been good, and the conversation loud. The stars were shining, the snow was melting, and so, like the whippoorwill at dusk, I burst into song. John joined me and the rails rang with "Dim, Dim the Lights," "Hearts Made of Stone," "Roll with Me, Henry" and of course "Heartbreak Hotel." After "Heartbreak Hotel," John and I finished our business and went back inside for coffee. About six minutes later the night freight rolled past. "Good God," the luminary said, "if you fellows had remembered Bo Diddley or Howling Wolf, all the ambulance men would have found of you would have been two hands with dicks in them." "They would have reckoned you were going fishing," a man at the next table said. "That's right," the fellow across from him added, "but just for minnows." Word of the fishing trip spread quickly, and when I showed up in the English Department the next afternoon, the first person to see me said, "Well, if it isn't old Izaac Walton."

I don't understand money matters, and while friends have made bundles on insurance and fried chicken, hospitals and self-rising flour, I have sputtered along, taking the standard deduction, and saying, "Pickerings weren't made to make money." This past fall, though, when a collection of my essays appeared, I forgot the family pattern and got greedy. When patrons of a local library invited me to read from my book, I suddenly saw the way to gold. The book sold for $14.95, but I could purchase copies wholesale. If I bought ten copies wholesale and sold them at the reading retail, I would make a nice profit. Including postage my ten copies cost $91.68. By the time I arrived at the reading, I had already sold the books—in my mind at least. Unfortunately, as I parked the car, I noticed the librarian carrying an armful of my books into the library. There was nothing I could do but leave my copies in the car. The patrons had invited Vicki to the reading; she came, and we left the children and twelve dollars at home with a baby-sitter. Because the reading did not start until fairly late in the afternoon, Vicki did not think she would be able to get back to the kitchen and slap dinner together before the children fell asleep, so before we left home, we ordered a large pizza, one half bare and the other covered with mushrooms and sausage. Along with two Greek salads, the pizza cost $11.42. Thinking the reading would be over at 4:45, we ordered pizza for 5 o'clock. The reading ended at 4:15, and so Vicki and I drove around to kill time. Unleaded gas was $1.04 a gallon, and we probably used a gallon and a half at a cost of $1.56. When all was added together—books, baby-sitter, pizza, and gas—the reading cost $116.66. At the reading I autographed, appropriately enough, ten books; for that number my royalty is about $9.00. Thus my loss on the day was $107.66. If my book ever became popular and I was asked to give many readings, I would soon be bankrupt.

Not even shock can fracture a pattern. "I wish your wife to breed in safely," a friend wrote last year from Syria, "I congratulate you in anticipation by son." Vicki and I had two boys, and, like my friend in Syria, I assumed the third baby would be male and had already named him Samuel Innis. I knew nothing about little girls and did not know what to say when the doctor told me we had a nine-pound eight-ounce girl. By the end of an hour, though, I had settled into a pattern comfortable for fathers of daughters. I began to worry about her meeting and marrying the right sort of man, and that night when I called John to tell him about Eliza, I said, "You and Cathy can come by to see the baby, but don't bring those nasty little boys of yours."

Preaching platitudes about discovery, self-realization, inhibition, and freedom, people who lead conventional lives often urge others to break out of patterns. During the first year we were married Vicki and I spent six weeks in the Dodecanese Islands. Because it could almost be stuffed in a thimble, Vicki carried a tank suit with her on the trip. As we wandered through the islands and discovered nude beaches, I urged her to leave the suit in her suitcase and "frolic unhampered by prudery." On Rhodes, Kos, Patmos, and Mykonos, Vicki wore her bathing suit. One day, though, while we were traveling to a small island off Paros, I noticed she did not have her suit. "You are not going to have much fun," I said. "You forgot your suit." "I haven't forgotten my suit," she answered, "and I am going to have a helluva time." "Oh," I said.

When we got to the island, Vicki went straight to the beach. A few people were there, most wearing suits. Vicki dropped her towel right in the middle of the people. Then without saying a word, she took her clothes off, shook her hair, stretched her arms toward the sun, and, after what seemed an age to me, ran splashing into the water. "Come on," she shouted, "the water is great." I hesitated; despite what I urged upon Vicki, swimming naked really wasn't my sort of thing. Still, after all I had said, I didn't have a choice; I sat down and, undressed, and made my way to the water as unobtrusively as possible. Once in, I squatted down and, paddling about like a floating toadstool, kept the water safely up to my chin. Not Vicki—she dove and splashed about in the shallows. For moments she would stay out of sight; then suddenly she would burst into the sunlight, white and pink and blowing mouthfuls of water at me. "What's wrong with you, old hide-under-the-surface?" she shouted, her breasts shaking and drops like rainbows all about her. Never again did I accuse Vicki of prudery. On Santorini, the next island, I even praised her suit, saying it offered good protection against sunburn and sharp rocks. Now, safe years later in landlocked Storrs, when the children are quietly abed and I am weary with writing, I sometimes think about Paros and see Vicki leaping into the sun, blue water falling from her in clean, bright streams.

"Everybody in the world needs watching," Josh Billings wrote, "but none more than ourselves." Studying the self can become a habit. Compared to most habits, though, examining the patterns of life is harmless. Love and laughter often lie at the heart of patterns, laughter at foolishness and love growing from appreciation of the world. Many years ago Beth, one of my first loves, visited me at my grandmother's house in Virginia. My step-grandfather ploughed his garden for vegetables—corn, butter beans, snaps, and tomatoes; my grandmother baked a yellow chocolate layer cake, and Peggy the maid cooked a country ham. The food was wonderfully satisfying; during those years, though, I had a big appetite, and not long after a meal I was usually ready for a snack. What I wanted to nibble on most was Beth; unfortunately, the house was full of people. To have some time to ourselves, we drove to Williamsburg. Scores of visitors were there, and as we strolled hand in hand along the streets it seemed we would never be alone. Then I remembered the maze behind the governor's mansion. Under its high hedges and along its twisting paths we could lose ourselves, and others. Happily the garden was practically empty, and warm with affection Beth and I plunged into the maze. For several minutes we searched for the solitary heart of the maze. When we reached it and Beth turned to me, her eyes big and brown, I put my arms around her and kissed her heartily. What I had forgotten was that the maze was sunken and that people walking nearby could see into it. As I got ready to kiss Beth again, cheering and clapping broke out. We pulled apart, looked around, then up, and saw a bus load of tourists waving at us. For a moment we were embarrassed, but then we laughed and, waving at the people, kissed again for their pleasure before we left.

Not long ago when I told Vicki about something I was thinking about writing, she said, "That's ordinary. Why write about it?" The question was good, and I guess I think and write about ordinary things like a boy kissing a girl in a maze because such is the stuff of patterns, not simply the love and laughter of my life, but the love and laughter of the lives of strangers. I have not seen Beth in over twenty years, but I heard that she like me has three children. If we were to meet in the maze tomorrow, we would sit in the quiet center and talk about our children. Maybe we would kiss, just once for old time's sake, because that too is part of a pattern.

Might as Well

L IKE MANY countrymen at the turn of the century, Wiley Trefry distrusted doctors, telling his wife Verna he would rather die behind a mule than be quartered in a hospital. And so when Wiley appeared in his office early one Monday morning, Doctor Sollows was surprised. "Wiley," he asked, "what brings you to Carthage?" Wiley, it seems, had eaten some ham that had skippers. "I have just the thing for you," Dr. Sollows said after hearing Wiley's symptoms. "Last week I got in a box of suppositories from Nashville. They are the newest thing and will cure those pains of yours." "You do know how to take them," Dr. Sollows continued as he handed Wiley some capsules, "you put them in. . . ." Before Dr. Sollows could finish his instructions, Wiley assured him he knew what to do and was out of the office on the way to Read's drugstore. There he bought a Coke and opening the capsules poured the contents into the glass. As soon as they were dissolved, he gulped down the mixture. At eight the next morning he was back at Dr. Sollows's office. "What's wrong, Wiley?" Dr. Sollows asked. "Didn't you take the medicine?" "Take it!" Wiley exclaimed. "Great God! Right after I left your office yesterday I went to Read's drugstore and took two of the damn things. By afternoon the pains were worse than ever. For all the good that medicine did me, I might as well have stuffed it up my behind."

Dr. Sollows then explained the mechanics of suppositories to Wiley, and after two nights of treatment Wiley was fine. Actually, he probably would have recovered just as quickly if he had not gone to the doctor. For most of life's occurrences "might as well" is good enough. For years I have tried to take things as they come and let them go the same way. The great exception to such behavior comes in medical matters, particularly those which apply to a sick child. With a sick child, the relaxed "might as well" soon becomes the tense "what if," and against all reason parents often find themselves rushing children to doctors. My family and I spent this summer in Beaver River, Nova Scotia. Like Wiley, our little girl Eliza ate something that disagreed with her. After several days of stomach pains, we decided to take her to a doctor. "We have to do it," I told Vicki, "but the doctor won't know anything more than we do and will tell us to feed her yogurt, rice, and apple juice. For all the good this will accomplish, we might as well stay home." Of course, we didn't stay home; in truth, I broke the speed limit in driving Eliza to Yarmouth. While a doctor examined Eliza in the out-patient clinic, I took Edward and Francis to the gift shop. While we were eating lollipops and looking at stuffed bears, the doctor who saw Eliza came in and bought a cup of coffee. After he left, one of the two women who worked in the shop turned to the other and said, "He didn't buy six candy bars today." "What do you suppose he does with all those bars anyway?" she added. "Give them to patients?" "Huh," the other woman grunted, "give them to patients? No, that doctor has to give them away to get patients." Shortly afterward Vicki appeared with Eliza in tow. "You were right," she said, "it's yogurt, rice, and apple juice."

My ancestors blessed me with a remarkable lack of athletic ability. On many a playing field, I learned early in life to be satisfied with things as they were. No matter how I struggled to master a sport, I never succeeded. Hours of training did not make me a better athlete, and I became content with the ordinary and even less than ordinary. By high school talk about excellence and being the best or "number one" struck me as silly. I knew I would never be best at anything, and I suspected none of my classmates would either. Even such attainments as they would achieve were bound to be fleeting and finally disappointing. How much better it would be, I thought, if schools taught children to go comfortably through their days in peaceful mediocrity. Locker room pep talks about giving one hundred and ten percent effort did not inspire me. Instead the impossibility of expending ten percent more energy than one was capable of made me want to assign coaches to classes in remedial mathematics. Two or three percent of my energy was all athletics deserved in high school; at least that's all I could give. Defeat did not upset me, and when talk was directed to "turning things around" in the middle of an enjoyable losing season, I stopped listening.

As might be expected, this attitude toward athletics was only part of my general view of life. Satisfied with the less than satisfactory, I have rarely been bothered by society's problems. Without reform and reformers, this world and its inhabitants would probably behave worse than they do, and if someone caught me before I stopped listening, I might praise folks with fiery social consciences. Still, reform is not for me, and whenever I meet a reformer I behave much like Sodus Rutledge when his wife and Reverend Harbottle founded the Carthage Methodist Improvement Society. "Lady" Rutledge enlisted most of the Methodist wives in the Society, and they passed bylaws encouraging regular church attendance and fining parishioners for such things as cursing and spitting in public. The restrictions were not too popular with male Methodists, but rather than upsetting things domestic they lay low and waited to see how the wind would blow. It wasn't long before a breeze began puffing. The first person fined was Sodus, ten cents for using strong language after barking his shins with a posthole digger. The fine made him so angry that he bought a jug of whiskey from Earl Hodges, drank it off in an afternoon, and fell out drunk across the grave of Willis Smotherman in the Carthage Community Cemetery. Dr. Sollows found him there the next morning and took him home in a wagon. When Lady saw him, the first thing she said was "fifty cents." When Sodus heard that, he refused to get out of the wagon and made the doctor drive him back uptown, where he bought another jug from Earl. The last anyone ever saw of him was sitting on a bench outside the railway station in South Carthage, drinking and waiting for the afternoon train to Nashville. Shortly after Sodus decamped, the Improvement Society folded.

Being a minister is not a happy life. Always trying to better people takes something out of a man. Deacon Priddle, who never cared for Reverend Harbottle, always said that the preacher would have been better off if he had grown tobacco around Dixon Springs like the rest of his family. "Old Harbottle," Priddle claimed, "got educated out of common sense and became a preacher so he could have an easy life feeding on milk and honey from the collection plate." Things worked out differently than the preacher expected, Priddle added: "People looking for a way to heaven without dying or doing a lick of good deeds have aggravated the hell out of Harbottle for his entire life."

I have no quarrel with religion, even that religion which under the surplice of selfless concern stirs crudely about in people's doings. In fact, I enjoy singing old hymns which show concern for others, hymns like "Where Is My Boy To-night?" "Where is my wand'ring boy to-night," it begins, "The boy of my tend'rest care, / The boy that was once my joy and light, / The child of my love and pray'r?" Despite my enjoyment of rollicking old hymns, my faith is quieter. Instead of prodding me to reform, it leads to calm, and many are the hours I spend in graveyards. Two miles down the road from our house in Nova Scotia is the Port Maitland cemetery. Often when something gnaws at me, I walk to the graveyard and wander about, reading tombstones. The cemetery is isolated and lonely. Rising in small terraces above a lake, green family plots are stacked above green family plots. In July yellow cow lilies bloom along the shoreline and loons call through the blue morning fog. Except for robins picking through the terraces looking for worms, little moves in the cemetery, and when I visit I take Francis and Edward, aged five and three. The boys bring life to my visits and keep me from becoming melancholy.

In the cemetery I am drawn to the graves of small children, particularly those with lambs carved atop tombstones. Sometimes the inscriptions on the stones are poignantly simple. In 1858, when their fifteen-month-old daughter died, Mary and David Corning had "Little Rosabella" engraved on the stone. The small stone over the grave of a two-year-old boy reads "Our Baby." Verse appears on many stones. "These little buds were called / To bloom in fairer climes" is written above two sisters, aged three and one. Over "Our Little Carrie" is engraved "Jesus came for Carrie. / Mamma's work is done. / On His loving bosom, / Rests our little one." "How do the babies get out from under the big stones?" Edward asked when I told him that lambs marked the graves of children. "Daddy," Francis said, "you read only sad things. They will drive your heart crazy." Along the road to the cemetery grow yellow and white ox-eyed daisies, and one day before we left Francis picked an armful. On our arriving home, he gave them to Vicki, saying "Happy Anniversary." Some five weeks earlier, on our anniversary, Vicki and I had gone to dinner at the Golden Lamb, a fine restaurant in a red barn in eastern Connecticut. We laughed and ate a glittering meal. We even drank wine, something rare for us. Yet the sparkle of that evening faded alongside the daisies and "Happy Anniversary."

Whenever I remark that poking about in people's lives rarely accomplishes much, somebody always tells a story about a friend who would have been a different person if he had been put on the right path early in life. I am suspicious about such claims. Well-meant direction might color the inessentials of a person's life, but I doubt it would influence anything important. Whenever I hear somber accounts about reform just missed, I think of Bunyan Healy, the oldest son of Eben Healy, a furniture maker in Carthage. Bunyan was slow, and town idlers nicknamed him Doodlebug. Old Mr. Healy was a hard-shelled believer, so much so that he refused to attend any of the churches in town and every Sunday conducted family services at home. His favorite book was *Pilgrim's Progress,* not the bible. Besides reading selections from it to his family every day of the week, Eben took the names of his four boys from its pages: Bunyan, Good Will, Faithful, and Evangelist. There were not many temptations to yield to in the Healy household, and as soon as they were old enough, the younger boys set out for the City of Destruction and changed their names, probably not, though, as story had it, to Tom, Dick, and Harry.

Doodlebug wasn't quick enough to get away and, until one summer morning when he was about thirty-five, he lived an uneventful life in Carthage, being the butt of jokes and working in his father's shop. On this day, though, he got the notion that he was Christian, and taking a knobby stick, a can of sardines, and a box of crackers, he left Carthage saying he was headed for the Celestial City. That night he got as far as Gordonsville and the Clendennin place, a farm owned by three maiden sisters and their bachelor brother Lemuel. Although Lemuel was in Nashville selling hogs, the sisters invited Bunyan to eat dinner in the kitchen. All went well until Bunyan learned two of the sisters were named Prudence and Piety. "Praise the Lord," he shouted. "I knew I would meet you." Then taking the third sister by the hand, he said, "This is Charity and don't nobody tell me different." In Enigma recently a clerk in W. H. Moody's hardware store became convinced he was Samson and ran amok with a sugar-cured ham, killing a dog and four cats. "Amen, amen," Prudence said quickly. "Truly you are among the elect. Sister's name is Charity, and this is the Palace Beautiful." "Come along this narrow path," she continued, taking Bunyan's hand and leading him out of the kitchen, onto the screen porch, and up the back stairs to the spare bedroom. "Enter the Chamber of Peace," she said, opening the door and pointing to a six by four foot painting hanging on the far wall. "Here are sweet gospel sights to help you on your journey. Enter and behold goodness." As soon as Bunyan stepped into the room to look at the painting, Prudence slammed then locked the door. Aside from setting Otis, the hired man, outside in the hall, the sisters did not know what to do, so they decided to keep Bunyan confined until the next morning when Lemuel returned from Nashville on the early train.

Bunyan was a model prisoner and, if he had not lit the oil lamp, the room would have seemed empty. "The painting must have struck him speechless," Piety said. "Labelle should be here to explain it." An active

Mason, Lemuel was a "Prince of Jerusalem" in the Zerubbabel Lodge in Gordonsville. Each year on March 11, the anniversary of Jacques de Molai's martyrdom in Paris, the lodge held a picnic and raffle. Because proceeds from the raffle went to the Masonic Widow and Orphans' Home in Knoxville, Lemuel bought a bushel of tickets. The items raffled were donated, most of them by "Heroines" of the Eastern Star: pies, cakes, samplers, even quilts, and one year a grandiose painting by Labelle Watrous. At the time Labelle was Conductress of the Harmony Chapter of the Eastern Star, and some members whispered that she hoped the picture would oil her way through the ranks to Worthy Matron.

"All cosmetic, the work of a painted woman," Prudence said acidly and enviously because, for once, her sampler was not the talk of the raffle. Envy aside, however, the Watrous farm was next to that of the Clendennins, and when Lemuel won the painting, it had to be hung. "We put your painting in the guest bedroom, Labelle, dear, because we are so proud of it," Prudence said. "We want it to be the last thing visitors see at night." "Like a pillar of fire," she said, folding her hands and bending her head as if in prayer, "may it guide the lost and the weary to the fold." The painting itself depicted Moses receiving the Ten Commandments on Mt. Sinai. From an orange cloud at the top of the painting God's arms reached down, the right hand holding two gray tablets and the left resting benevolently on the head of Moses. On God's left hand was a ring decorated with the Masonic sign of square and compass. From the ring rose golden ladders on which angels climbed to heaven, blowing trumpets and playing harps. God's arms were dark and bulky. "Clearly those of Hopp Watrous," Lemuel said. "See the scar above the wrist. That's where Hopp cut himself with a scythe while mowing the grass behind his cow shed." The painting was filled with Masonic symbols. From the middle of Mt. Sinai stared an eye, a dull blue pupil around which red veins coursed like great gushing rivers. "That's Hopp, too," Lemuel said. "That's how he looks after going to Carthage and drinking at Enos Mayfield's."

On one side of Mt. Sinai stood three columns; on each Labelle had painted a word, first "Wisdom," then "Strength" and "Beauty." On the other slope of the mountain was an ark, beached under a tall sheltering cedar tree. Resting on a ledge above the tree was a beehive surrounded by a cloud of industrious bees. In the sky not far from God's right hand was a five-pointed star. The points were different colors: blue, yellow, white, green, and red. Just beyond each point was a plant the same color: a blue violet, then a sprig of yellow jessamine, a white lily, a green fern, and finally a red rose. "Without Interpreter," Piety said, "Bunyan will fall into the Slough of Despond, trying to figure out Labelle's meaning." When Bunyan stepped out of the bedroom the next morning, he was a changed man. He had a rod in his back and fire in his eye. It was not, however, the painting which changed him but a stack of westerns on the bedside table, all of them about Wild Bill Hickok. Bunyan lit the oil lamp not to look at the painting but to read the westerns. Later when he was on the porch talking to Lemuel, he asked to borrow the books. Since they had read them, the Clendennins gave him the whole batch. Later that day Otis drove Bunyan and the books back to Carthage. Not long afterward Bunyan started growing a mustache. Once the mustache was well underway, he went to Nashville and bought chaps, cowboy boots, and a ten-gallon hat. For the rest of his days, he wore cowboy outfits and was known as Doodlebug Bill.

Although different books might have changed Bunyan's dress, they would not have had much effect upon his character. And in truth to go through life as Doodlebug Bill seems as good a way to go as any. Of course, some folks might argue that Bunyan was deluded and should have been set right. Believing that absolute truth exists, such people are usually fervent advocates of education. We study history, these people lecture, in order to learn from the past. For me, most history is fiction; certainly if the history of nations resembles that of families it has little to do with actual happenings. Some years ago a distant cousin of mine killed himself. A believer in the good and the true, he decided to take an active part in community affairs. What he saw didn't aggravate the hell out of him like it did Reverend Harbottle, it deranged him. One morning, so I was told at the time, he went into the toolshed and blew his brains out, not before, however, leaving a note in the kitchen which he signed Franklin Roosevelt. At a family gathering this past fall I was told he hanged himself in the garage and signed the note John Foster Dulles. A decade from now I will probably hear that Alger Hiss jumped off the Cumberland River Bridge with cinder blocks strapped to his calves.

In recounting this story, I don't mean to imply that education is useless. It is just that claims made for education are exaggerated. Once upon a time I read shelves of important books. On looking back, the reading seems to have had no influence upon me, and I might as well have spent my time sitting in a closet reading dime novels. Great literature rarely attracts me now. Our house in Nova Scotia is almost a library in itself. In the study books are stacked from floor to ceiling while book-shelves blanket walls in the bedrooms and flow out along the halls, making walking difficult. On a bookshelf somewhere in the house can be found a complete set of every major English author.

Although we stayed two months in Nova Scotia, I rarely read books from the shelves. What I read were books I found in the barn in three wooden boxes labeled "Womens Dorothy, Ideal F, 25 Pairs." Several books were temperance hymnals flowing with fervor and song, songs typically entitled "Cold Water," "Drink Water Every One," and "Flowers Drink Their Morning Draught." "Round the Spring," a hymn by the same name urged, "laugh and sing, / Water makes us merry; / Water makes our lips and cheeks / Red as ripest cherry / Wakes the sunlight in our eyes, / Fills our mouths with gladness, / Alcohol we'll never touch, / That brings pain and sadness." "Round the spring," the refrain echoed, "laugh and sing, / Every son and daughter, / Alcohol we'll ne'er extol, / Give us clear cold water." On the title page of *Alexander's Gospel Songs Number 1* was written "Beaver River S. School. Kindly use with care." Inside was page after page of stirring hymns: "He Leadeth Me," "Shall We Gather at the River," "Tell Me the Old, Old Story," "Love Found a Way," "My Faith Looks Up to Thee," "Work for the Night Is Coming," "Blest Be the Tie That Binds," "No Burdens Yonder," and "Nearer, My God, to Thee." I kept the *Gospel Songs* in the bathroom, and whenever the children bathed I sat on the clothes hamper and sang.

Unlike a study in which books are organized and displayed, often to create an impression of their owner, the volumes in the boxes fell into no pattern. Beneath the *Field Exercise and Evolutions of Infantry* "as Re-vised by Her Majesty's Command" in 1867 lay *Paul at Ephesus* (1846) and *Tuwarri: A Story of the Coral Isles* (1848), books which had once been the "Property of the American Seaman's Friend Society." Many books intrigued me, almost always for quirky reasons. One afternoon I spent forty minutes looking at the St. Paul's School Yearbook for 1928 and cal-culating what college was the most popular with seniors. Attracting twenty-five seniors, Yale was most popular, followed by Princeton with nineteen and Harvard with fifteen. Two students planned to attend Pennsylvania, while Dartmouth, Williams, Lehigh, Cornell, and West Point each attracted one.

I spent an evening looking at *Jane's Fighting Ships* for 1918. Initially I read about the navies of the major powers. In World War I, according to Jane, the British lost twelve battleships, ten armored cruisers, and sixty-one destroyers. In contrast, the United States lost only two destroyers, a submarine, and five or six auxiliaries, three of which were armed yachts. The only big American ship sunk was the *San Diego,* an armored cruiser mined off Fire Island. After a while, though, the long lists became repetitive, and I turned to the navies of lesser countries. If there wasn't much romance in their lists, there was individuality. Jane had trouble remaining current during the war. Before the war, though, Jane stated, Natal owned a tug the *Sir John* and a surveying ship, the *Churchill.* Although Jane said the *Susa,* a 36-ton patrol boat might exist, the editors knew with certainty of only three ships in the Persian navy: the 400-ton imperial yacht *Seleukia,* the 378-ton *Mozaffin* armed with two or three Hotchkiss guns, and the *Persepolis,* 1,200 tons and carrying four 2.7-inch guns and two machine guns.

The book which I enjoyed most described the Chicago fire of 1871. Written by one Frank Lucerne and published in 1872, the book was entitled *The Lost City! Drama of the Fire-Fiend! or* CHICAGO, *as It Was, and as It Is! and Its Glorious Future!,* containing "STARTLING, THRILLING, INCIDENTS, Frightful Scenes, Hair-Breadth Escapes, Individual Heroism, Self-Sacrifice." Lucerne's prose burned with purple heat. "The Conflagration of Chicago, will, in the records of future ages," he wrote, "figure as the crowning disaster of the Nineteenth Century,—a disaster not like that which over-took Herculaneum and Pompeii, for they still lie buried beneath the ruins of their grandeur,—but as the holocaust of that wonderful City which sprang into existence at the behest of the very Aladdin of enterprise, and exhaled before a cloud of flame like the unsubstantial fabric of a vision, that like the Phoenix, has already arisen from her ashes, and is pluming herself for still grander achievements." Amid the destruction left by a fire "more implacable than the demons of the Herodian massacre," Lucerne found much that was positive. At times the fire seemed a cleanser, purging Chicago of the effete and the corrupt. "The vilest crusts," he wrote, "have now become morsels to the pampered children of luxury; and the fop of yesterday, who criticized his tailor without mercy for the slightest wrinkle in his fashionable habiliments, accepts in charity a soiled and thread-bare coat as a priceless boon."

Chicago contained illustrations. One of the first woodcuts showed the "Young Ladies of Chicago Distributing Sandwiches to the Poor Children." Ideals borrowed from Currier and Ives, the young ladies were soft and big-eyed, while the children were angels in rags. Many of the books in the boxes were illustrated. I passed over most illustrations quickly, but occasionally one made me pause. In Robert Sears's *An Illustrated Description of the Russian Empire* was a plate depicting an "Esthonian Woman Abandoning Her Children to the Wolves." While her horse rolled his eyes in fear and plunged frantically through the cold winter snow, the woman sat bundled in the sled, almost casually tossing her children behind to ravenous, pursuing wolves. Despite her attempt to slake the brutes' appetites, the fate of the woman was inevitable. Although she was much tougher than her cherubic offspring, she was destined for the main course.

Inside the house sets of books stood in long rows. In the library little was out of order. Shakespeare's works were on one shelf, those of Conrad and Milton on another, those of Henry James on yet another. No *Roderick Random* was stuffed between *As You Like it* and *A Comedy of Errors*. Instead of being jammed in on its side, *Tom Jones*, unlike the novel's hero, stood upright, exuding rectitude. Because a glance revealed their contents, the shelves lacked mystery and excitement. Far better were the boxes, full of the unexpected with books piled atop books. In one box I even found three bottles. Originally they must have been part of a ship's medicine chest. All three contained medicines dispensed by "Pollock & Fripp, Chemists, 133 Fenchurch Street, London, E.C." A tall, thin bottle with a stopper held "Blue Pills" while the two large bottles contained "Black Draught" and "Flowers of Sulphur." Finding the bottles was exciting and I brought them back to Connecticut and put them on the mantel in the living room. My living room is informal and very different from those in the houses where I grew up in Tennessee. Much as great books no longer appeal to me, so I prefer to furnish my house with the conversational and the odd. Since I cannot afford the formal or the stately, I may be making virtue of necessity, but necessity is the source of most virtue anyway.

Years ago I sold my grandmother's piano; in its place now is a cabinet organ, manufactured in the nineteenth century by Chute, Hall and Company. The organ is broken and can't be played. I bought it, however, not for music but for what is written on one of the foot pedals: "Mouse Proof Pat. 88." Sitting on top of the organ are five coffee cups, sold as gifts in the nineteenth century. On three of them, raised purple letters, outlined in gold, say "Present," "Remember Me," and "Think of Me." Around the rims of the two other cups are pink roses and blue violets; in gold on their fronts are the names of their owners: D. Roach and Dorie Cottrell. Hanging on the wall over the cups is a large three by three print entitled "Pity," published in the late 1860s. Three girls appear in the print. Not far from their feet and lying at the edge of a frozen stream is a small bird, eyes glazed with exhaustion. While two girls hold her coattails to keep her from falling onto the ice, the third girl is leaning over and reaching toward the bird. Once I hankered after good taste, even formality. But like skill in athletics, good taste is something I can do without. My house is comfortable, and if the furnishings don't impress visitors with style, they are sources of conversation. Instead of watching manners and behaving like puppets, guests relax and talk sprawls.

Learning to be satisfied with the ordinary did not come so easily as learning to be comfortable with athletic mediocrity. Years ago when I started to write, fresh from a regimen of great books, I hoped for big things and wanted the landmarks I built in the literary world to stand out. Somehow, though, I never got around to writing about King Lears and Hamlets. Instead I wrote about turtles, cicadas, and birds, not bald eagles either but robins and starlings. For a while I was irritated at myself for accomplishing so little, but then I quit fretting and decided I might as well be satisfied with lesser things. Once I decided this, writing became fun, and I began receiving rewards, not fame or fortune, but the occasional appreciative letter.

Last summer *Reader's Digest* printed a piece of mine on dandelions, and I received a bouquet of letters, not a bouquet with hothouse flowers but one filled with wildflowers: primroses, meadow sweet, columbine, and asters. An eighty-nine-year-old woman sent me her picture and wrote that when she had gone to Niagara Falls on her honeymoon in 1917 dandelions were blooming. "When our three children were growing," she recounted, "they heard their Dad and me say it was truly a beautiful sight and they began bringing us bouquets. Now my grandchildren and young great-grandchildren do the same every spring. This has become a tradition of love and for me the lowly but beautiful Dandelion has become a glorified flower." A man in Missouri sent me a song he wrote in honor of the dandelion, while several people sent poems. A woman from Arizona sent poems on various subjects. One which she wrote in the fifth grade appealed so much to Vicki that she is sewing it on a sampler. When Vicki finishes, we will probably hang the sampler in the living room next to "Pity." "If stars are really the windows of Heaven," the little poem reads, "Why are they small like a pin? / And why are the Angels allowed to peek out / And we're not allowed to peek in?" "Your article," a woman wrote from Michigan, "sent my mind back about sixty-eight years. My older sister had bro't measles home from school, and passed them around to younger sisters. When we were re-covering from the measles, our yard was covered with the yellow blos-soms. They were the most beautiful things I had ever seen. We wanted to go outside and pick them but our Mother would not let us go outside yet. I'm seventy-two years old now and still think of the memories, each spring when the lawn turns yellow." "Last fall," she continued, "my home of forty-five years burned down. All I had left was the clothes I had on when I had left home. My family cut logs (home grown) and had them sawn. Now rising out of ashes and rubble is a very pretty log house. Next spring I plan to look out of windows of my new home and enjoy the dandelions."

In general, taking things as they come makes life pleasant. Occasion-ally, though, a person can imagine a situation which can't be borne. Shortly after they married Thomas and Helen Sudley moved from Car-thage to St. Louis. After living in St. Louis for almost fifty years they returned to Carthage and bought the Hull place on Main Street. Sup-posedly the Hull place was haunted, and after the Sudleys had lived in it a while, Dr. Sollows asked them what it was like to live with ghosts. "Oh, we don't mind," said Thomas. "They use the back stairs and stay mostly in the attic and guest bedrooms. The only time we see much of them is in winter. On cold nights they sometimes come in the parlor and sit in front of the fire and read." "Besides," Helen added when Thomas paused, "they are folks we used to know. Of course things would be different if they were strangers. We just couldn't abide strang-ers wandering through the house."

Among the books I found was *The Choral Harmony: A Collection of Hymn Tunes, Chants, Sentences, Motets, and Anthems* published in 1859. The book contained home truths put to the music of familiar tunes. For their part, most of the tunes were named after cities and counties in New England. The truth associated with Windham County, near which Vicki and I live in Connecticut and in which we do most of our shop-ping, was fairly grim. "Broad is the road that leads to death," *The Choral Harmony* declared, "And thousands walk together there; / But wisdom shows a narrow path, / With here and there a traveler." Taking things as they come, I confess I prefer the broad road. Although not so scenic as the narrow path, the broad road usually has more conveniences. Still, times do crop up when a person ought to detour off onto the narrow path.

Recently I flew from Pittsburgh to Nashville on USAir. I sat in an aisle seat in the No Smoking section. Sitting next to me was a doctor. Sweeter than candy coating on a pill, she was a divorcee, traveling to a convention in Nashville. I introduced myself and soon learned she was a radiologist and had two children aged nine and seven. We got along well, and I told her about my philosophy of taking things as they come. Just before we landed, she told me that, although she was not planning to marry again, she had decided to have another child. "Won't that interfere with your career?" I asked. "No," she said, "I am making so much money that I can afford home care. I could even buy the baby-sitter a Mercedes. Actually, I could buy the baby-sitter." "Anyway," she continued, "I thought I had picked out the baby's father. But you are fun, and I like your attitude toward life." "How about being the father?" she asked, her hand dropping down upon my thigh like warm rain. In the heat of the moment all philosophy evaporated, and with a stomach tighter than that of Wiley Trefrey after he swallowed the suppositories, I stumbled about and then summoning up a hundred and ten percent effort said, "You are mighty attractive, and I wish I could oblige. But I am the sort who never strays from the straight and narrow." With that I buckled my seatbelt, and, praying for a fast safe landing, shut my eyes and silently began singing "Cling to the Bible, My Boy" and "Yield Not to Temptation."

Summering

I HAVE BEEN a summer person for a long time. During the late 1940s and 1950s, when polio raged through southern cities, I went to my grandfather's farm in Virginia as soon as school ended in June. I did not return to Nashville until September when cool weather brought an end to the polio. When I was in high school the farm was sold, and my grandmother rented a house at Wrightsville Beach, North Carolina. Every July we drove to the beach from Virginia and Tennessee, cars heavy with books, barbells, fudge cakes, cousins, and great aunts. During college I spent summers as a counselor in a boys' camp in Maine. Later, when I began teaching, I went to London every May to study in the British Library. In fact, as I look back over the years, I seem never to have spent summer at home. For the past decade I have summered in Nova Scotia. Since the 1930s my wife's family has spent summers in Nova Scotia. For almost twenty-five years Vicki's grandmother ran the Green Tree Inn in Hebron, a small town north of Yarmouth on the Gulf of Maine. In the 1940s Vicki's parents bought a farm in Beaver River. Five months after she was born in 1953 Vicki traveled to Nova Scotia. In May 1981 my little boy Francis was born; that July he made his first trip to the farm and became a fourth-generation summer person.

Neither tourists nor residents, summer people are always outsiders. We are edgy about our place, quick to say how long we have gone to Nova Scotia and to assert that Nova Scotia is more than a second home. During the summer we read the weekly newspaper carefully and, laboring to create the fiction that we belong, attend local events: agricultural exhibitions, ox hauls, and flea markets. Of course, summer people don't belong and as a result are always uneasy. The unease shows up in strangely opposite ways. Sometimes it drives us toward silent retirement, making me wish I could fold anonymously into the green landscape and not be noticed. At other times it makes me aggressive and superior. Each summer we attend the Seafest, a week-long festival in Yarmouth celebrating the bounty of the ocean. During the week Vicki and I and the children roam dock and street, looking, listening, and tasting. On Saturday there is a parade in downtown Yarmouth. The parade is gentle and informal, and we sit on the grass in Frost Park and watch participants stream by: realtors in red and white carrying a dollhouse, senior citizens square-dancing on the back of a flat-bottomed truck, Shriners on small motorcycles, an all-girl fife and drum corps, a pickup decorated to resemble a giant lobster trap, clowns, bagpipers, old fire engines from the town museum, members of the Yarmouth Association for the Blind playing country music, and draft horses pulling a wagon of little girls all dressed as fishes. While our children stood on the curb and gathered candy thrown to them by marchers, Vicki and I sat in the sun, ate strawberries, and for a while felt a warm part of things. But then suddenly and almost irrationally we sensed we were outsiders and our mood darkened. "Next year," I said, "let's enter the parade. We could paste dollar signs on the car and put a poster on the hood reading 'From our pocket to yours. Big Bucks, the Basis of True Friendship.'" "Right," Vicki answered, "we could wear bathing suits and put a lawn chair on top of the car and on it hang beach towels and a sign saying 'Keep Nova Scotia Clean—For Us.'"

Little could sweeten our mood, not even the pockets of candy the children collected, and, driving back to Beaver River after the parade, we criticized alterations made in Victorian houses along the road. No matter that picture windows let in more light during brown winter days, they violated, we said, the integrity of a building. In Nova Scotia my taste is more refined than in Connecticut. In Connecticut I shop in malls and hardly notice when pastures become fields of asphalt. In Nova Scotia I dislike seeing the modern replace the old, in part perhaps because it makes me aware of mortality. Since I am away from Nova Scotia for nine or ten months each year, change strikes me as frighteningly sudden. Gradual and everyday, change probably does not startle residents of Yarmouth. For me, too, the business of business, tearing down and pushing up, seems emblematic of all the vague forces washing under me and eroding the stability of my life: economics, disease, the children's growth, the dissolution of friends' marriages. Moreover, changes in the physical landscape seem part of larger social change. Because we don't belong, summer people are able to indulge in easy familiarity, priding ourselves on being able to associate with all sorts of Nova Scotians. This familiarity, however, has little to do with liberality, for summer people are deeply conservative. Much as we want our countryside scenic and undeveloped, so we want Nova Scotians "unspoiled," that is, comparatively poor and tied to the land and sea and the occupations of their fathers. In our desire for social stability is, of course, an element of self-interest. As development occurs and people are pulled off farm and boat toward easier, better-paying, safer jobs, summer people have difficulty finding caretakers to watch houses during the winter and then mow meadows in late spring.

I am not sure why I go to Nova Scotia each summer. In part I go to escape my workaday existence in Connecticut. In part I go for the continuity, simply because I am a member of a family who has always gone. Then, too, I am middle-aged, in that time of life when traveling to some place different, New Mexico or Ireland, for example, looms insurmountably difficult. I also go to Nova Scotia for the long clear summer light and the salty air off the Bay of Fundy. I go for the streams of lupin purple and pink along the highway and for the flowers in our fields in late June: smartweed hip-high and brownish red, buttercups above the knee, yellow goatsbeard just below, beneath that yellow rattle, red clover, the small white starry blossoms of lesser stitchwort, and winding through the grass vetch just turning purple. Along the ground, its creamy green blossoms almost hidden, is lady's mantle. Shaped like cloaks worn by wealthy women in the Middle Ages, its leaves seem always silver with balls of dew, a sign for me not simply of its value but in my quiet moments of the value of the ordinary and unobtrusive. During the Middle Ages lowly lady's mantle was a treasured herb. Not only could it stay bleeding and vomiting but it could heal bruises and cure ruptures. For childless women it was a blessing; drinking its juices for twenty days promoted conception, while bathing in them prevented miscarriages.

Our first days in Nova Scotia are busy. We clean the house, shoveling up dead mice and sweeping out a bushel of animal droppings. Wood has to be split for the stove and part of the old chicken house chopped up for kindling. After a week, though, there are not many duties aside from watching the children, and I spend much time dabbling. This past July, for example, I found a small green balloon on the rocks along the beach at Beaver River. Printed on the balloon was "Huckleberry Frolic. East Rockaway, New York." I carried the balloon home and that night wrote a letter to the director of the Frolic, saying I thought they might be interested in how far one of their balloons traveled. The next morning I mailed my letter and the balloon to East Rockaway. I enclosed my address in Storrs, and when we returned to Connecticut two letters awaited me. One from the village clerk of East Rockaway thanked me "on behalf of the Mayor and Board of Trustees and all of us at Village Hall" for "taking the time to write." The other from the director of the Frolic explained that the festival was held to raise money for the village museum, an old mill building. The building would be three hundred years old in 1988, and, the director wrote, "We expect to have a big wing-ding." Containing clippings about the museum and the huckleberry celebration, the letters were just the sort of slow, friendly thing to appeal to a summer dabbler.

Along the beach in front of our farm great boulders squat in the sand, and streams of ancient lava run out into the bay, half buried yet still sharp like broken jetties. Tides are high and what washes ashore in the early morning usually is gone by midnight. Consequently I don't spend so much time wandering the beach as I do the soft fields. In them I find flowers which attract me, lady's mantle or, as in this past summer, orange hawkweed, a slender flower six to twenty inches high with a small dandelionlike blossom, orange and red like the last moments of the evening sun, below the horizon but burning vivid against the clouds. Hawkweed got its name because people once believed hawks ate its leaves in order to better their vision. The belief that plants were responsible for good eyesight was widespread. While eagles supposedly ate wild lettuce and linnets, eyebright, swallows fed celandine to their young. Actually, there may be truth in the belief, not applicable so much to birds as people. Perhaps the person who notices or takes the time to look at eyebright or blue-eyed grass, as it is more commonly known, sees more of what matters in life than the person rushing to and fro, mind forever focused on the important. Certainly that is what I want to believe.

When friends in Connecticut ask why we spend every summer in Nova Scotia, I say, "In Nova Scotia the children range free, far from television and traffic, studies and measurement. They wander about, digging and rooting, growing green and weedy, somehow getting in touch with things that matter." "Whatever those things are," I add in inarticulate self-consciousness. In the summer I am a sentimental environmentalist, believing that bigness, be it industrial or social, undermines the good, the true, and the beautiful. Alas, if our sprawling technological world with its supermarkets and power plants collapsed, my family would starve. For my children I want a modest life and in summer preach the virtue of simplicity. Yet when school begins this fall Francis, my first grader, will have little time to dabble and observe. His Saturdays will be filled by a computer course for talented students. Paradoxically I want my children to opt out of modernity while at the same time I want them to master it. Be this as it may, however, we dabbled in Nova Scotia. Francis and I searched our fields for orange hawkweed or devil's paintbrush. We filled an envelope with seeds and bringing them back to Connecticut scattered them in the side yard near the screen porch.

Besides fields I roam through barns, taking away not seeds to make my lawn bloom but furnishings to brighten my writing. In the loft of our barn, I found a hat tub. Pink with brown stripes around it like waterlines, the tub resembles a policeman's cap turned upside down. In days before hot water heaters, people bathed in hat tubs in the kitchen, filling them with water from tanks on the sides of wood stoves. Someday in an essay I will paint the tub blue and yellow and sticking a rubber plant in it will turn it into a planter. On a kitchen table will sit a Class II Salter's Improved Family Scale with a brass face and the capacity to weigh up to fourteen pounds. On the wall in the study will hang a pair of ice skates with wooden soles and upper leather parts joined like sandals by buckles over the toes and around the ankle. In lamplight the tempered steel runners, a quarter of an inch wide, will shine silver and make me think of red apples, hot chocolate, and snow swirling white over the fence and through the spruce. Not all the things I find in Nova Scotia become matter for imaginary houses, however; I carry some things home to Connecticut. For four years our doorbell has been broken. In the backhouse this past summer I found a cowbell. After bringing it back to Connecticut, I hung it outside the back door. One shake and all the dogs in the neighborhood jump; two shakes and they howl and I am at the door.

Much as I fill fictional houses with furnishings from Nova Scotia, so I people Nova Scotia with an imaginary populace. Living almost entirely within their families, summer people have few friends. When Vicki and I visit, we don't visit people but places, landmarks of personal experience—Smuggler's Cove where Vicki and her family gathered raspberries and picnicked when she was a little girl, Yarmouth Light and the great rocks nearby from which her grandmother's ashes were tossed into the ocean. Although I know almost nothing about any native's private life or personal history, I have begun writing tales about our corner of Nova Scotia. Writing may, perhaps, be my way of making the summer and indeed Nova Scotia itself live. Now whenever I drive past the Shore Grocery in Port Maitland and glance down Cove Street toward the wharf, I see more than a row of Victorian houses, neat and silent in the white sun. I see "Raisin" Nubbin walking toward the store, his history garish in my mind and splashing over the quiet houses in great swatches of lively natural color: mulberry, apricot, peach, and plum.

Born on Burn's Point, Raisin went to sea as a carpenter's assistant on the bark *Thistle,* bound for Natal, along the way calling at ports in the Indies, South America, and Japan. At first the voyage went smoothly; Raisin quickly got his sea legs, and the waters around Cape Horn were calm. When the *Thistle* sailed near Angelica Reef in the Flores Sea in the East Indian Archipelago, however, it was caught in a typhoon and driven north past Kalatoa toward the Tiger Islands, so named because, uncharted and unknown, they were the subject of fearful tales about long-toothed tigers and cannibals with feathers in their hair and bones in their noses. Near one of the islands a wave broke over the ship, sweeping the deck clear of barrels, spars, and Raisin. In the storm the *Thistle* could not come about, and Raisin was given up for lost. Fortunately for Raisin, though, the wave that swept him overboard pitched him high on a beach. For fourteen hours he lay insensible. When he woke, he was hungry and thirsty. Pulling himself to his knees, he noticed smoke rising from the edge of the jungle, just beyond a bend in the beach. Although terrified of cannibals, Raisin was so hungry he crawled to a clump of trees near the smoke in order to study the savages. Kneeling at the trunk of a giant palm, all he heard at first was rough mumbling. Then suddenly a harsh voice that made the hairs on his head stand straight up roared, "Why the hell did you play that card?" "Praise the Lord," Raisin exclaimed, raising his hands toward the heavens, "they are Christians!"

Being lost at sea made Raisin's fortune. Since childhood he had kept a coin or two sewed in the lining of his trousers for just such emergencies. After drinking a gourd of coconut milk and eating a pile of mangoes and a helping of boiled python, Raisin perked up considerable and, ripping the lining of his pants, extracted the coins and asked to be dealt in. Raisin was a humdinger of a cardplayer, and in fact had been expelled from the Port Maitland school for gambling. By the time he and his compatriots were rescued, he had won everybody's money, enough to sail back to Port Maitland first class and to buy an eight-room house on

Cove Street and a quarter interest in Mothersole's tannery at Cann's Brook.

The man who could turn the sands of the Tiger Islands into gold was not likely to be satisfied with but a single business, and, not many years after coming home, Raisin bought half interest in Eleazer Gawdry's store. An advertisement for 1917 declared that Gawdry dealt in groceries, flour, feed, fisherman's supplies, gasoline, parts for gas engines, fresh and pickled fish, shoes, and dishes. Shortly after Raisin became his partner Gawdry started selling coal, and Raisin built a shed for storing coal near the south wharf in Port Maitland. Although Raisin eventually bought into several businesses up and down the coast, even in Yarmouth itself, he was especially fond of the store, and most mornings he could be found there, sitting on a wooden lard tub, eating candy: Sweet Marie chocolate bars or suckers like Honeymoon or Ladies' Choice.

Raisin became so successful and well known that the Yarmouth paper kept his obituary on file and updated, ready to print at a moment's notice. Unfortunately, this zeal led, as zeal so often does, to a mistake. When Mr. Ralph Newbern, grocer at Short Beach died, a reporter, recently down from Halifax, was assigned the obituary. Not familiar with the names of prominent local people and not hearing the editor clearly, the reporter found Raisin's obituary in the file and, confusing one grocer with another, ran the obituary on the front page. Raisin had just sat down to a breakfast of kippers and fried green tomatoes when he saw his obituary. The announcement put him off his food and, going to the telephone, he rang the store. "Eleazer," he said, "this is Raisin. Have you seen the notice of my death in today's paper?" "Yes," Eleazer answered, pausing and then finally speaking tentatively. "Yes, I've seen it. Where, Raisin, where are you calling from?"

Although I have not filled them in, several years would pass before Raisin's obituary appeared again in the paper. One day I spent an afternoon walking around Port Maitland, deciding where Raisin's children would live and whom they would marry. Although no one spoke to me, Port Maitland seemed friendly, and I didn't think myself a summer person. I did not write anything else about Raisin, however, because my parents suddenly sold their house and bought a condominium. They needed me to help them move, so Vicki and I cut our summering short. She and the children returned to Connecticut, and I flew to Tennessee. In the attic of my old house in Nashville with the temperature always above ninety, Nova Scotia melted out of mind, and real summer, searing and sad, began. I dug through trunks and cabinets, throwing away life-times as if they were dried bulbs, long past a last flowering. Into the garbage went linen tablecloths, Panama hats, dolls, rounded half moon–shaped bricks used for ballast by colonial sea captains in the eighteenth century, diaries and love letters, those written by Father to Mother in the 1930s and those written to me by my first love thirty years later. Through my hands the spring of my life ran and turned into hard sum-mering as I threw away the big Blue Horse notebooks I used in the first grade. Over three boxes of framed pictures I stopped to look at my fourth-grade photograph. I had just entered Parmer School and was in Mrs. Bonnie's class. I thought about keeping the picture, but knowing I would never clear the attic if I started sifting I threw it and the other eighty or so photographs away.

Later I paused over a snapshot of myself and my great-aunt Lucille at Wrightsville Beach. One night at dinner, I remembered, Aunt Lucille's husband Uncle Frank lost a tooth, but thinking it a piece of gristle he chewed it up and swallowed it. I remembered that the next to last time Aunt Lucille came home from the hospital, her cleaning woman greeted her and after making her comfortable said, "You don't know how I envy you." "Why?" Aunt Lucille asked. "Because," the woman answered, "you are going to see Jesus before I do." Silently I laughed and then threw the picture away. Seasons had changed and Aunt Lucille was gone from my life. Still later I found a copy of the *Carthage Courier* for May 1919. On the front page was an announcement for an All Day Service at the Gaines-boro Methodist Church. I had never been to Gainesboro, Tennessee, but I remembered a story Father told me about it. Gainesboro was an out-of-the-way red clay and tarpaper town in Jackson County. About the only people who traveled to Gainesboro regularly were drummers, and they usually traveled by horse, staying at a small hotel run by Miss Polly Gittings. One wet fall day just as Miss Polly stepped out on the porch to ring the lunch bell, a drummer splashed up, his horse caked with mud. A smart aleck, he stopped in front of Miss Polly and said, "Ma'am, could you tell me where Gainesboro, Tennessee, is?" Miss Polly took her hand away from the bell rope and turning around looked the drummer up and down. Then, as people began to gather for lunch, she said, "If you'll just jump down off your horse, you'll be up to your ass in it right now."

I wanted to stop and roll memory back and forth, letting associations rise in the mind, sweet and tangy. Unfortunately, I did not have the leisure to savor the past. The house had been sold, and I had to shovel the attic clean. By the end of the week the attic was bare except for some bits of red clay, items which had tumbled out of boxes or had long been lost behind old suitcases and trunks. Some of these I examined and a few I kept: a hairbrush belonging to my grandmother Pickering, covered with silver roses and with the name "Fannye" engraved on it, and a diploma awarded to my great grandmother Nannie Brown on June 7, 1860, by Minerva College, located, the diploma stated, "Near Nashville, Tennessee." The degree was signed by S. E. Jones, "President and Professor of Biblical Science," as well as by the governess and teacher of English and French, the professor of Ancient Languages and Literature, the instructress in Mathematics, the instructress in Fancy Work, the mistress of the Preparatory School, and the professor of Instrumental and Social Music.

Reading came almost naturally to me. Every night my parents read, and, when I was a boy, doing anything other than reading after dinner was abnormal. As I look back, my childhood seems marked not so much by physical awakenings or developing abilities as by books: the travels of Richard Halliburton, the novels of Edgar Rice Burroughs, and the adventures of the Hardy Boys; the animals of Ernest Thompson Seton, biographies of great Americans, some national heroes like Washington and Lincoln, but many southern—James K. Polk, Stonewall Jackson, Sam Houston; then the comic novels of Mark Twain and Booth Tarkington, the westerns of Zane Grey, and the histories of Winston Churchill. Now as an adult I read almost unconsciously and in the attic was pulled toward objects with writing on them. Not the silver and raised roses but the odd spelling of "Fannye" drew me to Grandma Pickering's hairbrush.

When I cleared cupboards and emptied file cabinets, a few papers spilled out on the floor. Among them was a copy of a letter Father wrote in 1948. That October he and Mother and Dewitt Tate, a friend from Nashville, drove to Sea Island, Georgia, and spent a long weekend at the Cloister. While there they met the Brellsfords, a couple from Richmond, stopping at Sea Island for a few days while on their way to Florida. The Brellsfords, Mother and Father, and Dewitt Tate made a gay fivesome and during their last evening together drank heavily, so much so that the next day Tate remembered little that occurred. "My God, Dewitt," Father said, seizing the chance to enliven the tedious drive back to Nashville with fiction, "my God, man, don't you recall flirting with Grace Brellsford, whispering something, and then leaving the table? She followed soon after, and Lyndon was furious." When Dewitt said he could not remember anything about the evening but assured Father he was not the sort to fool around with another man's wife, Father just grunted and said, "Well, we shall see."

Back in Nashville Father wrote a letter and sent it to a friend in Richmond instructing him to mail it to Tate. "Dear Sir," the letter began, "No doubt you will be surprised to receive this communication from me and to learn that I have canceled my trip and returned to Richmond. Furthermore, you will be interested to know that I left my wife in Florida and I am now making arrangements for a divorce. While my reasons have been cumulative over the months, the events of Monday evening, October 11, were the final straw. As best I could I tried to forgive and overlook the happenings at the table. After all I hoped what transpired had been induced by alcohol and though objectionable and disgraceful was not necessarily vicious. However, after my wife left the room for a rendezvous I could stand no more. Through the medium of the hotel staff I found whom she met and where. Need I say more?"

"Mr. Tate," Father's letter concluded, "you may wonder why I have troubled myself to write to you. It is simply that I am extending you the courtesy of forewarning you so that you may be prepared—which incidentally is more than you did for me. You may expect to hear from me in a more formal and legal vein within a very few days—when the papers are served. Yours, very truly, L. W. Brellsford." Written in the spring of spirit, the letter made me chuckle and then long to play jokes myself. Unfortunately, my friends and I are deep into the summer of life, that cautious time beyond misbehaving, when disruption, even playful disruption, brings worry and visits to the doctor, not laughter. The best I could do was write stories about Nova Scotia. Raisin Nubbin was not the sort to drink, but his son Clarence, the one who sold Fords in Moncton, could probably be persuaded, I thought, to dip into the flowing bowl.

Not all the objects I took away from the attic had writing on them. In a box I found the figurines which stood on Mother's wedding cake. Slender and elegant, they were seven inches tall and made in Germany. The groom had blond hair, blue eyes, red lips, and a Roman nose. He wore a black swallowtail coat, white tie, carnation in his lapel, and patent leather shoes. The bride also had blue eyes but her hair was brown, cut fashionably short like a boy's with a wreath of flowers holding it down over her forehead. Over her face was a veil and in her arms she carried a bouquet. Stuck to the train of her dress and the groom's shoes was icing from the cake. Someday I hope the figurines will again stand elegant and dignified, sentinels of sweet order on top of a cake, this one, though, baked for the marriage of my little Eliza. For my children I want harmony and decent formality: veils, swallowtail coats, carnations, and wedding cakes.

Actually, I may people Nova Scotia with imaginary characters not so much because I want my summers to live but because I want the illusion of controlling life. Writing about tanneries and grocery stores I forget the present with its weapons and poisonous waste. Of course, I can't completely escape the present, for it lies in the past, even in a hot, bare attic in Tennessee. Among the objects I found was a game I played with in 1945 or 1946. Manufactured by the A. C. Gilbert Company of New Haven, the game consisted of a small four by three by one inch box with a sealed, clear glass top. Under the glass at the bottom of the box were a drawing of Japan and two capsules, each with a BB inside. While Japan itself was black, spiky yellow flames exploded from the islands and burned across the drawing. Falling down from the top of the drawing was an object clearly labeled "Atomic Bomb." The names of three cities appeared on the drawing: Tokyo, Hiroshima, and Nagasaki. At the locations of these last two cities were two small indentations, and the object of the game was to shake the box so that the two "bombs" tumbled into the holes and stuck straight up. Sometimes at night I wake up, frightened for my children, convinced that years won't bring Eliza figurines and instruction in fancy work but fire and ashes. Yet the Atomic Bomb game delighted me, and I played with it in the attic until I became an expert bombardier. On my return to Connecticut I showed it to people whom I knew it would upset. When an acquaintance whose feelings on peace run deep looked closely at the game, his hands began to shake. "No, no, that's not the way. This is how you do it," I said, jerking the box out of his grasp. "You have to keep your eye on the target," I added, "and shout Kaboom! Kaboom!"

Before leaving Tennessee I spent an afternoon wandering about our yard, looking at flowers and bushes. In the back was a bed of pink, frilly July lilies. They originally came from Grandma Pickering's house in Carthage. When she sold her home and moved into an apartment, Father dug up bulbs and planted them in Nashville. The lilies would be pretty, I thought, in the lawn outside my screen porch. Chances of the hawkweed growing were small; besides, I reckoned, the lilies had been part of my family for three generations while the hawkweed was only a summer flower. Behind a box of kindling in the toolshed, I found a rusty trowel, the picks and shovels all having been sold. For three weeks there had been no rain in Nashville and the ground was dry and baked. As a result I could not dig up a single bulb. Leaning over the trowel, I scraped and pushed until the handle snapped off. Returning to Connecticut without the flowers, I felt dissatisfied. Eight days ago, however, Mother telephoned. "I knew you wanted some of those July lilies," she said, "so I sent Philip over to dig up a few. He got a couple and I have mailed them." The lilies arrived yesterday. This morning I put the Atomic Bomb game in the attic, and this afternoon Edward and I planted the lilies by the porch. If they thrive, I will take bulbs to Nova Scotia and plant them around the well. On warm evenings after dinner Vicki and I sit by the well. While she watches birds—catbirds and warblers hunting insects and swallows cutting and dipping over the eaves—I people the evening, imagining Eliza an endless summerer, wandering down Cove Street, children bright about her knees like flowers: goatsbeard, lady's mantle, orange hawkweed, and frilly July lilies.

Having My Way

I DON'T GET my way much now, but I think a lot about it. What I
think most about is going on a journey, the sort I used to take before
I had a family. Sitting in some far-off place I once turned thought loose
to run and play, to circle foolishly and leap about trying to follow mysteries spinning through the breeze. Nowadays I rarely wander far from
home, and, when I do, I leave distracting thought behind, taking with
me only attention, tightly leashed and snapping at the heels of my
children. I shun the attractions of the passing world, and for people who
come too familiarly close I have ready hackles and a snarl. Years ago I
behaved differently. When strangers approached I wasn't immediately
suspicious and, instead of growling, smiled and listened. "The square
across the street is named after Franklin Roosevelt. Do you know why?"
a man asked after dropping down next to me on a park bench in Budapest. "The Russians named it," he said after I shook my head. "They
named it after Roosevelt because he gave them this country."

I tell my children never to accept presents from strangers. "If someone
offers you candy," I warn, "back away and say 'No thank you.' If the person insists, yell 'Go away' and run." Years ago strangers approached me
bearing gifts. Instead of refusing them because I suspected a dark bitter
motive lurked under the wrapping, I tore the gifts open, eager to sample
the sweets of life, strange though they might be. One day as I sat in an
outdoor restaurant in Tiblisi, a bowl of strawberries and a bottle of champagne appeared on my table. One bottle led to a second and then more
and an afternoon of dancing Georgian folk dances and toasting Joe
Stalin. For Georgians, Stalin was not just a local boy who made good, he
was the man who harvested Russians like Nebuchadnezzar chewing
grass. After the toasting and dancing came song, and eventually I went
on the warpath, setting off up the street chanting "Bring on the damned
old KGB." Shortly afterward my request or something like it was granted;
a car drew alongside, and two soberly dressed, pleasant men got out and
offered to drive me to my hotel. Befuddled beyond direction, I accepted

and got into the car, and, without my volunteering or their asking the name of my hotel, they drove me straight to where I was staying and saw to it that I got quietly to my room.

Those days of champagne and trenchcoats have lost their mysterious fizz. Still, whenever I think about traveling, they bubble through memory. On my imaginary travels I am always alone. When one travels with someone, events and places exist only in relation to the other person, not as themselves. With another person the long climb from Wadi Mousa to el Deir, carved into the soft mountains above Petra, does not lead to an appreciation of the monument itself but to feelings earthy and love among the ruins. The oleanders at the mouth of Wadi Siyagh bloom full, red and white, like a woman's breasts, and amid the stones broken like dry bones under el Deir, one wants to gather his companion to him, as a sign that in the powdery waste some bones live and flower. Although one neglects the monumental for the moment when traveling with another person, one is better off with a companion. Alone one sees too much and startled by the sublime, imagination can bound headlong past flesh and reason toward the suicidal. From el Deir the hike back to Wadi Mousa seems a return to the low littleness of life: bowels, a room in the guesthouse, postcards, and bedouins selling Pepsi-Cola. How much better, one thinks, to leap from the mountain, for a moment golden in the air, like the Deir at sunset.

Today there's not much chance of my doing a half-gainer off some mountain. Most of the ruins I visit are not ancient monuments but my contemporaries, broken not by water or wind but by disease. Long climbs are now beyond my strength, and when I go on a journey I don't travel far and I go down rather than up. My wife Vicki and I and the children spend summers in Nova Scotia. In a field close to our house is an old cellar hole. We planted raspberries in it, and some days when I dream of traveling I walk over and, on the pretext of seeing how the berries are doing, climb down and sit on a rock. Over stones at what was the front of the house grows a bank of roses, always heavy with bees. Where the sides of the cellar have tumbled down, mallow and yarrow have squeezed through to bloom. On the floor of the cellar are purple knapweed and ox-eyed daisies. Garter snakes live in the foundation, and if I sit long and quiet enough I see one pull like green twine through the rocks. Usually, however, my stay is short. Mosquitoes and black flies drive me slapping back to the house and porch before I begin dreaming about distant lands or see a snake. Still, much as I have given up mountains for cellars and, I suppose, the Iron Curtain for screens, so I have forsaken faraway places for out-of-the-way knowledge.

Because they drove me from the cellar and were on more than mind, I began reading about insects and learned a few curious and useful things. Each spring I swat the first wasp I see. That brings good fortune and insures that people who don't like me will stay away all summer. If the unlikely occurs and I go on a long trip and have to spend a night in a Hilton or Hyatt-Regency, I won't be bothered by bedbugs. Bedbugs, I discovered, won't bite the traveler who puts a jar of cold water under his bed before going to sleep. Instead of wasting time calling neighbors when a cow disappears, a farmer ought to search the walls of his barn for a daddy longlegs. If asked politely, the daddy longlegs will lift one of his front legs, pointing out the direction taken by the cow.

Much of the knowledge I have picked up concerns the origin and appearance of insects. Suspecting he would be busy navigating and searching for olive branches, Noah didn't think he would have time for small things, and so when the wood tick crawled aboard the ark Noah pinned him to the railing. Although he did get a little thirsty toward the last months of the cruise, Mr. Tick was not really inconvenienced. Even at the landing when Mrs. Noah pulled out the pin and set him free, leaving a white scar on his back, the tick did not complain. He had enjoyed himself at sea. During the day he dozed in the sun or kept score while other animals played shuffleboard. A busybody interested in creatures' private affairs, he relished being on deck at night. Lying low and looking like a chip of wood, he wasn't conspicuous. The other creatures forgot about him, and he saw some highly entertaining things, things which if he had been talkative might have gotten the rabbits and goats, in truth a whole zoo of creatures, kicked off the ark.

Actually, Noah was responsible for more than just the spot on Mr. Wood Tick's back. Blame for my being unable to stay long in the cellar hole can be laid squarely on Noah's shoulders. Busy nailing the tick to the railing, Noah didn't notice an extra snake crawl on board the ark. By the time he found out, the floods had begun and Noah was too soft-hearted to pitch the snake overboard; besides, snake-handling had not received official sanction from above and Noah wasn't certain if the snake was poisonous or not. "That serpent would not be here," he told Mrs. Noah, "if He hadn't willed it." "Now," he said, "stop pestering me. Navigating isn't any piece of manna, you know." As far as navigators go, Noah was pretty good but he was no Phoenician. Moreover, in his six hundredth and first year, he wasn't young, and by the time the flood-waters began abating, he was tired and made mistakes. One cloudy night while sailing along what today is the border between Turkey and Iraq, the ark struck the top of Mt. Cilo and sprang a leak. By ordering the elephants and hippopotamuses to gather at the stern and then jump up and down in unison so that the bow lifted into the air, Noah got the ark off Cilo, but then he could not figure out how to plug the leak. Since the accident occurred at night when most of the creatures were occupied with the sort of doings Mr. Wood Tick observed, there were few animals about to whom Noah could turn for advice.

Not having a mate made the lone snake bitter but it also gave him time to study the leak. The ark was made out of gopher wood, and the snake had spent his boyhood crawling through the roots and along the branches of gopher wood trees, hunting for mice and chameleons. After sloshing about in the hole of the ark, eyeing the leak with first one side of his tongue then the other, the snake said he would save the ark if Noah promised him a banquet of human flesh once the deluge ended. With the water rising in the hole and threatening the granaries, Noah had no choice but to go along with the snake's wishes. As soon as Noah agreed to the banquet, the snake slithered into the side of the boat. Twisting and coiling, he wedged himself into the ark and plugged the leak like a cork pushed into a bottle. And there he stayed, silent and stoic during the long, cold sail from Cilo to Ararat.

Once the ark was high and dry and the animals had begun traipsing off into the bush, he uncoiled and, after stretching and pulling his ribs about, went to Noah and demanded his due. "Have you forgotten your pledge?" he hissed. "Good gracious," Noah exclaimed. "Certainly not. For you I am going to put the big pot in the little pot, as the Canaanites say. I just wanted to get shuck of all these beasts, fowls, and creeping things before I settled down to fancy cooking. Slither down to the stern and look over the railing. You will see the makings of a big bonfire." "Mrs. Noah thinks it's an altar for an offering, but, good buddy," he continued, stroking the snake behind the venom glands, "it's for her. I know you are not used to having your meals cooked, but Mrs. Noah is sour and might give you acid indigestion if you ate her raw." "I am not about to let that happen to such a regular guy," Noah ended, running his hand down the snake's back all the way to the tip of his tail. Not used to such gentle handling, the snake practically shed his skin in pleasure.

While Noah piled on the faggots, once in a while stopping to wave and smile, the snake stretched out in the grass, its fangs dripping in anticipation. Finally after the bonfire had been lit and the flames seemed to reach the clouds, Noah picked up the snake and, walking over to the fire, lifted him high in the air, so, as he said, "his pal could be part of the action." And so, alas, the snake was, for although Noah was one of the Giants of the Earth, he was not above stooping to a lie. When he got close to the flames, he pitched the snake right in the middle of the fire without so much as a thank you or a good-bye. Before he could even hiss in astonishment, the snake was incinerated. Noah, however, was not able to wiggle out of his promise, and his word was redeemed. From the snake's ashes swarmed a cloud of fleas, lice, mosquitoes, and black flies, all the bloodsuckers who have preyed upon Noah's descendants ever since the flood and who make it impossible for me to spend much time in my cellar hole in Nova Scotia.

Out-of-the-way knowledge doesn't provide much pleasure unless it is shared with someone. In truth, the more I think about insects or even going on a trip, the more I want to be with my children. This past November I received a letter from Henry, a friend teaching at another college. I had read a novel he wrote and had written him, praising the book and asking about his family. "Beverly and I have been divorced for over a year," he replied, "and since August Martha and Sally have lived with her in Ohio. Beverly works for an insurance company in Akron." Henry missed his girls, and he ended the letter, writing, "Your family sounds terrific. Treasure those kids." Not only do I treasure the children but I have shared my hoard of bug knowledge with them. I want them to be ready for school and classes in science and religion. Things are more complex than theologians and scientists make out, and I don't want the children to fall for threadbare theories about evolution or biblical creation. I haven't got all the answers myself, but I am working on them and I tell the children almost everything.

Of course, like a good researcher I am selective and don't reveal all my findings, particularly those which might raise doubts about any of my previous discoveries. Just the other day I read an account of the origin of the botfly. Because it would lead to questions about Noah and the snake and Noah's responsibility for noxious insects, I have not told the children about the botfly. According to this account, the botfly is St. George's not Noah's responsibility. Knights were not particularly tidy, and after freeing the maiden and wiping the smoking blood off his lance St. George rode away, leaving the remains of the dragon sprawled out in front of the cave and stretching down through a nearby valley and over three or four hills. The local turkey buzzards did yeoman work, but the amount of dragon to eat was monstrous, and before they could dig their way to the sweetmeats, the botfly had been generated by the decaying entrails and let loose upon the world.

Spading up buried knowledge and thinking about going on trips do not so much, perhaps, reflect a desire to have my way as they do the wish to escape pettiness. Today bigness and growth are too important, and few people appear interested in the good small things of life. Committed to becoming, as administrative officials say, "one of the top twenty research institutions in the country," my university, the University of Connecticut, has decided to plough under four hundred acres of woodland, farm, and meadow and raise an "Industrial Park." Last fall a pond was drained; and warm April will no longer bring the bright song of spring peepers. Deer and groundhogs will have to find water elsewhere or die. As gray, boxlike buildings rise where cattails stood, not only sight but language will be impoverished. No longer will the dragonfly pitch and dart above the water, flashing blue and green, iridescent with color and names: flying adder, snake doctor, horse stinger, and devil's darning needle. Instead low buildings will squat, heavy metallic letters stamped on their sides. When a dragonfly is killed, an old story says, death will follow, and indeed it will, here not the death of a person but the death of feeling. Before such buildings the heart contracts. Instead of reaching out to embrace the world with affection and concern, one turns away, hardened and uncaring, and becomes a user not a conserver. Last week only three people attended a meeting of faculty members concerned about peace and the threat of war. People stayed away, not because they didn't care but because they knew they could no more slow the grind toward destruction than they could stop bulldozers from pounding pond and field into Industrial Park. Discouraged, I left the meeting determined to burrow deeper into the cellar of out-of-the-way knowledge.

The best plans and strongest determinations go astray not because of human weakness but because of the infinite variety of life. Flashing like a silver lure near the surface of a pond, life pulls one up from the cold depths of most self-imposed narrowness. As black flies drove me from the cellar hole in Nova Scotia, so the student newspaper drew me out of depression. The next day, I read, had been designated UConndom Day. In the library a film on "the proper way to use a condom" was going to be shown while condoms themselves would be given away at various locations around the campus. "I am going to that film. This is not to be missed," I thought, imagining condoms tumbling out of great boxes, like Gummi Bears, yellow, blue, and green. Of course, I didn't get my way. Instead of seeing the film, I spent the day at the aquarium in Mystic, looking at fish with Vicki and the children. Actually, I was happy to be at the aquarium; despite the smile provoked by UConndom Day, ponds, fish, and children are more my sort of thing. The discrepancy between thoughts and deeds is great, and although I often think about trips I once made alone, I am now Domestic Man, so much so I begrudge moments spent away from the children. This year Francis entered kindergarten. On the first morning Vicki and I stood at the end of the driveway with Francis while he waited for the bus. We thought he might be nervous about getting on the bus and going to school. We were wrong. When the bus stopped, Francis leaped on board, laughing. Not Francis but Vicki and I found it difficult to let go and, as the bus disappeared around the corner, we held hands and cried. For his part, Francis probably wishes he could take a trip, for when the bus brings him back at noon, I am waiting on the steps, ready to ask, "What did you do at school today?"

Having one's way may just involve getting out of other people's ways or simply getting out of the way. "Someday," Brother Ardent McIneery said at a meeting in the Methodist Church in Carthage, Tennessee, "the lion and the lamb will lie down together." "Maybe," a voice responded from the congregation when Brother McIneery paused to give profundity a chance to adhere to his words, "maybe, but the lion will be the only one to get up." Such lions as there are around the University of Connecticut are mostly literary and toothless; in any case, I am not about to lie down with them or, for that matter, with anybody other than Vicki and the children. Still, I don't approach within roaring distance of some people.

I especially avoid hiking through the high savannah of social life with ideologues, certain a particular way of thinking provides answers. When confronted by the doctrinaire, I try to shift the grounds of conversation, behaving like the old rogue harangued at a cocktail party by a good-looking feminist. "Sweet thing," he said, "could you be quiet?" "Haven't I a perfect right," she began, whipping up energy to charge into the argument that she was free to say whatever she wished. "Yes, indeed, Sugar, you certainly have," the old boy nodded in agreement, "and your left's not bad either." Besides shifting the grounds of conversation, one can take the bite out of sharp controversy by avoiding certain words. I, for example, never say "precedent"; once a person pulls precedent into a discussion, all chances of someone else's getting his way vanish. Renaming things, however, is more fun than avoiding words and is probably more successful in helping a person have his way. When Brother McIneery rented a small house he owned in South Carthage to Farr Stonebridge, he stressed that no animals were allowed. Showing up to help Farr move in, he was astonished to see a goat tethered in the front yard. "Farr," he said, "what's this goat doing here? I told you animals were not allowed." "Oh, that's no animal," Farr answered, "that's a crate of country butter."

Farr's cousin Maury Stonebridge owned a farm near Lebanon on the Nashville road. On Saturdays people from Nashville often drove into the country for pleasure. One spring Saturday just after Maury finished spreading manure on his fields, a carload of city tourists passed on the road. Seeing Maury standing at the edge of his fields near the road, the woman driving the car stopped, backed up, and rolled her window down. "Excuse me," she said, "but what's that I smell?" "Fertilizer," Maury answered. "Oh, for land's sakes," the woman exclaimed. "Yes, lady," Maury replied. Having one's way brings responsibility. I would like to have my way for the sake of the land but, like the woman driving the car, I don't know anything about farming. Although I have read through libraries, I am book-ignorant and would not know where to begin. I don't know how to make a plough, and I have never planted crops or slaughtered animals.

Although contemporary man has been educated into helplessness and perhaps never has his way about any of the major things affecting his life, he sometimes gets his way with little things, most frequently when he is young and life is relatively uncomplicated. When I was a student at Cambridge I played water polo. Since the referee has trouble seeing what happens under water, the game can be rough, with victory going not to the skillful but to the dirty. At the beginning of a game fists and elbows splash about as players test each other. When league games began I decided that not only I but those who played against me were going to play my way. In the first game, when the referee looked away, a player on the opposing team elbowed me in the chest. As he started swimming off, I grabbed his hair and, climbing over his back, chewed his ear, mangling it so badly that he had to leave the game. Because of the incident players thought me slightly mad and nicknaming me "cannibal" put on visiting manners whenever they played against me.

In those youthful days I frequently got my way without thinking; now thought unfortunately blocks action. Every noon I try to exercise in the university pool. The pool is crowded with undergraduates who stand in the shallow end and gossip, preventing people like me from turning around at the end of the pool and swimming laps. Crashing into them, arms flailing, doesn't bother the students. "Sorry to be in your way," they say and continue talking. Biting would make them move, and, if I were twenty-two again, I would gnaw on the first navel I found blocking my lane. So far, though, I haven't even bared my teeth. Not sure whether I would get in more trouble for munching on a male or female, I heave myself out of the water like a toothless old lion when undergraduates begin to gather in the shallows.

Many times, of course, when I got my way, the way didn't turn out to be exactly what I expected. Because someone told me Lawrence had lived there, I avoided the new tourist hotels and sought out and stayed in the Baron Hotel in Aleppo. Although Vicki was with me, I walked into the Baron dreaming about Allenby and Feisal, Akaba and the Hejaz Railway. I left carrying a jar of rose petal jam given to Vicki by a waiter. When I think about Aleppo now, Lawrence does not come to mind. Instead I remember the jam and imagine bushes of sweet red roses. The days when I exerted myself to have my way are gone. Actually, it's not the days so much as the ways which have gone. The unexpected contents me, and the wish to have my way rarely arises. Still, if I no longer try to impose a way upon experience, others attempt to force ways upon me, pressing me into a mold baked in the hot kiln of zeal.

For generations religion has run through my family like a quiet brook, rising occasionally to wash silt over the lowlands but until now never flooding, pushing stony doctrine through the even gentleness of life. My grandmother started the water rising. Not until the death of her son, my uncle, was she particularly religious. My uncle was survived by his wife and my cousin Sherry, then three years old. Kept away from the funeral, Sherry did not visit the cemetery until ten days after her father's burial. The first time she went to the cemetery, my grandmother accompanied her. No one told Sherry, Grandmother said, where they were going, but as soon as the car stopped and the doors were open, Sherry ran through

the grass and winding through the headstones went directly to her father's grave. "Daddy's here," she said, "Daddy's here." Shaken by what
happened, six months passed before Grandmother took Sherry to the
cemetery again. Once again, as soon as the car doors were open, Sherry
ran to her father's grave. This time, however, she stopped and turning
her head to one side, said, "Daddy's not here anymore."

The first time Grandmother told me the story she was seventy-five
years old. Clearly, though, her faith was built upon the two visits to the
cemetery with Sherry. As Grandmother grew older, she told me the
story more often and her faith seemed to grow stronger as she tried to
press it upon me. Her last words to me were "Don't forget your God,"
words which she repeated to Mother, urging her to concern herself with
my spiritual welfare. Long having found more matter for my spirit
under the open heavens than within a building, I am recusant insofar as
formal religion is concerned. Once Grandmother's words would have
trickled silently away down the spillway of time. Now pitched forward
by the fervent spirit of the age, they have washed over my family, digging channels through the green plain of daily life. While Mother telephones urging me to take the children to Sunday School, a cousin who
gave his father a leather-bound, rhinestone-covered, folio-sized bible for
Christmas writes when he hears that I have a bad back, "Jesus will heal
your pain."

In September I will enroll the children in Sunday School. Letting
mother have her way doesn't bother me much; I don't see the children's
attendance as a matter of principle. In truth, I rarely see principle in
anything, for "principle" like "precedent" is a word which I avoid. Moreover, there are occasions when letting another person have his way
makes life easier. In the fall telephone conversations with Mother will
be more pleasant. Sometimes, of course, the choice of whether or not to
accede to another's wishes does not exist. Several years ago I taught in
Syria for a year. Examinations took place long after classes ended. When
classes concluded at the end of the second semester Vicki and I left
Syria and traveled in the Dodecanese. After six weeks we returned to
Syria, so I could grade examinations. In our absence visa regulations
changed, and although my passport stated I was an employee of Tish-
reen University in Latakia and contained a reentry permit, appropriate
when we left the country, immigration refused us entry, saying we had
to sail back to Cyprus and obtain a new visa. Until I mentioned that
several important members of the army would be angry if Vicki and I

were denied entry, the official at the port refused to let us off the boat. Even after he allowed us off the boat, he took our passports, saying we could not leave the compound without them and would have to return to Cyprus that evening. With that he departed, and Vicki and I talked our way out of the compound and went to the university. Saying "the law was the law," the dean of the college refused to help us. The man, however, who would have been obliged to grade my three hundred or so examinations if we returned to Cyprus took matters into his hands. Together we visited a series of officials. Initially we had little success and were treated rudely, but as we climbed the ladder of rank and officialdom the treatment got better. By late afternoon we were in a suite at the top of a building, the office, I was told, of the military commandant for northern Syria. While my colleague told my story, shaking his head and waving his arms, I tried to look affable and naive. When my colleague finished, the commandant made a clucking sound, then reached over and made a telephone call. An hour later we were in our apartment, passports in hand.

That night my colleague brought the examinations to the apartment. When a student finished an examination, he wrote his name at the top; a flap was then glued firmly down over the name. Only after the registrar received the graded examinations was the name revealed, thus insuring that favoritism played no part in the results. After putting the examinations on the dining room table, my colleague said that he told the commandant that two influential generals would be pleased if Vicki and I received visas. "Of course," he said, "I must now speak to the generals and tell them I used their names. That would be easier if I had some good news for them." From the pile of papers he picked up the top two examinations, flaps still glued over the students' names. "This," he said, looking at one paper, "is the examination taken by the daughter of one general; the other is that of the niece of the second general. I have read both. Neither, I am afraid, is quite up to passing, but perhaps you could find enough points somewhere to get the girls through." When I looked a little startled, he added, "Use your conscience, of course, but if the girls passed, things would be easier for me." With that he got up, saying as he walked out the door, "It certainly is good to have you back. For a while I didn't think I could get you in, but then I thought of the generals."

Fifty is a passing grade in Syria; on an ordinary examination anywhere from a quarter to three-fifths of the students pass. I read the girls' papers; both made about thirty-five. I wasn't sure what to do. I didn't believe that the papers had been written by relatives of prominent generals. Most likely my colleague had his own reasons for wanting the students to pass; perhaps they came from his village or were kinsmen or maybe he owed favors to their families. Whatever the reasons, they had little to do with me. All I had to do was mark the papers. Before writing a grade on the papers, I paused. If my integrity wasn't at risk, which it probably was, at least, I thought, some principle was at stake. But as I sat in my comfortable chair in my comfortable apartment, eating a pomegranate, integrity and principle seemed beside the point, even silly and intrusive. What was important was that Vicki and I were not steaming toward Cyprus, perspiration running off us in rivers. "When in Syria, do as the Syrians," I thought to myself, and picking up my pen wrote "51" boldly across the top of both examinations.

The day had been tiring, and I slept well that night. The next morning, though, the grades bothered me. Throughout the year I treated students equally, and I didn't want to leave the country having acted badly, albeit only a little badly. I fretted all morning until suddenly a simple solution came to me. Grade inflation was rampant on American campuses. Why not import a little bit of America into Syria and curve the marks so that everyone who scored thirty-five or more passed the examination? That, of course, is what I did, passing an unheard of eighty percent of the class and feeling good about it, too.

No person goes through life without occasionally having his way. The occasion, however, usually does not last long. For some time I have dressed informally, wearing hunting boots, floppy sweaters, and rough trousers. Recently, though, Vicki has decided to change my appearance. Favorite sweaters and jackets have vanished and been replaced by crisp, clean clothes with colors firm, not yet aged into richness by tea, chocolate ice cream, and juice from a grove of oranges. I have let Vicki have her way with my wardrobe, although having favorite clothes suddenly disappear can be dislocating. "What's wrong?" Vicki said one morning not long ago on coming back from her shower and finding me sitting half-dressed on the edge of the bed. "Why aren't you dressed?" she asked. "I can't remember where I left my brown jacket, the one Grandmother bought me at Miller and Rhodes in Richmond," I said. "It's not in the closet; I looked twice. Maybe I left it on a table in the library the other night. If I did, it's probably gone." "Oh, it's gone all right," Vicki answered, pinching her stockings out from her calves so they wouldn't cling but would run smooth and neat, "long gone. That jacket was a disgrace, and I threw it away."

I have kept only one piece of clothing away from Vicki, a winter coat made by the Woods Bag and Canvas Company of Toronto and Winnipeg. I bought the coat in 1970 and have worn it through every winter since. Because the coat is filled with down, it has never been cleaned, and Vicki says it smells like "mutton fat." The coat hangs to my knees, and its pockets are swollen and convenient. In them I stuff books, papers, tangelos, Mounds Bars, bathing suits, goggles, cartons of milk, whatever I need for a day and sometimes whatever I need for a week. Although practical, the coat isn't stylish and often when I have it well loaded and walk across campus people stare and even say things. "Sam," a dean said the other day, "you look like a bagman." "What do you think of that remark?" I asked Vicki later. "The dean's blind," she answered. "You don't look like a bagman; you look like one of those people dug out of a peat bog in Denmark, fatter than most but still a peat person." Vicki's answer pleased me. How nice it would be, I thought, to be a walking bog: pitcher plants in my pockets, sundew behind my ears, and cranberries in my hair.

Actually, if I had my way my house would resemble a pond, rooms teeming with possessions. Each room would be different. The living room would be sunny and green smacking of yellow iris, pickerel-weed, water parsnip, arrowhead, and bur-weed with patches of the great pond snail's eggs stuck to it. Through the narrow halls would rush diving beetles, back swimmers, water boatmen, and whirligigs, while flatworms, caddis fly larvae, sticklebacks, and an occasional horse leech would hang from walls or sit on shelves in my study in the dark back of the house.

Vicki likes rooms clear and orderly. She doesn't blame Noah for fleas and lice, and last summer when I spent a whole afternoon swatting flies she became exasperated after I explained that I had accidentally killed a crab spider. Killing a spider, I said, brings bad luck. If, however, a person swats fifty-three flies, bad luck turns good. Vicki is slightly inconsistent though. Not only does she oppose the Industrial Park with its windowless neatness but she also opposes my attempts to make our house resemble a pond. Before a dinner party last week I removed a silver rolltop dish from the middle of the dining room table. In its place I put a ten by seven inch wooden box, rounded at the top like a loaf of bread and covered with orange and brown paper so that it looked like a clothes trunk. On front of the box was an imitation mailing label on which was printed "From the Brantford Starch Company." The box once contained six pounds of Lily White gloss starch. Lining the inside of the box like paper lining a trunk was a drawing of Lily White. A round little girl about eight years old with puffed cheeks and curly hair, she was the image of purity, surrounded by lilies and wearing a bonnet, a white dress, and ribbons. In the box I put an announcement which I found in an old cookbook in Nova Scotia. About the size of a postcard, the announcement was for a "Baptist Men's Rally" at the Temple Church in Yarmouth. The Yarmouth Male Choir would sing, and a minister from Liverpool, Nova Scotia, would speak. The meeting, the card proclaimed in black type, was "the Kind of a Meeting Men Like." "Objective" it urged, "200 Men—Be one of the 200!"

I hoped the box and card would enliven conversation. By the time guests arrived, however, the rolltop dish was back in the middle of the table, and box and card were in the attic. Never, though, am I upset when I don't get my way. Still, sometimes I stage a symbolic revolt, usually telling a wondrously and, to Vicki, embarrassingly bad joke. "Did you read in the *Willimantic Chronicle* about that poor man whose business was failing?" I interrupted when someone started talking about the differences between the ways men and women talked. "He went to Agway," I said, "and bought half a pound of birdseed. Then he spooned as much of it as he could into his mouth and went outdoors and took a deep breath." "He did it," I said, "because he wanted, more than anything else in life, to suck seed."

Whatever the differences between the speech of men and women, Vicki has never embarrassed me while I am a continual embarrassment to her. Perhaps embarrassment is the price a woman pays when her mate gives up having or even wanting his way in important matters. Saying and doing silly things is deeply satisfying and keeps me content. At Mystic we usually eat at McDonald's after visiting the aquarium. On UConndom Day Vicki wanted to go somewhere different, so we ate at a restaurant called the Steak Hut. With a high ceiling and big beams, the interior of the Steak Hut resembled a barn and the children were thrilled. I wasn't so happy. The dolphin that we had come to see at the aquarium was having a baby and all the shows were canceled. Inside the restaurant every table was occupied; the service was slow, and the kitchen had run out of french-fried potatoes. When we were ready to go, I told Francis and Edward to put their coats on four times before they moved.

"You must learn to obey, boys," I said loudly. "If I had been disciplined as a child I would not have gone to jail." At the word "jail" everyone around me sat up straight, except, of course, Vicki, who hung her head. "But now I am out of jail," I cautioned, speaking louder, "and I am not going back again and I don't want you ever to go." "Jail," I said, almost shouting, "is no fun, no fun at all."

Vicki tolerates my doings, telling friends that "it's just his way." Unfortunately, I have come to suspect that odd behavior may not be my way but the way of the blood I inherited. Generous and charming, my grandfather was also peculiar, so peculiar that the more I think about it the more convinced I am that he, not my uncle's death, drove my grandmother to religion. Throughout his life he refused to kiss or be kissed. "For a while," Grandmother told me, "this bothered me, but then I adjusted to his ways." Grandfather wasn't cold; he was simply frightened of germs. When Grandmother had to have a mastoid operation, one which doctors told her could be fatal, he sent her to the hospital in a taxi. Every day he sent bundles of flowers to her room, but he refused to visit. He was a florist and loved flowers, and each spring he went to Europe to see the flowers. Grandmother stayed at home, and one day while she and Mother sat in the living room thinking he was in Italy, he walked through the front door. On the day he landed in Southampton he suffered from indigestion. He walked down the docks, bought a ticket on another ship, and sailed home that afternoon. "Traveling with indigestion," he explained, "is certain death."

Grandfather owned huge greenhouses in which he grew the flowers he sold. Convinced that most fruit sold in groceries, particularly bananas, was unclean, he decided to grow his own bananas. He bought some small banana trees and nurtured them carefully until they produced bananas. Mother was at the breakfast table when the first ripe banana was served to him. He took a single bite, she said, then spit the banana out, screaming, "Jesus, I'm poisoned. Cut down the trees." On another occasion he decided to grow grapes and make his own wine. From New York he brought an expert to Richmond to supervise planting the vines. Later, when the time came to harvest grapes and make wine, he brought in another expert. The wine was put into small wooden casks which he imported from France and stored in a wine cellar which he had constructed in the basement. After the wine had aged for what he had been told was an appropriate time, he breached a cask. He took but one sip. "Great God Almighty," he yelled, blowing the wine out of his mouth. "Vinegar. This will kill us all." The next morning farm workers carried the casks away and smashed them in a gully deep in the woods. "My God," he exclaimed, "the fumes from that poison could pollute all the milk in the dairy. If someone drank a glass of it, he would be paralyzed or go blind. Then I could be sued for everything and we would end up in the poorhouse."

After complaining vociferously and in the process enjoying himself immensely, Brother McIneery let Farr Stonebridge move into the house with the goat. Farr was Ardent's drinking companion, and Ardent was not about to let a little country butter spoil Saturday nights. At about nine-thirty one cold winter evening Ardent stumbled into Enos Mayfield's "Inn" in South Carthage. "Have you seen Farr this evening?" he asked Enos. "He was here an hour ago," Enos answered. "Are you sure?" Ardent asked. "Did he have a goat with him?" "He left the goat outside but it was Farr all right," Enos answered. "Well then," Ardent asked, fixing Enos with a wandering blue eye, "was I with him?" Grandfather, I suspect, has been with me in more places than the Steak Hut. But when I remember the cannibal, willing to gnaw like a goat upon ears or anything coming within biting distance or when I think about that boy weaving along the sidewalk in Tiblisi, serenading the KGB, I wonder if I was with them. Whatever the case, their ways are certainly not my ways, reading about bugs and writing so that when "Daddy's not here any more," the children will have word and tale to push away from and start them on their ways.